From Mandate to Blueprint

FROM MANDATE TO BLUEPRINT

LESSONS FROM INTELLIGENCE REFORM

Thomas Fingar

STANFORD UNIVERSITY PRESS
Stanford, California

STANFORD UNIVERSITY PRESS
Stanford, California

Printed in the United States of America on acid-free, archival-quality paper

Library of Congress Cataloging-in-Publication Data

Names: Fingar, Thomas, author.
Title: From mandate to blueprint : lessons from intelligence reform /
    Thomas Fingar.
Description: Stanford, California : Stanford University Press, 2021. |
    Includes bibliographical references.
Identifiers: LCCN 2020048156 (print) | LCCN 2020048157 (ebook) |
    ISBN 9781503628670 (paperback) | ISBN 9781503628687 (epub)
Subjects: LCSH: Fingar, Thomas. | United States. Office of the Deputy
    Director of National Intelligence for Analysis. | Intelligence service—
    United States. | Administrative agencies—United States—Management. |
    Administrative agencies—United States—Reorganization.
Classification: LCC JK468.I6 F54 2021 (print) | LCC JK468.I6 (ebook) |
    DDC 353.1/70973—dc23
LC record available at https://lccn.loc.gov/2020048156
LC ebook record available at https://lccn.loc.gov/2020048157

Cover design: Kevin Barrett Kane

Typeset by Kevin Barrett Kane in 11/14 Adobe Garamond Pro

WITH GRATITUDE TO THE COMMUNITY OF ANALYSTS

The dedicated men and women of the United States Intelligence Community who protect our nation and advance American interests by transforming data into insight and providing objective analysis of potentially consequential developments

Contents

Preface

Bureaucracies exist to perform two critically important but very different functions. One is to perform thousands of routine and mostly mundane but often highly specialized tasks reliably and without drama. The second is to prepare for unlikely and unforeseen developments that require rapid and effective responses to limit unwanted consequences. When bureaucracies, bureaucrats, and the officials who lead them perform as expected, organizations and the procedures that enable them to function are almost invisible and largely taken for granted. We expect them to work and, most of the time, they do. When breakdowns occur and problems arise, they can be identified and fixed before causing extensive disruption or damage. Well-functioning bureaucratic organizations are more boring than flashy and generally prize routinization and predictability more than innovation and uncertainty. This makes them easy to lampoon but essential to life as we know it and expect it to be.

What is true of bureaucracies and bureaucrats in general is—or was—true in spades for agencies and activities of the American federal government. The scope and importance of federal government missions and responsibilities are mindboggling. Hundreds of millions of people in the United States and around the world unthinkingly rely on unknown agencies and faceless bureaucrats to ensure that aviation, food, pharmaceuticals, and myriad other everyday essentials are safe, and that banks, insurance, telecommunication, and hundreds of other industries meet minimum standards and comply with applicable laws and regulations. They also ensure that mining and cattle grazing on federal lands, use of agricultural chemicals, national parks, and the environment are managed for the benefit of all, and that social security checks, unemployment benefits, and bridge and power plant safety inspections are provided on time and to the right recipients.

We used to take for granted that federal agencies would do what they are supposed to in the way that they are supposed to, and that they would do so efficiently and reliably. Americans have long had a somewhat schizophrenic propensity to complain about federal spending and decry bureaucratic bloat while at the same time defending the (sometimes expensive and inefficient) services important to them. Everybody wants cuts in general but more money (and often more people) for the programs from which they derive concrete benefits. We could joke about "bureaucracy" and "bureaucrats" because we were confident that, most of the time, they would deliver the services on which our nation depends. That is no longer the case. Our government, especially but not exclusively executive branch agencies, is now widely—and often accurately—perceived to be badly broken and in desperate need of repair, and often more of the problem than the solution.

Performance problems, politicization of government functions, and failure to reform and reengineer institutions and procedures to meet twenty-first-century requirements antedate the election of Donald Trump, but the way his administration mishandled the missions of governance has made the situation almost incalculably worse. Successor administrations will face monumental challenges as they tackle overdue and unavoidable requirements for reinvention and rebuilding of government capacity and public confidence in institutions that can no longer be taken for granted. Responsibility for determining what can and must be done and how to achieve priority objectives will fall primarily to the few thousand senior appointees who will head specific components of the federal government. I intend this book to help them negotiate the daunting transition from "Wow, we won" through "What do I do now" to "Here is what we are going to do."

In "normal" times, the transition from one administration to another is—or was—a time of renewal and reinvigoration in which new appointees took command of reasonably well-functioning and fully staffed agencies and other components of the federal government and tweaked them to implement campaign promises and/or address specific problems. Career bureaucrats generally welcomed the once-in-four-years opportunity to fix problems, adjust priorities, and rekindle enthusiasm. They anticipated that most things would continue more or less as before after they had educated new appointees and explained how organizational structures, procedures, and workforce capabilities were tailored to meet the requirements of their primary missions. There was a bias for continuity tempered by recognition that some change was unavoidable and desirable. With briefings from their predecessors, most appointees to most positions could expect to get up to speed quickly and focus on a relatively small number of problems and objectives. That was then, but we are not in a normal situation and the challenges facing every new appointee will be more numerous, complex, contentious, and consequential than those confronted by their predecessors.

When I began this book, I thought of its scope and purpose as describing the unusual, unique, even idiosyncratic challenges encountered in the course of standing up new organizations (the Office of the Director of National Intelligence and the Office of the Deputy Director of National Intelligence for Analysis), implementing the most far-reaching reforms to the national security establishment since 1947 (mandated by the Intelligence Reform and Terrorism Prevention Act of 2004 and a presidential directive to implement most recommendations of the Commission on the Intelligence Capabilities of the United States Regarding Weapons of Mass Destruction), integrating the analytic work of sixteen agencies, and transforming the way intelligence analysis is performed in the United States national security establishment.

Describing what made the challenges I faced unique, or at least unusual, was a significant motivating factor and goal of the first draft, which was largely an insider account aimed primarily at past, current, and future members of the Intelligence Community. Developments since I started the book, however, convinced me that my own experience and challenges might be more common in the future than they were in the past, and therefore germane to future appointees to a wide array of federal positions. Indeed, growing recognition of how rapidly events were moving toward the situation described in the opening paragraphs of this book persuaded me to recast it to use lessons from the way I perceived and implemented the tasks of intelligence reform to illustrate general principles or guidelines for all new appointees. The result is much less than a checklist or template of what to do and how to do it than it is a guide and cautionary tale for appointees certain to discover that the tasks they have assumed are bigger and more complex than they anticipated.

Acknowledgments

Acknowledging the contributions of friends and colleagues is a humbling and hazardous undertaking. It is humbling because recalling specific undertakings and interactions underscores how much I have benefited from the assistance of talented and generous colleagues. It is hazardous because explicitly noting the contributions of some risks inadvertent omission of names that should be acknowledged. If you think your name should have been included, you are probably right. I apologize for the oversight.

The adventure described in this book was a collective undertaking. I was privileged to play a leading role, but the ideas, enthusiasm, diligence, and bureaucratic skill of others on the team were at least as important as anything that I contributed. Many sentences in the book could begin with "we" rather than "I," but that would unfairly suggest that others should be held accountable for decisions that I made. Their contributions were extremely important to me and to what we did, but I alone am responsible for the errors that I made and for any critical omissions and shortcomings in the way I have told our collective story.

An entire chapter is devoted to the recruitment of deputies and other members of the Office of the Deputy Director of National Intelligence for Analysis (ODDNI/A) senior team, and the names of many key members appear there and in other portions of the book. They also deserve special recognition here. Those named in this section were courageous (or foolhardy) enough to cast their lot with a new and unproven organization with an ambiguous mandate and skeptical workforce. Some were the first to hold a position; others joined the team when their predecessors accepted new assignments. All were critical to the task of standing up the ODDNI/A and are listed in alphabetical order. They are Joe Garten, David Gordon, Craig Gralley, Richard Immerman, Steve Kaplan, Jan Karcz, John Keefe, Captain Ron Rice, Nancy Tucker, Mike Wertheimer, and Colonel Jon Wohlman. Other key members of the team were Sherry Hong, Sandi Jimenez, Caitlin Meehan, Brian O'Callaghan, Andy Shepard, Kelley Shreffler, and Becky Strode.

The context and decisions described in this book were shaped by colleagues and counterparts in the Office of the Director of National Intelligence (ODNI). Most of their activities occurred in parallel to those in my directorate, but our tasks and initiatives intersected, had to be coordinated, and affected my ability to achieve ODDNI/A objectives. Both of the Directors of National Intelligence for whom I worked, Ambassador John Negroponte and Vice Admiral (retired) Mike McConnell, gave me enormous leeway and support. I appreciate their trust, confidence, and encouragement. Other members of the core ODNI team included Lieutenant General Ron Burgess, Glenn Gaffney, Mary Margaret Graham, General Mike Hayden, Pat Kennedy, Don Kerr, Mike Leiter, Al Munson, and David Shedd.

The third important group that played critical roles in formulating, selling, and implementing the measures we adopted to implement mandated reforms and transform analysis first came together as an informal collection of Intelligence Community (IC) analytic managers determined to fix problems we all recognized but lacked clear authority to address. After I was named Deputy Director of National Intelligence for Analysis (DDNI/A), this group morphed into more formal advisory bodies for the *President's Daily Brief* (PDB) and the Analysis and Production Board. This group included Jim Buchanan, Robert Cardillo, Paula Causey, Peter Clement, Kate Hall, John Kringen, Wayne Murphy, Earl Sheck, Dave Shore, and Caryn Wagner.

Colleagues too numerous to mention individually but critical to the effort to transform analysis in the Intelligence Community include the dozens of National Intelligence Officers (NIOs) and Deputy NIOs who worked with me at the National Intelligence Council, former colleagues in the State Department's Bureau of Intelligence and Research (INR), and the hundreds of analysts and analytic managers in IC component agencies. They were an invaluable source of ideas and feedback. More important, their willingness to try new approaches and work collaboratively across agency boundaries and dedication to providing objective and useful analytic support to policymakers and military commanders validated our transformation agenda.

Like every successful leader or manager, I learned much from the people who promoted me to positions of greater responsibility and taught me by instruction and example. I was fortunate to work with many truly exceptional mentors, including all of the INR Assistant Secretaries with whom I worked: Mort Abramowitz, Carl Ford, Toby Gati, Doug Mulholland, Phyllis Oakley, and Stape Roy. Other mentors at the State Department taught me to understand what policymakers want and need from the Intelligence Community. They include Rich Armitage, Marc Grossman, Tom Pickering, Colin Powell, and Stobe Talbott.

Writing this book fifteen years after the events it describes would have been impossible without the assistance of friends and colleagues who shared the experience and provided comments on earlier drafts. They are Roger George, Richard Immerman, Steve Kaplan, John Keefe, Bo Miller, Mike Wertheimer, and Jon Wohlman.

As a former government official, I was eager to publish this book as quickly as possible, but as an academic, I wanted it to have the validation of quality provided by the thoroughness and peer review process of an academic press. When the manuscript was nearing completion, I sent a précis to Stanford University Press director Alan Harvey. Academic presses are notoriously slow, but my positive experiences publishing four previous books with Stanford and Alan's enthusiastic reaction persuaded me to submit a fifth manuscript. Thanks to Alan, Caroline McKusick, Jessica Ling, Kevin Barrett Kane, and David Horne, and to the outside readers who reviewed the draft and provided many useful comments with exceptional alacrity, this book was produced more quickly than I would have thought possible.

Last, and by no means least, I want to acknowledge and thank my wife, Orlene, for her patience and support during the long days and seven-day workweeks that were a constant in our lives during the period described in this book. She has provided comfort and moral support on every step of our more than five-decade journey together.

Abbreviations

ADDNI	Assistant Deputy Director of National Intelligence
AIS	Analytic Integrity and Standards
ARC	Analytic Resources Catalog
CI	counterintelligence
CIA	Central Intelligence Agency
CIO	Chief Information Officer
CMS	Community Management Staff
DAS	Deputy Assistant Secretary
DCI	Director of Central Intelligence
DDNI/A	Deputy Director of National Intelligence for Analysis
DHS	Department of Homeland Security
DI	Directorate of Intelligence
DIA	Defense Intelligence Agency
DNI	Director of National Intelligence
DOD	Department of Defense
DC	Deputies Committee
FBI	Federal Bureau of Investigation
FSO	Foreign Service Officer
HPSCI	House Permanent Select Committee on Intelligence
HUMINT	human intelligence

IAPB	Intelligence Analysis and Production Board
IC	Intelligence Community
ICD	Intelligence Community Directive
ICPM	Intelligence Community Policy Memorandum
INR	Bureau of Intelligence and Research (State Department)
IRTPA	Intelligence Reform and Terrorism Prevention Act (of 2004)
LNI	Library of National Intelligence
NCPC	National Counterproliferation Center
NCTC	National Counterterrorism Center
NIC	National Intelligence Council
NIE	National Intelligence Estimate
NIM	National Intelligence Manager
NIO	National Intelligence Officer
NIPF	National Intelligence Priorities Framework
NIU	National Intelligence University
NSA	National Security Agency
NSC	National Security Council
ODDNI/A	Office of the Deputy Director of National Intelligence for Analysis
ODNI	Office of the Director of National Intelligence
ORCON	originator-controlled
PC	Principals Committee
PDB	*President's Daily Brief*
RASER	Rapid Analytic Support and Expeditionary Response
SFRC	Senate Foreign Relations Committee
SHARP	Summer Hard Problems program
SIGINT	signals intelligence
SSCI	Senate Select Committee on Intelligence
TS	Top Secret
USG	United States Government
USIA	United States Information Agency
WMD	weapons of mass destruction

From Mandate to Blueprint

Purpose and Perspective

WRITING THIS BOOK was an unnatural act because it required greater attention to transparency than to accuracy and objectivity. As a career-long analyst who considers accuracy and objectivity to be absolute requisites if not the *sine qua non* of good scholarly research and intelligence analysis, writing a book that focuses more on my perceptions and thinking about the subjects it explores than on the completeness and accuracy of those perceptions is unnatural and uncomfortable. It also is uncomfortable because it puts me at the center of the narrative in ways that exaggerate my importance and understate the ideas, influence, and impact of many others.

Why, it is reasonable to ask, have I decided to do something that I find unnatural and uncomfortable? The answer, in brief, is that more than a decade after retiring from the concurrent positions of Deputy Director of National Intelligence for Analysis (DDNI/A) and Chair of the National Intelligence Council, I've found that colleagues and students are more interested in *why* I approached the challenges of intelligence reform as I did than in the "reforms" themselves. Thinking about why I did what I did forced me to be more analytical about the considerations that shaped specific decisions than I was at the time. It also forced me to disaggregate the interconnected tasks involved in setting up a new organization (the Office of the Deputy Director of National Intelligence for Analysis [ODDNI/A]), implementing reforms mandated by the Intelligence Reform and Terrorism Prevention Act of 2004 and relevant presidential directives, rebuilding morale and restoring confidence in the Intelligence Community (IC), and implementing transformational reforms to improve the quality and utility of intelligence analysis.

Answering such questions proved more interesting to me than describing or boasting about the content of what we attempted and accomplished. Moreover, and more important, I somewhat vainly concluded that describing how I thought about and defined the objectives of reform, how I perceived the bureaucratic and political environments in which I operated, and why I made the decisions that I did might be more useful than a descriptive or defensive narrative.

The preceding sentence raises the obvious question, "More useful to whom?" Stated another way, why should anyone care about what I was thinking almost fifteen years ago? The passage of time had undoubtedly diminished the interest or curiosity of IC colleagues who shared and/or were affected by the things we attempted, but the evolution of intelligence analysis from a job to a career to a profession has, I surmise, fueled interest in how it became what it is today.[1] This suggests a large but specialized audience comprising government employees and both former and aspiring public servants who work in the national security community but are employed by private firms. Writing for this audience required a fair amount of "inside baseball" detail that will be too esoteric for some readers but clarifying and, I hope, interesting to IC professionals who lived through the period and events at the center of this book.

The second target audience is the large and growing contingent of students enrolled in courses on intelligence and/or national security, or with a more general interest in what it is like to work in the federal bureaucracy and how to get things done in Washington. There is a large and growing literature describing what the Intelligence Community and intelligence analysts do, and this book does not rehearse descriptions of organizations, missions, and methods that have been well covered by others.[2] Rather, it attempts to complement existing descriptions of products and processes by focusing on how and why they took the forms that they had in 2009 and, in some cases, have today.

The third target audience was initially an afterthought but might be the most important one. As I was completing work on the case study portion of the book, I realized that many of the challenges I faced as the first Deputy Director of National Intelligence for Analysis had unique aspects but were manifestations of more general challenges faced, *mutatis mutandis*, by new appointees to senior positions in all components of the federal government. That prompted reconceptualization of the book to explicate some of those general challenges in a way that would provide a rough "checklist" of things that new appointees should think about as they take up new assignments. The generalized considerations presented in Part II were written for this audience. They do not constitute a checklist of the kind used by pilots before takeoff or by an increasing number of healthcare professionals, but I would have found it helpful to have had such a list of things to consider as I embarked on the bureaucratic journey described in Part I.[3] The amount of detail and specific considerations in Part I will be of less interest to appointees to positions outside the Intelligence Community, but the examples presented there illustrate and help to clarify the general points made in Part II.

Describing the considerations summarized in Part II as a checklist exaggerates their coherence or completeness. At best, they are a starting point designed to alert new appointees to the importance of context, team-building, and prioritization, and to identify other challenges they are likely to encounter. The challenges discussed here were not drawn from academic studies or "how to" guides for newly appointed officials. Indeed, if such studies or manuals exist, I did not consult them either before undertaking the tasks described in Part I or when writing this book. What I have labeled challenges are efforts to categorize and generalize the many different but often interconnected decisions I encountered after accepting the job of standing up the ODDNI/A, implementing provisions of the Intelligence Reform and Terrorism Prevention Act of 2004 (IRTPA) that pertained to analysis, overseeing and reforming the *President's Daily Brief* (PDB) and the National Intelligence Council (NIC), improving the quality and utility of intelligence analysis, and continuing to provide world-class analytic support to the national security enterprise.

The magnitude and complexity of interconnected responsibilities and organizations involved were greater than those facing most new appointees, but they were similar in kind. Every new appointee experiences some variant of the "What do I do now?" challenge that follows hard on the heels of "I'm honored to have been given this opportunity" euphoria. The general considerations and specific examples in this book do not provide an answer to that question. What they try to do is more modest but perhaps more important, namely, to provide guidance on how to think about the common challenges and particular clusters of considerations all new appointees must navigate.

Some will read the first part of the book with an eye toward evaluating the choices I made and conclude that some were better than others. I certainly do not mind and would actually welcome such an examination, but my objective in writing the book was not to prove that I did the right thing or did everything in the right way. I already know—and knew at the time—that such was not the case. Rather, my primary objective was to be as explicit as possible about why I made the decisions that I did because I believe that helping others to understand how problems and opportunities were perceived, prioritized, and addressed is more useful than a self-serving history of what I did when given the opportunity to integrate, restore, and transform intelligence analysis in the United States.

Genesis of the Book

When I was first urged to write a book about implementing the analysis-related portions of the Intelligence Reform and Terrorism Prevention Act of 2004, I planned to write a descriptive history of the Office of the Deputy Director of National Intelligence for Analysis during its first four years (2005–2008). Had I written the book in 2009, it would have been less egocentric and more focused on what we did than on why we did it. Although it would have been relatively easy to write such a book during the first year after my return to Stanford in 2009, I was more eager to resume my academic career by working on subjects of greater interest to me than describing what I had been doing during the preceding four years.[4] Other interests, and writing and/or editing four other books, caused me to defer writing about intelligence reform for nearly a decade.[5]

The passage of time eroded my memory of steps taken, the sequence of events, who proposed or opposed specific actions, and the constantly changing political environment in Washington. In retrospect, I probably should have made and retained notes or a daily journal summarizing what we did and why we did it, and I probably should have urged my senior staff to do likewise. But I didn't and they didn't. As a once and future scholar, I certainly understood the value of preserving notes and other contemporary accounts, but my team and I were so focused and so busy "doing" things that we did not make time to record what we were doing or thinking.[6]

Insufficient time and other priorities were not the only reason that I did not keep a log of debates, decisions, and developments. Perhaps unreasonably, I worried that doing so would become known, trigger demands to share the chronicle, invite second-guessing, and in other ways make it more difficult to accomplish what we had decided to do. I also worried that chronicling everything we did might tempt me or others to "grandstand" or make decisions on the basis of how they would "look" instead of focusing more narrowly on efficacy, efficiency, and implications for other parts of the transformation agenda.

The final reason for eschewing a formal record is that I thought it important—even essential—to create an environment in which colleagues on my own staff and across the Intelligence Community would feel comfortable sharing concerns, complaints, and suggestions. Very soon after accepting the DDNI/A position, I recognized that the list of tasks in my portfolio included many with the potential to create or exacerbate divisions and rivalries in the IC.[7] I did not want to discourage frank dialog or make it harder to achieve priority objectives by keeping a record that would exacerbate fears and suspicions about the ODNI and what I was trying to do.

As I thought about the challenges and virtues of writing a "why"-focused book, I concluded that the most useful way to do so was to be as explicit as possible about my analysis of the situation, how I defined and prioritized tasks, how I drew upon aspects of my own experience and proposals recommended by others, how I assessed and attempted to use individual and institutional resources, and numerous other dimensions of "why I did what I did." Recreating the context and calculus of decisions made more than a decade ago proved to be easier than remembering the precise sequence and interplay of specific elements of the transformation agenda. Somewhat to my surprise, recalling what we did almost always triggered memories of why I thought it appropriate or necessary to take a particular step at the time we took it. Further reflection convinced me that it would be more useful to more readers to approach this book as a case study of one man's perceptions, priorities, and choices with respect to institutional and behavioral change affecting multiple organizations, thousands of people, and the personal and political interests of powerful players in Washington.

Describing what I was thinking at the time puts me, uncomfortably, at the center of the narrative. This is, in important respects, one man's story, but I hope readers will focus on why we did things as we did and not on who made the decisions. Another person with different experiences might well have made different choices and nudged intelligence reform along a different trajectory. I certainly do not claim that what I did was the "right," "only," or "best possible" course of action. Others must judge the wisdom and efficacy of what we attempted. My goal is not to justify what I—we—did but, rather, to describe the factors and considerations I thought were important, how I assigned priorities, and how my decisions were shaped by inputs and reactions from my staff and colleagues. My goal is not to persuade readers that I made the "right" decisions or to self-assess the wisdom and effectiveness of those decisions more than a decade after the fact. Rather, it is to be as transparent as I can about how I conceived the mission I was asked to undertake, defined and prioritized steps designed to achieve the goals of intelligence reform, and navigated the political and bureaucratic seas in which I had to operate. No one will face the same conditions or pursue the same objectives, but I hope that the pages that follow will help others to meet their challenges and cope with the environments and constraints in which they operate.

INTRODUCTION

From Mandate to Blueprint

EVERY NEWLY APPOINTED GOVERNMENT OFFICIAL enters office with excitement, trepidation, and a mandate to achieve prescribed and personal objectives. For some, the appointment is a long-desired opportunity to apply the lessons of experience and academic study. For others it is a welcome but somewhat unanticipated reward for political activism or loyal service on the Hill or in an electoral campaign. A third type of appointee reaches the new position after years of service and demonstrated achievement in lower-level bureaucratic assignments. No matter how they ascended to the new position, their excitement and self-confidence are soon confronted by the need to address two critical questions: "What am I supposed to do, and What is the best way to achieve those objectives?"

The content and character of these questions are shaped if not determined by the mission and responsibilities of the position, its political profile, promises made during the electoral campaign, and the priorities of the administration and higher-level officials. But regardless of the specific parameters, every new appointee must quickly decide what he or she wishes to achieve, what can or must be done, how to prioritize and sequence interconnected objectives, and how to structure and staff arrangements to achieve organizational and personal objectives. Appointment to the new position is an opportunity, but it is also a challenge. It sometimes—or to some degree—carries with it a mandate subsuming specified requirements and authorities, but it virtually never comes with a blueprint detailing the steps that must be taken to enhance performance, perform new missions, minimize disruption of continuing missions, overcome bureaucratic resistance, or manage the expectations and involvement of oversight bodies.

The situation confronting every new appointee is unique, and there is and can be no "one-size-fits-all" prescription or checklist for making the transition from mandate to blueprint. But there are important commonalities that shape and constrain possibilities and prospects for success. I was aware, albeit often only dimly, of some of the factors that would facilitate, complicate, or impede my ability to define and perform the missions of the Office of the Director of National Intelligence for Analysis when I accepted the position of Deputy Director of National Intelligence for Analysis. For the most part, I was navigating without a map and with imperfect understanding of how the numerous component tasks subsumed by my mandate to reform intelligence analysis did or should fit together. Part I of this book describes how I thought about, defined, and linked specific subtasks to achieve overarching objectives. Although I did not have a master plan or conscious strategy, discussions with my senior team, feedback and lessons learned in the course of implementation, and discovery of new problems and opportunities that became apparent only when our ideas were tested in real-world application provided enhanced retrospective understanding of how component factors did and should fit together. This introduction will frame the specific decisions and developments described in Part I and identify broad questions and challenges the guidance in Part II is intended to address.

Mandate and Mission

All appointments come with a mix of specified and assumed tasks, responsibilities, and opportunities. Sometimes they are spelled out clearly in legislation, executive orders, or campaign promises, but such enumerated goals are always and inextricably linked to ongoing missions and responsibilities. It is almost never possible to stand down an agency or bureaucratic element while devising, implementing, and perfecting desired reforms. Old missions must continue unless and until they are explicitly terminated or transferred elsewhere. Stated more simply, attempts to make improvements cannot jeopardize performance of ongoing missions. Some, perhaps many, of the continuing responsibilities will be as or more important, at least to some customers and constituencies, than the new agenda items a new leader is expected to undertake. This means that one of the first jobs of any new appointee is to determine which prescribed and suggested tasks are mandatory (must dos), which ones are possible and/

or expected but are not formally mandated (desirable), and which ongoing tasks are critical to mission performance (essential).

Clarification and categorization of tasks and responsibilities is a necessary prerequisite for prioritization. Some tasks are more important, more urgent, or more foundational than others. Some tasks will be easier to achieve than others and might be placed near the top of the agenda in order to build experience, confidence, and momentum. Others will be judged more difficult to achieve and to entail greater risk of failure or diversion of resources needed to achieve other goals. Most organizations have a bias for continuity and reluctance to undertake new missions, but many contain individuals or components with strong ideas about what can or must be done to meet the requirements of key customers. There is no magic formula or algorithm for prioritizing constituent and interconnected tasks, but failure to prioritize is almost certain to preclude focus, concentration of effort, and ability to get things done. Stated differently, specification and prioritization of tasks is essential for development of strategies and plans to achieve them.

Prerequisites and Enablers

Defining and prioritizing objectives and responsibilities must both precede and be accompanied by determination of what is necessary to achieve them. Do the requisite conditions (for example, staff, information, authorities, funding) exist or must they be obtained? Will acquisition of foundational conditions be easy or quick to achieve, or will expected delays jeopardize undertakings with high priority and political salience? Are specific mandated or other high-priority goals sufficiently important to the President, key Members of Congress, or influential constituencies that they will help to overcome identified impediments? Should you push ahead even if you doubt your ability to achieve goals important to others (or to you) and hope for the best, or should you advise key players early on that favored or priority objectives are at risk? Posing and exploring such questions are both derivatives of and integral to the prioritization of mandates and mission objectives.

Next-step considerations must address such derivative and enabling tasks. For example, if some tasks require skills that are not currently available, it is desirable if not essential to identify and recruit people with the necessary skills and experience. If building the capacity needed to achieve enabling and/or priority goals requires restructuring the existing organization and reassigning personnel, doing either requires steps to protect or deemphasize legacy activities. This, of course, requires investigation and judgments about the relative importance of multiple responsibilities to the overall missions of the organization, national security, economic performance, and so on, and to powerful political actors

Inventory and Use Personal and Political Capital

Appointment to a position bestows a certain amount of authority and ability to command attention and consideration of proposals, but it does not ensure success. "Do it because I'm the boss" is seldom an effective way to secure buy-in. To maximize the likelihood of compliance and cooperation it is prudent to identify and exploit all the leverage you can marshal. Obtaining clarity about legal imperatives and constraints, the intentions and expectations of key players in the executive and legislative branches, and the limits and possibilities of authorities delegated to the position is important for the design of any blueprint. So too is awareness of the strengths (and limitations) of your own reputation and those of your senior staff. Winning benefit of the doubt is often critical to securing at least tentative support for innovative steps. Obtaining buy-in can be easier if key constituencies and individuals judge that you—and therefore your proposals—are worthy of respect.

Building Support and Managing Opposition

Bureaucratic organizations generally welcome the arrival of new officials and the opportunity to revitalize existing structures, procedures, and priorities. But they are also skeptical of *arrivistas* presumed to lack in-depth understanding of agency missions, routines, and capabilities. Career bureaucrats can be a rich source of information and support for goals they embrace. But they can also be a formidable obstacle to changes they deem inimical to agency mission or individual career prospects. Striking the right balance between utilization of all that experienced bureaucrats can contribute and willingness (and ability) to lead them out of their comfort zones is an early and unavoidable challenge. For both obvious and nonobvious reasons winning their acquiescence if not heartfelt support can be critical to achieving instrumental and overarching objectives. They want their organization to succeed and, for that reason, most will want the new leader to succeed. The challenge is to align their definition of success with that of the new leader.

Transparency, Feedback, and Flexibility

Winning cooperation and staving off criticism from opponents and people who support what you are trying to do but believe they could do better requires finding an acceptable balance between transparency (telling others what you intend to do, why you are doing it, and how you plan to achieve enunciated goals) and flexibility (willingness to make course corrections in response to feedback). Members of the senior team, subordinates, superiors, members of oversight bodies, the media, and other constituencies have an interest and a stake in the organization's performance. The more one telegraphs intentions and intended actions, the greater the likelihood of criticism and complaint before efficacy can be determined and the harder it is to make adjustments. Conversely, the more that specific intentions are withheld, the greater the likelihood of misunderstanding or judgments that the leader has a hidden agenda or lacks a clear plan.

Perceptions are often as important as performance. Having observers judge that one knows what he or she is doing is as or even more important than actually having a detailed blueprint for achieving announced goals. Helping constituencies to understand what one is trying to do and reporting often on progress and problems can build support and buy time. Knowing what to report and when to report it, and describing actions in ways that demonstrate flexibility and response to feedback without conveying an image of irresolution and lack of a strategy, require both forethought and continuous reassessment. They also require judgments about how long to stick with innovative actions in expectation that they will work eventually and when to admit failure and try something different.

Blueprints need not—and often cannot—be fully fleshed out before one begins efforts to secure buy-in and implement key elements. Indeed, large parts can be more visionary than detailed. But the vision must be clear, easy to explain, and truly reflective of what the new appointee plans to do. Feedback and flexibility are invaluable for judgments about what to continue for at least a bit longer and what to modify or jettison right away. We captured this with a bumper-sticker-size motto that was also our modus operandi: "Think Big, Start Small, Fail Cheap, Fix Fast."

PART I

What Was I Thinking?

Why I Did What I Did to Implement Intelligence Reform

A CASE STUDY

Intelligence Reform
Unique Opportunity or Fool's Errand?

MOST CHARACTERIZATIONS of the Intelligence Community are as diverse and erroneous as the descriptions of an elephant provided by six blind men in the classic story from India. Almost every description is true of some part of the community at some time or with reference to some set of issues, but almost no gross generalization is completely accurate or helpful. The perspective of outsiders is limited by both secrecy and the fact that most individuals "touch" only a small piece of the large, multifaceted, and ever-changing IC enterprise. The perspective of most insiders is limited in other ways (for example, to knowledge of only parts of their own organizations, and limited interaction with and often negative characterizations of other agencies). The longer one serves in the IC, the more experience one has working with and in different components, and the higher one rises in the IC hierarchy, the broader and better one's understanding of the enterprise as a whole. This being the case, at least in my perception of the situation, it is not surprising that most critiques of IC structures, procedures, and performance are based on partial and/or faulty understanding of reality. It follows that most diagnoses of putative problems are at least partially flawed and most measures prescribed to correct them turn out to be ineffective or detrimental.

Notwithstanding the description above of the situation and dismissal of gross characterizations as inaccurate and unhelpful, I will assert with confidence that the IC is neither as good nor as bad as its defenders and critics claim. It is, in my opinion, the best intelligence enterprise in the world, but it is not as good as it could or should be. Components are wildly diverse in size and mission, there is much real and even more apparent duplication, and compartmentation and competing bureaucratic cultures inhibit effective collaboration. The list of actual and imputed maladies is long and consequential, but the even longer list of problems alleged to require the transformative effects of intelligence reform was not the primary driver of demands in 2004 to "fix" the Intelligence Community.

Much has been written about the genesis and evolution of the Intelligence Reform and Terrorism Prevention Act of 2004 (IRTPA), virtually all of which was published long after I had formed the perception and interpretation of events that shaped my approach to implementation.[1] Key factors shaping my understanding and view of the intelligence reform legislation included a judgment that the impetus for reform came primarily from a political need to do something in response to widespread public concerns triggered by the events of 9/11, Congressional ire caused by flawed IC (which largely equated with the Central Intelligence Agency [CIA] assessments of Iraq's weapons of mass destruction), and growing public dismay and disillusionment about the war in Iraq.[2]

The IC certainly had problems, many of which probably could not be addressed satisfactorily without structural, budgetary, and administrative changes, but recognition of real and alleged deficiencies was not the driving force for intelligence reform. Indeed, I considered the IC's internal problems to be only the fourth most important driver and shaper of reform legislation. Those I considered more important were the political imperative to reassure the public that its elected officials had taken steps to prevent another 9/11, the political incentive to redirect public anger about the Iraq war from the misguided decision to overthrow Saddam Hussein to alleged intelligence errors that misled members of the executive and legislative branches, and the political skill of 9/11 Commission members determined to ensure that their findings did not suffer the ignominious fate of virtually all previous studies calling for IC reform.[3]

Rank ordering the factors driving intelligence reform in this way is not intended to minimize the importance of the IC's structural and procedural problems; it is to note that, in my opinion, the impetus for reform and content of the legislation did not originate with a rigorous analysis of IC strengths, weaknesses, missions, and imperatives. The path to intelligence reform began with the 9/11 Commission finding that what happened on that watershed day was the result of multiple failures across many agencies. The commission recommended intelligence reforms, but its report made clear that Intelligence Community deficiencies were part of a much broader problem.[4] Fixing everything was clearly a more ambitious and demanding task than the White House and Congress were willing to undertake in the tense and uncertain post-9/11 environment. Intelligence reform was not the only response, but focusing on the IC offered a "silver bullet" solution that promised to improve the performance of the United States Government as a whole by improving the quality of intelligence support provided to all agencies with roles to play in what was soon called the "war on terror."[5]

Intelligence gaps, failures of imagination, and analytic caution before the events of 9/11 and flawed Intelligence Community judgments about weapons of mass destruction in Iraq certainly warranted serious attention and efforts to improve performance. But even in 2004 it was hard to make a credible case that the United States had gone to war in Iraq because of flawed intelligence.[6] Perhaps I was—and am—overly cynical, but I thought at the time that outrage over IC performance was exaggerated in order to shift blame for an unpopular military adventure from policymakers to intelligence professionals. To the extent that this was the case, it was consistent with the axiom that in Washington anything that is not a policy success is an intelligence failure.

Like many other IC leaders, I bristled at what I considered unfair criticism but hoped that it would open the door to more serious efforts to address Intelligence Community shortcomings and enhance IC performance through means other than the normal Washington solution of throwing more money and more people at the problem. I was hopeful, but not optimistic, at least not until members of the 9/11 Commission embarked on a campaign to ensure that their recommendations did not suffer the fate of so many earlier calls for reform. The efforts of Commission members to make "their" cause an issue in the 2004 election and enlistment of 9/11 victims and victim families to promote intelligence reform were as effective as they were unexpected. I believe that their campaign to put intelligence reform on the national agenda was decisive. It forced the White House to take the Commission's recommendations more seriously and spurred the preparation of numerous Congressional reform proposals in advance of the election. The trifecta of 9/11, ire fueled by the war in Iraq, and the bipartisan efforts of the 9/11 Commission made it possible, if not inevitable, that intelligence reform legislation would be passed and signed by the President.

From Unlikely to Inevitable

The three factors discussed above created an atmosphere that made it imperative for the White House to engage to control the process and/or to demonstrate that it recognized the need to "do something" about the intelligence
problem. By mid-summer, it was becoming increasingly clear that the latest
calls for intelligence reform could not and would not be consigned to a file
drawer and forgotten.[7] Public anxiety fueled by incessant warnings of potentially catastrophic terrorist attacks and growing anger traceable to events in
Iraq and the administration's changing explanation of why it was necessary
to remove Saddam Hussein made it politically imperative to do something.
Under the circumstances, the Intelligence Community was an obvious target
for blame, recrimination, and "reform."[8]

Blinking Red, Michael Allen's history of how outrage, fear, and political
maneuver shaped the most significant intelligence reform legislation since
1947 provides extensive detail on key protagonists, issues, and compromises.
At the time, I knew little about most of the developments he describes, but I
was a participant in some of them and, more important for the purposes of
this book, what I heard, saw, and experienced had a profound impact on the
way I thought about intelligence reform.

The first change in my thinking occurred when I realized that public ire
and political expediency made reform of the Intelligence Community virtually
inevitable. That realization came in early August 2004—approximately one
week after publication of the 9/11 Commission report and recommendations.
Until then I had assumed that "reform" would consist of little more than harsh
criticism of the Intelligence Community in general and CIA in particular, the
replacement of a few senior officials, and firmly stated admonitions to break
down barriers, share information, and fix problems identified by the Senate
Select Committee on Intelligence (SSCI), the 9/11 Commission, and the
Commission on the Intelligence Capabilities of the United States Regarding
Weapons of Mass Destruction (WMD Commission).[9] My agency, the State
Department's Bureau of Intelligence and Research (INR), was unlikely to be
in the crosshairs or significantly affected by whatever cosmetic changes were
mandated. That being the case, I initially had only limited personal or bu-
reaucratic interest in the content of reform proposals.

My assumption and attitude were reinforced, briefly, when I attended
a White House meeting on intelligence reform chaired by Fran Townsend,
the President's Homeland Security Advisor, in late July.[10] The purpose of the

meeting, which was attended by senior officials from most intelligence agencies, was to discuss the 9/11 Commission recommendations. More specifically, it was to inform us that the White House planned to praise most of the recommendations, declare them to be exactly what was needed to correct identified shortcomings, and assert that many or most were already being implemented by the Intelligence Community. During the discussion, we were requested to provide examples to illustrate what was already being done to achieve the goals of the 9/11 Commission recommendations.

I interpreted this exercise to mean that the White House hoped to preclude legislation mandating the recommended—and probably other—reforms by claiming that legislation was unnecessary because the problems were already being addressed within the executive branch. To my knowledge, no one at the meeting characterized this as disingenuous or a sham. We—agencies and officials of the Intelligence Community—had identified essentially the same problems in our own postmortems of events, and individual agencies were already making changes to correct or alleviate problems within their purview. Some of us, acting informally, were beginning to work across agency boundaries to enhance collaboration and other forms of cooperation.[11] We were motivated by chagrin at the shortcomings of the Iraq WMD estimate, awareness that we had to address an increasingly serious morale problem among the vast majority of analysts who had been tarred with the brush of incompetence because of errors made by the small number of people who had worked on that now infamous estimate, and recognition that improving performance was our responsibility. At the time, this seemed to be a low-cost and appropriate response to demands for reform. The President might issue an executive order codifying and mandating changes that we were already implementing, but "reform" would be achieved without major structural changes or negative impact on our ability to provide support to policymakers and military commanders.

If that was the intended course of action, it quickly proved unviable. Within days—it might even have been the next day—we were convened again to begin drafting input for an administration bill to reform the Intelligence Community. My sense of the exercise was that it was in part a genuine effort to "fix" specific problems and enhance IC performance, but that it was also, perhaps primarily, an attempt to limit the scope and disruptive impact of reform legislation. Although I do not recall discussing the scope or purpose with others at the table, I suspect that most shared my concern about the danger that reforms intended to improve IC performance could, in the short term, disrupt and degrade the ability of individual agencies and the Intelligence

Community as a whole to provide the kinds and quality of intelligence support required to address the more salient and more serious threat of transnational terrorism, wage wars in Iraq and Afghanistan, and support all other missions of the national security enterprise. In the event, we paid more attention to minimizing disruptive change than to seizing opportunities for fundamental transformation of the intelligence enterprise.[12]

At the time, that did not strike me as inappropriate. In retrospect, it was probably inevitable, a classic case of short-term responsibilities trumping long-term possibilities reinforced by personal and bureaucratic comfort with continuity and discomfort with change of unknown proportions. What I did find striking was the degree to which discussion and drafting efforts focused on authorities and jurisdictional issues and how little attention was devoted to cultural, bureaucratic, and operational impediments to collaboration. I certainly recognized that the issues addressed were important to other agencies and participants, but the authorities and jurisdictional questions being debated were not very relevant to the Bureau of Intelligence and Research. INR had far more interest in lowering barriers to collaboration. On many of the issues debated, I simply did not share the passion of the most active participants (usually from CIA, DOD, and the FBI) or care which view prevailed. It wasn't my problem or my fight.

Perhaps I should be faulted for my relative disinterest and minimal participation in the effort to craft an administration bill on intelligence reform, but my approach was shaped by both the agenda and the political adage that if you do not want anything, get out of the way. I did not and do not know who set the agenda and determined the focus of the drafting effort, but I was comfortable with the fact that the areas for potential reform that I cared about most (expertise, analytic tradecraft, outreach to non-IC specialists, collaboration, and so on) were largely ignored in these sessions. From my INR perspective, existing practices prevented the IC as a whole from performing as well as it could or should have but allowed INR to operate largely according to its own rules. I was more interested in protecting arrangements that enabled INR to perform well despite its small size and paltry budget than in pushing with uncertain success for reforms to make other agencies and the Intelligence Community better. Had I judged circumstances to be more favorable for serious consideration of issues I did care about, I would have raised them. Since neither the "process" nor other participants raised issues that, depending on how they were resolved, might make it more difficult for INR to perform its core missions, I was content to live with existing arrangements.

In other words, I did not want to initiate a process that I could not control and was unlikely to win.

Although I was more curious spectator than active participant in these White House meetings, listening to the debate reminded me of lessons learned in graduate school that shaped my thinking when I became DDNI for Analysis.[13] More active participants were not fighting over matters that concerned me, but they were fighting over issues important to them. Some of the fights were shaped if not triggered by personal passions and animosities, but most reflected the competing bureaucratic interests of the protagonists and/or vigorous defense of prerogatives judged essential to the performance of assigned missions.[14] Many of the contentious issues remained unresolved even after passage of the intelligence reform legislation and subsequent executive orders. Participating, albeit on the margins, of these fights during the summer of 2004 was entertaining but it also instilled lessons that helped me to avoid at least some feckless undertakings and to understand why my Office of the Director of National Intelligence counterparts had greater difficulty than I did when designing and implementing reforms.

Where I Sat Determined Where I Stood

Washington is in many ways still a company town in which rumors and repetition of putative "inside information" are endemic.[15] By the spring of 2004, assertions and speculation about the findings and recommendations of the soon-to-be-released reports on intelligence (and other) failings related to the attacks on September 11, 2001, and the decision to invade Iraq in 2003 had become impossible to ignore.[16] Everyone anticipated that the reports would be highly critical of the Intelligence Community, and that they would make sweeping recommendations to address identified and imputed shortcomings. However, although there was certainly much that warranted both criticism and reform, I was skeptical—even doubtful—that the reports would actually lead to meaningful changes in the structure, culture, or operating procedures of the Intelligence Community.

Calls and proposals to reform the US intelligence establishment have a very long history and many similarities. Use of the term "intelligence establishment" is deliberate, as it was when the organizational structure that became today's "Intelligence Community" was conceived in 1947. Then, and to a considerable extent thereafter, the agencies and organizations comprised in the intelligence establishment were designed to function as a confederation in which each enjoyed a high degree of autonomy to achieve the specific mission requirements of their parent departments and primary customers.[17] The Central Intelligence Agency was assigned certain overarching responsibilities, but there was little effort or intent to integrate the components or exploit opportunities for synergy.[18]

Perhaps the most consistent attribute of the many reform proposals commissioned prior to 2004 was their minimal impact on the structure and working arrangements of intelligence organizations. Indeed, there is considerable validity to the observation of WMD Commission members that "[t]he Intelligence Community is a closed world, and many insiders admitted to us that *it has an almost perfect record of resisting external recommendations.*"[19] We know now that the reform initiatives of 2004–2005 had a far greater impact on the Intelligence Community than did any of the previous calls for change, but we—or at least I—certainly did not know that would be the case when the 9/11 Commission issued its report and recommendations in July 2004.

Although I expected the reports to be highly critical and demand sweeping changes, experience and knowledge of history persuaded me that what actually happened would fall far short of what was recommended and, more important, what was needed to significantly enhance intelligence support to the national security enterprise. My expectations were low not only because earlier reform efforts had failed, but also because I sensed that the Bush administration had little appetite for disruptive reform of the Intelligence Community while fighting intelligence-dependent wars in Iraq and Afghanistan and pursuing its crusade against international terrorism.

Seeing little prospect for achieving the kinds of reform I thought necessary, I was disinclined to embark on a fruitless quest for desirable but unachievable outcomes. My disinclination to do so was reinforced by concern about the possible consequences of an INR-led campaign to correct deficiencies in the Intelligence Community. INR was and is a first-class intelligence organization, but its ability to perform its missions is inextricably tied to its ability to work effectively with counterparts in other parts of the Intelligence Community. Rightly or wrongly, I judged at the time that if I—and therefore INR—attempted to lead the charge for reform, it would be resented and resisted by IC analysts and agencies whose collaboration was essential to INR's ability to support its customers and missions. This was not simply a hypothetical concern because a portion of the buzz in the spring and summer of 2004 drew critical, even invidious comparisons between INR and other components of the Intelligence Community. Though it was flattering to be praised for having been less wrong on some of the judgments in the 2002

Iraq WMD estimate, I saw great risk and little potential upside to leading the charge in what was likely to be an unsuccessful effort to remake the IC in the image of the Bureau of Intelligence and Research.[20]

The flip side of my decision not to seek a high-profile role as a champion of intelligence reform was increased recognition that it might be necessary to "play defense" in order to ensure that whatever changes were considered or attempted would not disadvantage INR or impede its ability to collaborate with colleagues in the IC, the State Department, and experts based outside the US Government. I soon learned that counterparts in other agencies were pursuing a similar strategy.

One of the benefits of working in the Intelligence Community is that it is seldom necessary—or desirable—to take public positions on controversial issues. I would have been happy to stay as far below the radar as possible while members of Congress and the administration developed positions on intelligence reform, specifically the question of whether to create a cabinet-level director of national intelligence. But my ability to do so was constrained by serendipity. I had been Acting Assistant Secretary of INR for almost nine months when finally scheduled for a confirmation hearing on June 14, 2004.[21] This meant that my open confirmation hearing took place in the midst of heightened commentary on intelligence reform and just a few days prior to the release of the SSCI and 9/11 Commission reports. As I prepared for the hearing, I was certain that I would be asked what I thought about intelligence reform and, for the first time, began to think more systematically about what might be achieved, what must be avoided, and how best to pursue changes that, if achievable, would produce the greatest benefit for the IC and the national security enterprise it supports.

Though prepared for many possible questions, in the event I received only one on intelligence reform. Senator Richard Lugar noted that some of his colleagues had proposed establishing the position of Director of National Intelligence to oversee and integrate the Intelligence Community and asked what I thought of that idea.[22] I responded that I thought the integration and performance of the Intelligence Community could be achieved by strengthening the authority of the Director of Central Intelligence (DCI) and that it was therefore unnecessary to create a new position and bureaucratic support structure. There were no follow-up questions, and I did not volunteer additional observations or justification.[23]

The reason I responded to Senator Lugar's question as I did was a matter of bureaucratic self-interest informed by my judgment that even a DCI with more authority to manage and integrate the Intelligence Community would still have to split his or her time and attention between managing CIA and managing the IC. Under the bureaucratic regime that had existed since 1947, INR and other department-based IC components enjoyed a high degree of autonomy and were essentially accountable to only one boss. For INR, that one boss was the Secretary of State.[24] The DCI did—and could do—little to help the Bureau, but he, or more accurately members of the Community Management Staff acting in the name of the DCI, could and did levy demands on the Bureau and its personnel that forced zero-sum choices between responding to DCI requests and fulfilling obligations to our primary customers.

As the prospective next Assistant Secretary, I judged that a DCI with greater authority would have less inclination and ability to interfere in the affairs of INR than would a Director of National Intelligence with more narrowly focused responsibilities and greater authority to manage all components of the IC. From my perspective, INR functioned better than did many other components of the IC and was more likely to be hurt by efforts to standardize, integrate, and redirect the work of the Intelligence Community than it was to benefit from any new arrangement. This was, of course, a narrow and parochial perspective, but it was also one that I suspect was shared by many senior managers in other IC agencies.

The confirmation hearing was not the only prod to think more systematically about opportunities and risks of intelligence reform. A second, and more important motivator was the nudge I received from Paula Causey, a long-time friend and INR colleague who many times rescued me from my natural proclivity to focus too narrowly on substance at the expense of relationships with colleagues. This time the prod took the form of a question and follow-on statement. "When are you going to tell the Bureau what you think about the criticism of the IC and proposals for intelligence reform? People are confused and concerned about rumors of impending change. They assume you know more than they do and they really want to know what you think is going to happen."

Though I doubted that I actually "knew" much more than anyone else who read the newspapers and heard the endless chatter that served as a principal means of rumor dissemination before social media replaced word of mouth, I recognized at once that I had an obligation to organize my thoughts and share them with my staff. I also recognized the importance of listening to their concerns about and ideas for intelligence reform. Although I still considered it unlikely that Congress and the administration would adopt and implement significant reforms, it seemed prudent to pay more attention to what such reform might achieve and how to shape the reforms and their implementation.

By the winter of 2004, what once seemed unlikely had become unavoidable, or so it seemed. Virtually all action—or at least all action of which I was witting—had shifted to the Congress. What little I learned about deliberations on the Hill involved jurisdictional issues with few significant implications for the State Department. The one important exception to this generalization concerned the status of departmental intelligence units in the prospective new organizational structure. Virtually every bureaucratic player and commentator on intelligence reform recognized the need to improve information sharing and collaboration across administrative boundaries, but there was major disagreement over how best to achieve those objectives. As Secretary Colin Powell and Deputy Secretary Richard Armitage made clear when I was representing the Department at White House meetings on intelligence reform, State would oppose any proposal that jeopardized their ability to "command" their own in-house intelligence unit and ensure timely, tailored intelligence support to diplomacy.[25] Secretary of Defense Donald Rumsfeld took essentially the same position and aggressively pressed his case with key members of Congress.

By the time action on reform legislation had shifted to the Hill, Secretary Powell was comfortable with provisions of the draft legislation that preserved the role and authority of the Secretary of State in selecting and supervising the Assistant Secretary in charge of the Bureau of Intelligence and Research. He endorsed the president's reform proposals and summarized his intelligence requirements as Secretary of State in testimony before the Senate Governmental Affairs Committee on September 13, 2004.[26] His testimony also outlined what he considered to be critical aspects and characteristics of intelligence support to policymakers.[27] I extrapolated from his remarks that senior policymakers in other parts of the national security establishment would have similar needs and concerns.

For a number of reasons, including the refusal of department and agency heads to surrender control of "their" intelligence components and the reluctance of Members and the White House to risk degrading intelligence performance by making sweeping changes with troops on the ground in Afghanistan and Iraq and widespread fear of another terrorist attack, proposals for deep structural change had largely dissipated by late summer. The net result, as I perceived it, was that passage of reform legislation appeared increasingly inevitable but the prospective content of the reforms appeared less problematic and, to the extent it focused on improving tradecraft and reducing barriers to collaboration, more positive.

As summer segued into fall, I became convinced that any variant of the draft intelligence reform legislation approved by the Congress would be devoid of provisions that would threaten or degrade the ability of INR to support its primary customers and missions and that it was no longer necessary to "play defense" to avoid bad outcomes. I thought briefly about shifting to a more active stance of trying to shape process portions of the bill with the potential to improve tradecraft and IC performance. I probably should have been more active in pressing for provisions promoting expertise, facilitating collaboration, and expanding contacts with experts outside the Intelligence Community, but at the time I was pessimistic about achieving meaningful change.

While making the transition from defense of State Department and INR interests to passive but interested observation of developments, I began to pay greater attention to process elements of the proposed legislation, most of which derived from recommendations of the 9/11 Commission and expectations regarding what the WMD Commission would say when its report was issued.[28] Many were of little relevance or interest to me because they did not directly impact INR. I still viewed what was happening through the lenses of my position and responsibilities in the State Department. From that perspective, proposed changes affecting analysis were broadly consistent with existing INR practices and would, in my personal and bureaucratic opinion, be good for the IC and positive for INR. Since it appeared that developments were unfolding in ways positive for INR and I judged that the risks of attempting to make them better outweighed the likelihood of success, watching from the sidelines seemed the best course.

Although I chose to eschew attempts to play a leading role, INR was routinely included in meetings and data calls organized by the Community Management Staff to inform and influence the legislative process. Those participating in these activities wanted guidance but needed and received relatively little from me or others in the INR front office. In this respect, we followed normal procedures that assigned a high degree of authority and responsibility to those attending such meetings. They knew what was most important to the Bureau and were prepared to defend its interests if threatened and to endorse proposed changes consistent with INR's analytic tradecraft and perception of what did and did not work well in the IC as a whole. Given INR's historically outsized and activist posture on analytic issues, participants from other agencies often expected the INR representative to provide input or challenge the ideas tabled by others. Such expectations were seldom disappointed. INR representatives had opinions and were not shy about articulating them. Those attending for INR provided a quick debrief after returning to the Bureau, and I never saw a need to contravene what they had said. In most cases, Bureau participants accustomed to challenging analytic judgments proposed by colleagues in other agencies found themselves in the unusual position of agreeing with most of what was proposed.

Sliding Toward an Offer I Couldn't Refuse

I REMAINED an interested spectator as the legislation was finalized, passed by both houses, and signed by President Bush. There was much speculation—mostly unfounded, I suspect—about the search for someone willing to serve as the first Director of National Intelligence (DNI). Most of the speculation centered on factors that made the job unattractive, including its ambiguous authorities, unresolved questions about how the DNI would fare in bureaucratic wars with the Secretary of Defense and the Director of the Central Intelligence Agency, and hope of some, perhaps many, in the IC that the new organizational structure would fail quickly and allow things to return to pretty much the status quo ante. I have no direct knowledge of the search process, but the choice of career diplomat John Negroponte was fortuitous for the Office of the Director of National Intelligence and career changing for me.

John Negroponte was a five-time ambassador who had headed two of the largest embassies of the United States (Mexico and Iraq). His experience with the Intelligence Community was primarily as a consumer in Washington and leader of multiagency country teams in the embassies he headed. Some depicted his lack of direct experience in the Intelligence Community as disqualifying him for the job, but it also meant that he did not have bureaucratic loyalties or antipathies toward any of the fractious agencies he would oversee. His experience as a diplomat and leader of country teams with more players and competing priorities than the fifteen (soon to be sixteen) IC agencies was arguably more relevant to the task of implementing the Intelligence Reform and Terrorism Prevention Act than his lack of detailed knowledge about specific collection systems and liaison relationships. When he took the helm, the most pressing challenges facing the ODNI were organizational and administrative, not down-in-the-weeds intelligence problems.

I knew Negroponte, but not well. Our professional paths had crossed a number of times, and I regarded his repeated selection for demanding positions as indicative of exceptional ability. Negroponte's acceptance of the job convinced me that standing up the ODNI was a serious undertaking. This judgment was reinforced by the fact that he had already enlisted Pat Kennedy, a State Department administrative officer with an unparalleled ability to conceive and achieve managerial miracles. His immediately previous job had been to stand up (with Negroponte) the new—and huge—US embassy in Bagdad. Kennedy and I had been friends for many years. I was not at all surprised, therefore, when Pat called me almost immediately after Negroponte's confirmation to ask my advice on a number of organizational and staffing questions. I was happy to help because Pat was a friend and long-time colleague, but also because I anticipated working with the new ODNI as Assistant Secretary of INR. As important, I saw this as an opportunity to influence implementation of the analysis-related reforms mandated by the new legislation.

It would be an exaggeration to say that I had thought deeply and systematically about the challenges of standing up a new organization and implementing the demanding changes mandated by the IRTPA legislation and the President's endorsement of most of the WMD Commission recommendations, but I had thought about some of them.[1] Although implementation issues were not discussed in the meetings that I attended while the White House was formulating a response to the 9/11 Commission recommendations and, later, drafting its own intelligence reform bill, I found myself thinking, albeit in an unsystematic way, about how to achieve the objectives of reform and implementation of specific proposals. Doing so was the result of years of managerial experience that had taught me to consider "how" questions before endorsing proposals for change; it was also stimulated and shaped by informal discussions among IC analytic managers.

Long before the Senate Select Committee on Intelligence and the Commission on Intelligence Capabilities of the United States Regarding Weapons of Mass Destruction issued their reports assessing and criticizing the Iraq WMD estimate's many deficiencies, senior analytic managers—and many others in the IC—had begun to dissect the now infamous Iraq weapons of mass destruction National Intelligence Estimate (NIE) and the way in which it was produced.[2] First individually, then informally in pairs and small groups motivated by determination to correct systemic flaws, embarrassment, professional pride, and recognition that we had to rebuild morale and regain the confidence of national security policymakers, we undertook to identify and fix the deficiencies that had caused good analysts to produce a bad estimate.[3]

Our informal investigation of what had gone wrong was an exercise in self-criticism. We may not have been as objective as the large teams that came after us, but we had the advantage of inside knowledge and personal reasons for wanting to ensure that we—and our successors—would not repeat our mistakes. Whether because of shared chagrin or the fact that most of us had been colleagues and friends for many years, our dissections and discussions were both brutally frank and remarkably free of bureaucratic rivalry. More important, we were far more focused on fixing systemic and process flaws than on fixing blame.[4]

A third reason that I was more prepared than I might have been to respond to Kennedy's questions was that I had been forced to think about them by Paula Causey's earlier admonition to tell our INR colleagues what I thought about the reforms that were being bandied about and appeared increasingly likely to be adopted. Thinking about them with a "what might they mean for us" perspective led me to make judgments about whether to embrace or attempt to modify or contain specific proposals, and about how we might implement them in INR. Questions from INR analysts about implications for colleagues in other IC agencies prompted me to give at least preliminary thought to what it might mean for National Intelligence Council (NIC) products and even the *President's Daily Brief* (PDB).

At this point, I had no idea that I would acquire responsibility for the PDB, but I had been stimulated to think about the process by an exchange with my friend and Director of Intelligence (the analytic component of CIA) John Kringen, who visited my INR office in the summer of 2004 to ask what I thought about having INR analysts write for the PDB. I realized that this was a serious question because of prior discussions about what we (IC analytic managers) could do to address problems that we saw as well as or more clearly than did the critics and Commissions who were drafting proposals to fix IC problems. My immediate response was, "No. They were not going to write for a publication that they could not read or even know what else had been said on the subject." That part of our conversation did not go any further, but it prompted me, and I suspect John as well, to begin thinking about the question, "If the PDB were to become a community product, what would be required and how would we do it?" Several months later, that hypothetical question became real and immediate.

Among other questions and requests, Kennedy asked for a list of people that should be considered for senior positions in the Office of the Director of National Intelligence. This led to an interesting and probably inevitable exchange reflecting the fact that the ODNI at that point had only two officials (Negroponte and Principal Deputy DNI and former Director of the National Security Agency Lieutenant General Mike Hayden). It had no structure or organization chart. Kennedy later became Deputy DNI for Management, but at that point he was a member of the transition and startup team. He was collecting names of "good people" with only a dim idea of what they would be asked to do. I responded that it was hard to suggest names without knowing what the candidates were supposed to be "good at." We resolved the dilemma by settling on a list of people that I thought would be good at implementing mandates related to analysis.

I appreciated being asked for names but did not jump at a possible opportunity to nominate myself. I was not looking for a new job; indeed, I was looking forward to working with my good friend and new Secretary of State Condoleezza Rice and finishing my career in government as Assistant Secretary for Intelligence and Research.[5] Because Pat Kennedy was a friend, I took seriously his request for names. That required thinking more seriously than I had previously about the skills needed to implement provisions of the reform legislation and President Bush's directive that pertained to analysis. In other words, before I began to think about people, I attempted to define the job and its requirements. My approach was to consider first what was needed and only then to think about who possessed the requisite knowledge, skills, and experience. I did not think that I was designing a job for myself.

My initial list of requirements included knowledge of and experience in the Intelligence Community, proven leadership and managerial skills, and personal stature. The importance of experience in the Intelligence Community might seem self-evident, but criticism of IC analysis had been so scathing that I weighed the potential costs and benefits of appointing an outsider to "fix" the allegedly broken analytic community.[6] Recruiting a well-known outsider with superb academic credentials would signal to members of Congress, policy officials in the national security enterprise, and critics in the media that the new DNI took seriously his obligation to improve analytic performance. But playing to the external audience would likely have a disastrous effect on morale and self-confidence inside the IC analytic community. Given the already significant morale problems engendered by seemingly incessant disparagement of all IC analysts for the flawed work of the few (including me) who had worked on the Iraq WMD estimate and the separate and relatively small group of analysts who worked on terrorism prior to 9/11, I judged that bringing in an outsider to reassure outsiders would exacerbate retention and recruitment problems in the community.

Morale considerations were probably the most important reason I opted not to recommend recruiting an outside notable. They were not, however, the only ones. The two most important additional factors were my general conviction that expertise is essential to success in any complex undertaking, and the need to move with alacrity. My concept of expertise includes detailed knowledge about the Intelligence Community—the responsibilities and missions of component agencies, the quirks and cultures of groups working on specific issues, and the approaches and interpersonal relationships of key players. There was certainly a great deal that I did not know about IC elements other than INR, but I had years of experience interacting with counterparts at NIC coordination meetings, monthly gatherings of the "IC Deputies Committee," and the then recent informal discussions among analytic managers described above. At the time, I was not thinking in terms of my own suitability for the position, but I had concluded that it would be very difficult to get things done inside the IC without pretty good knowledge of where to go, who to talk to, and how to frame issues in ways that would resonate with IC professionals.

Outsiders can and sometimes do have clear ideas about *what* needs to be done, but knowing *how* to do it is equally important. Early in my career I had worked on technology transfer and export control issues and learned how important and how difficult it is to acquire "know-how," the intangible understanding or *Fingerspitzengefühl* essential for success when undertaking complex tasks. The Intelligence Community and its culture are significantly different from private-sector organizations and other components of the federal government, including other parts of the national security establishment. An outsider was unlikely to have the requisite "feel" for how to accomplish things in the Intelligence Community. People as experienced and clever as those who were my "models" for potential outsiders would know this and surround themselves with insiders who possessed the requisite understanding of the community.[7] But identifying the right people, establishing the requisite rapport, and developing effective ways to work together would take time and doubtless be plagued by startup problems and missteps.

Insiders would also have startup challenges and make mistakes, but my assessment at the time was that it would take outsiders longer to gain traction and demonstrate results because they would have to climb an additional learning curve. It can certainly be argued that insiders would be encumbered by organizational biases and attachment to aspects of IC culture and operating procedures that impeded implementation of precisely the kinds of change needed for sustained improvement. That is certainly a fair point and one that I considered. What tipped the balance in favor of recommending selection of an insider was my judgment that someone with inside knowledge and connections was more likely than an outsider to achieve early successes that would build confidence and momentum. Speed was an important consideration because confidence in the competence of IC analysts had fallen to a dangerous low. If the policymakers and military commanders supported by the IC lacked confidence in the products they received and the IC professionals who produced them, a key pillar of the national security enterprise would crumble.

Rigorous analytic skills and knowledge of the Intelligence Community were necessary but not sufficient to ensure success in the early stages of intelligence reform. In the course of my career in academe and government, I had encountered many brilliant scholars who were terrible managers, many political appointees who hovered above the bureaucracies they "led" but provided little leadership, and many Foreign Service Officers and intelligence analysts promoted on the basis of reporting or analytic skills who had little interest or ability in either leadership or management. In my opinion, the job of implementing reform of analysis required leadership and management skills.[8] Moreover, the assignment was too important to take a chance by appointing someone without proven skills as the head of a large, diverse, and often-querulous enterprise.

Although the importance of leadership and managerial skills may be obvious, I actually backed into this criterion by thinking first about what the first incumbent of the position later designated the Deputy Director of National Intelligence for Analysis (DDNI/A) would have to do. The list of essential tasks included building a leadership team with the specific skills needed to implement each of the mandated and desirable reforms and, collectively, knowledge of all IC components and analytic missions, providing strategic guidance while delegating substantial authority to members of the team, and ensuring that all members of the team understood how their responsibilities fit into an overarching approach or strategy. The person selected would also have to serve as morale officer for a dispirited workforce, public face of the analytic community, source and solicitor of ideas, and referee of last resort for the squabbles that were sure to arise.

The more I pondered these daunting requirements, the more I became convinced that expertise, leadership, and managerial skills alone would be insufficient. Simply being good at all of the skills required would not be good enough; the selectee would have to be seen to be good. I'd learned as a graduate student and reconfirmed repeatedly through my career that perceptions and expectations matter in politics, and doubtless other endeavors as well. The implication I drew from this lesson was that success—and perceptions of success—were more likely if the individual selected was expected to succeed because of personal stature and past performance.[9] Conversely, picking someone without a proven record of accomplishment and positive reputation might doom the individual and the new undertaking to failure.

Everyone has a reputation, and every reputation can be—and is—classified as one of three types: positive, negative, and unknown. Whether fully deserved or not, a positive reputation makes it easier to obtain a hearing and win support, and easier to start with benefit of the doubt. Conversely, anyone with a negative reputation starts in a hole or behind the eight ball. Having acquired no reputation, whether because of youth, newness to the arena, or undistinguished performance, is functionally the same as having a negative reputation because it does not bring benefit-of-the-doubt advantages. The challenges facing the inaugural DDNI/A were going to be formidable enough without compounding them by selecting someone unable to exploit the advantages of personal stature and reputation.

Personal stature was also important for another reason in my calculus because the position itself had no history or status. No one knew what the DDNI/A was, whether it was a meaningful or essentially hollow position, or why beyond the logic of bureaucratic organization charts anyone should support or even listen to the incumbent. In other words, the unproven and untested title would carry little weight, so bureaucratic heft would have to derive primarily from the stature and reputation of the person holding the position. This was sure to be an important factor with respect to the person's ability to recruit good people who would have to leave their current positions and career tracks to join a startup venture.

If I had had more time and greater incentive to think about the requirements of the job, I might have come up with a slightly different set of criteria. In retrospect, however, I still think the considerations I identified at the time were basically the right ones. Laying them out as I have here implies greater coherence than characterized my thinking at the time. This initial iteration of thinking about the job had the narrow purpose of establishing criteria I could use to identify possible candidates for an analysis-related position. But it also served as a helpful starting point a few weeks later when I was asked to become the first DDNI for Analysis. If I had not already thought about what the job would entail, I probably would not have accepted.

I shared some of my thinking about the position with Pat Kennedy and, later, with John Negroponte and Mike Hayden, but I also gave them a short list of names. As you might anticipate from the foregoing, most of those on the list were senior veterans of the Intelligence Community who had earned my respect as leaders, managers, and analysts. Before submitting my suggestions, I conferred with a number of people in and outside the Intelligence Community because doing so struck me as appropriate, even necessary to make an informed choice. That a number of people suggested I put my own name on the list was gratifying, but the amount of thinking I'd done about the job had not yet convinced me that it was something that I wanted to do more than to finish my government service as Assistant Secretary of INR.

I have no idea whether the position was offered to anyone before John Negroponte offered it to me. Before he did so, I had had several general conversations about the standup of the ODNI with Pat Kennedy and a few general inquiries about my own interest in joining the new team. I thought—and stated—that selecting someone from INR to integrate and transform analysis was logical from the perspective of the Bureau's track record and procedural conformity with many of the changes mandated in legislation and recommended by the 9/11 and WMD Commissions, but would likely be resented by the larger agencies and construed as a manifestation of State Department parochialism. Since Negroponte and Kennedy had come out of the Department, I argued that adding a third State Department official to the ODNI leadership team probably was not a good idea.

I have no idea what Pat, John, and Mike did with the lists I provided or who else was asked for names, but a few days into the process Kennedy called to say that Negroponte wanted to talk to me about implementing reforms affecting analysis and to observe that I had not put my own name on either of the lists I had submitted. My response to the latter observation was that I thought putting my name on the list would be presumptuous and that I planned to finish my career in government as Assistant Secretary.

As I recall it, my initial conversation with Negroponte was mostly substantive and focused on what I thought was necessary to improve intelligence analysis and better integrate analytic work across the community. That was followed by a separate conversation with Mike Hayden—a conversation that took place in the snack bar of the Old Executive Office Building because the cramped temporary space allotted to the DNI was too small to have a conversation there without disrupting what Negroponte and the tiny temporary staff were doing. Hayden showed me a hand-drawn "organization chart" with six boxes: the DNI was on top, the Principal Deputy Director of National Intelligence was below him, and four DDNI boxes were on a horizontal line below the DNI and PDDNI. The boxes were labeled collection, analysis, management, and customer outcomes, which was described as having responsibility for the integration of customer requirements. I had worked with Hayden for many years when he was Director of the National Security Agency, and he asked, "What do you think?" My response, in substance if not in actual words, was, "It's a start."

At this point I had a pretty good idea that I was on the short list for the DDNI/A position even though I had done nothing consciously to get there. What I had done, and continued to do in these meetings, was to outline thoughts about the position and the skills needed to succeed. The context for my remarks was John's summary of his thoughts on how to structure the ODNI and what he hoped to achieve. The follow-on conversation with Mike provided more—albeit still not much—detail.

We spent little time talking about Mike's chart and the proposed directorates. In retrospect, that is somewhat surprising because there was considerable buzz if not yet pressure to better integrate collection and analysis. One part of the mantra insisted "analysis must drive collection," an admonition that many interpreted as requiring structural changes that would effectively merge collection and analysis into a single bureaucratic unit within or across agency boundaries.[10] I fully supported the proposition that analysis should drive collection, which I interpreted to mean that since analysts had the most direct contact with policymakers and their requirements, and had the greatest awareness of what was not known about high-salience issues, they were the ones best able to provide guidance to collectors (for example, look for this, do not look for that; look here, do not look there, and so on). For me, and I suspect for Mike Hayden, this was largely a procedural issue, not something to be "fixed" through structural changes.

What we did talk about was the possible content of the "analysis" box—what it would subsume, the tasks it would perform, and the kinds of people and skills needed to implement mandated reforms and improve performance. I regarded the conversation as more brainstorming session than job interview. I continued to think about the challenges of designing and staffing a new organization to accomplish the tasks specified in the reform legislation, the President's directive, and Negroponte's vision as I returned to the State Department, where "in-box demands" precluded more extensive consideration of the challenges discussed at the Old Executive Office Building.

Although I probably should have begun to consider how to respond if I was offered the position, I have no memory of doing so. On the drive home that evening, I returned to consideration of "how" questions triggered by the conversation with Hayden but didn't think about "who" should lead the effort. The next day or perhaps the one after, I received a heads-up phone call from Kennedy telling me that Negroponte was going to call to offer me the job of Deputy DNI for Analysis. I had been in Washington long enough to know that this was a "If you intend to say 'no' tell me and he won't make the call" call and asked Pat whether he thought I should accept. I will not recap our conversation in detail; suffice it to say that we talked about the challenges of a "once in a couple of generations" chance to remake a major component of the federal government as a "how can you not take it" opportunity. The clincher for me was Pat's statement that he had decided to become the DDNI for Management.

The phone call from Negroponte the following day was not a surprise, but I had not given much thought to what I would say after "Thank you for asking." Since I generally spend very little time thinking about hypothetical possibilities, preferring instead to wait until I know that I actually have to make a decision and understand the concrete circumstances at the time, I had not prepared a list of questions, let alone requirements that I thought crucial for success.

I was, of course, flattered to be asked, and confess that I was confident that I could "do" it. Nevertheless, I was not yet ready to jump at the opportunity or even certain that I fully understood what that opportunity was. Participation in the White House sessions and contacts across the IC had sensitized me to the degree of concern, resistance, and defensiveness surrounding every aspect of reform. Whatever it turned out to be, accomplishing it was not going to be easy. I anticipated that some of my senior colleagues and some agencies would protest and resist every proposed change because change is always disruptive and changing anything is tantamount to acknowledging deficiencies in what was done previously. I feared this might be true even though a number of those same colleagues had participated in the informal gatherings in which we sought ways to address acknowledged problems within the existing organizational structure. Undertaking changes ourselves was one thing; having them imposed by a new organization was another matter entirely.

That the job might be difficult was only one, and probably not the most important, reason for my reticence to accept the position. A more important consideration was the opportunity cost of leaving INR, the State Department, and the chance to play a role in Secretary Rice's "kitchen cabinet." In some respects, this involved a choice between being a big fish in a little pond or a little INR fish in the big IC pond, but the role of the State Department in US diplomacy and national security policy is hardly a trivial one. In weighing my options, I had to calculate where I might have the greatest impact. In that calculation, the likely chances of success in the State Department trumped the smaller likelihood of success in a controversial and problematic effort to transform analysis in the Intelligence Community.

As I ran through these mental calculations, it did not take very long before I realized that I was constructing an argument to stay within my comfort zone instead of seizing a unique opportunity to transform and improve the intelligence component of the national security enterprise. The chances of full success (whatever that meant) were slim, but how many people ever get the opportunity to try? The thinking that I had done a few weeks earlier when considering what names to suggest for the position provided a yardstick against which to measure my own suitability for the job as well as a nascent sense of what it would take to succeed. In the end, I concluded that this was an offer and opportunity that I could not refuse. Maybe someone else could do a better job than I, but I was the one being offered the chance to address, if not correct, a host of problems that had bothered me for years. I had to try. I had to take the job.

My wife, Orlene, was the first person I told about my decision. As she has done many times throughout my career, she observed that I was probably crazy but should do this if I really wanted to. Condi Rice was the second one, not only because she was my boss but, more important, because I valued her take on administration views of intelligence reform and owed it to her because leaving would preclude working together in ways that were exciting to me and, I believed, important to her. Her response was quintessentially Condi: This is an important job and you should do it. But I do not want you to leave. Can't you find a way to do both? Also typical of my approach to life and our long friendship, I replied that I would see if that might be possible. The lawyers quickly informed me that it would not be possible. Thank goodness.

Before calling Negroponte to formally accept the position, I placed another call to Pat Kennedy to learn more about the consequences of accepting the job. Some of my questions were bureaucratic (such as what rank would the position have and how would moving to this new organization affect my status in the Senior Executive Service); others were idiosyncratic. For example, I wanted to know if the Deputy DNI for Analysis would be required to have a security detail. Pat replied, "Do you want one?" I said, "No. And if it is mandatory, I won't take the job." After a few seconds he said, "I don't want one either. The deputies will not have security details. Anything else?"[11]

Blank White Board and Ticking Clock

ACCEPTING NEGROPONTE'S INVITATION changed the way I thought about the challenges of intelligence reform. During the preceding months, my thinking had evolved from speculation about what structural and procedural changes might be mandated by Congress and the White House to consideration of how potential changes would affect INR to thoughts about how to organize and staff the Office of the Director of National Intelligence stimulated by Pat Kennedy's request for ideas. The further transformation that occurred when I began to consider the implications of having accepted responsibility for implementing reforms affecting all facets of intelligence analysis might not have been as dramatic as Mark Twain's observation that nothing so concentrates the mind as the prospect of being hung, but it was immediate. From that point on, every thought about what might be necessary or desirable was inextricably linked to considerations about how to achieve mandated and self-defined objectives.

The task of translating vague ideas about what needed to be done, how to accomplish specific goals, and what type of people I would need to help me was given greater urgency the day after I accepted the position when I returned to the Old Executive Office Building for the first meeting with my new boss and, more important, the first concrete discussion of tasks and priorities. This was not an abstract conversation about types of experience and people suitable to lead the new analysis directorate. To the contrary, it very quickly homed in on the disparate set of mandated reforms and continuing activities (and people) transferred to the ODNI by the reform legislation. When thinking about qualifications for prospective candidates and the implications of reform for INR, I had focused almost exclusively on mandated reforms, but this conversation forced me to think about specific and immediate challenges involving ongoing activities.

Arguably the most important of the transferred tasks was responsibility for the *President's Daily Brief.* I understood that the reform legislation had transferred responsibility for the PDB from CIA to the Director of National Intelligence, but I had not even considered the possibility that it would be included in the portfolio of responsibilities assigned to the DDNI/A, and certainly had not given any thought to how I would handle that responsibility. That changed during the conversation with Negroponte when he said, "The PDB is yours." I accepted that, and we quickly moved on to other topics. Reflecting on this conversation fifteen years later, I realize that it will seem strange to some readers that we did not spend more time discussing what many considered the Intelligence Community's most important product.

The reason, I believe, is captured by the sentence quoted above. John Negroponte is a superb manager who has led many large multifaceted organizations.[1] When he said, "The PDB is yours," that is exactly what he meant. He would retain ultimate responsibility, but he was delegating day-to-day responsibility to me. That is the way I heard him, and that is the way we interacted on this and the many other tasks assigned to my portfolio. I understood that I could go to him if I had a problem I could not solve, and that I needed to ensure that he knew generally what I was doing. But he was not going to micromanage. I had enormous leeway and delegated authority in addition to responsibility for managing that part of my account. Though a bit daunting, I welcomed this because it conformed to my own sense of how government should work and underscored the need to build a staff of my own to whom I could delegate responsibility for specific tasks. To further emphasize the need to delegate, Negroponte returned to the subject of the PDB near the end of this conversation when he said, "You are responsible for the PDB. But you cannot spend much time on that." My response was something like, "I've got it, boss," meaning both that I understood that he would hold me accountable for the quality and utility of the PDB, and that he expected me to spend more of my own time on other tasks in my portfolio. I welcomed this implicit clarification of his priorities with respect to my responsibilities.

The topic on which we spent the most time in this conversation was the National Intelligence Council. The IRTPA had transferred the NIC from the Director of Central Intelligence to the DNI. Like the PDB, the NIC had continuing responsibilities and could not be "taken down for repairs" as part of the transition to DNI leadership. Fortunately, also like the PDB, the NIC had many superb people and well-established relationships and responsibilities and could function quite well with limited strategic guidance. Negroponte told me that he planned to offer the position of the NIC Chair to an experienced and well-regarded academic. I knew of but did not personally know the individual he had in mind, but John was not seeking my approval of his choice. The NIC has often been headed by outside luminaries, and I considered that a strength, not a problem and I said so. Negroponte's response was, "Good. The chairman of the NIC will report to you."

The remainder of the conversation was devoted, in very general terms, to other responsibilities in my account, to the timing of my move from State to the ODNI, and to assembling a staff to oversee the disparate functions assigned to the analysis directorate. My key take-aways from the meeting were that I would have considerable leeway to decide all matters within my assigned purview, that Pat Kennedy's transition team had assembled lists of people interested in working for the ODNI, and that I needed to get started. The need for speed was to become a recurring leitmotif. The meeting ended with a question from John. After summarizing my principal responsibilities, he asked, "What are you going to do?" My response was, "I'll get back to you in a few days."

As I walked back to the State Department, I realized that our conversation had left me staring at a metaphorical white board with a long list of largely unprioritized tasks and an organization chart consisting of one box (the DDNI/A) and one appointee (me). This realization was sobering and more than a little intimidating. My first reaction was to think, "What have I done?" and to facetiously question my sanity. Before I reached my office, I had begun to tell myself "I can do this" with greater confidence than was warranted because at this point I had only the dimmest notion how to do it.

Many years in Washington had taught me that when Congress passes legislation, Members think a problem has been solved and that implementation is largely a mechanical process requiring little more than diligent execution. They are not the only ones inside—and outside—the Beltway who act as if the challenges of implementation are mere administrative "details" that bureaucrats can resolve quickly unless they are recalcitrant or incompetent.

That, unfortunately, is seldom the case.[2] Working out the details—defining and prioritizing tasks, identifying people with the skills and personalities to lead and manage those tasks, devising structures and procedures suitable to the tasks and the people involved, and obtaining buy-in and compliance from multiple constituencies—is not a trivial exercise. In the case of the ODNI, such standard difficulties of implementation—the devils in the details—were compounded by ambiguities about authorities and other matters in the legislation and the need to perform all "old" missions of the Intelligence Community while building entirely new institutions and procedures. For me, as for everyone else on the team entrusted to stand up the ODNI and implement mandated reforms, the number one question was, "Where—and how—do we start?"

I was mulling that question (while still serving in my "day job" as assistant secretary and working on transition arrangements for INR) when John Negroponte asked me to double-hat as Chair of the NIC. I agreed without hesitation. I do not know why he changed his mind about appointing an outsider but guessed that his original choice had declined or asked for a long transition. Adding the NIC to my portfolio would ensure early implementation of high-profile mandated reforms and facilitate the transfer of responsibility for high-level briefings from CIA to the ODNI (see further on). Some of my friends told me I was crazy to add yet another full-time job to my already unwieldy portfolio (by my count I had already taken on responsibilities previously shared by three senior officials, plus the new responsibilities of intelligence reform). Others worried that splitting my time between NIC and DDNI/A responsibilities would be detrimental to both. Such concerns were not unreasonable, and I might have said the same thing a few weeks or even days before I was asked to double-hat. What changed my mind was the thinking about potential sources of leverage and how to implement reforms that I had done since accepting the DDNI/A position.

I will have more to say on this, but the point I want to make here is that although the reform legislation gave the DNI greater authority than was ever given to the DCI, and the DNI had delegated a portion of that authority to me, my new position had no history, unproven bureaucratic clout, and many "enemies" with a vested interest in limiting its success.[3] Precisely the opposite was true of the Chair of the NIC. I readily accepted the new title because I thought I could leverage that position to achieve DDNI/A objectives. I was less concerned than some about the possibly detrimental impact of double-hatting on the performance of the NIC because I had great confidence in the

institutional capabilities and resilience of the NIC, and because I was prepared
to delegate considerable day-to-day responsibility to a deputy.[4]

Developing a Game Plan

During the nineteen years prior to becoming DDNI/A, I had been promoted
into a series of established United States Government (USG) positions with
existing staff, structures, and routinized procedures. In all cases, I had the
opportunity to observe and interact with my predecessors and was able to
ease into the new position without disrupting routines or having to make
immediate changes. The situation I faced in the spring of 2005 was very
different. My position was new, and it was embedded in an entirely new organization. I had legacy institutions and staffs (the PDB and the NIC), but
I also had a small number of legacy employees without clear responsibilities
(for example, those previously assigned to the Assistant Director of Central
Intelligence for Analysis and Production), and a long list of new tasks (mandated and desirable reforms) lacking both structures and staff. I obviously
needed deputies and other key staff to whom I could delegate responsibility
for developing and implementing changes that would improve performance
without jeopardizing the ability of the Intelligence Community as a whole
or the PDB and NIC in particular to sustain the high levels of support they
provided to national security decision makers. But to recruit good people, I
had to have a reasonably clear vision of what I would ask them to do, which
meant that I needed to devise at least a rough and ready organization chart
for the directorate. In part, it was a classic chicken-and-egg problem; I needed
structure in order to recruit people with the right skills for that structure
but, since much of what we were enjoined to do was inchoate, I needed
creative people to design the structures needed to improve and transform
the analytic enterprise.

    If time had not been a factor, it would have been possible to devise alterna-
tive ways to tackle these challenges and to test-drive them before making final
decisions. But time was not just a factor, it was a critical factor. It is not too
much of an exaggeration to say that Congress thought it had "fixed" urgent
problems in the national security enterprise by passing legislation to fix the
Intelligence Community. The legislation had been passed and signed in December 2004, but six months later, the ODNI was still a paper organization
with few people, no building or computer systems, no structural changes to
the IC or new regulations to integrate and reduce duplication among agencies,
and no detectable improvement in intelligence support to policymakers. That

it had taken the President two months to nominate and the Senate another two months to confirm the first DNI was glossed over by those demanding immediate results.[5]

I decided to deal with the chicken-and-egg problem by dividing my key tasks into preliminary bins or categories. One bin was for legacy institutions and responsibilities, specifically the PDB and the NIC. Each had been running largely on autopilot since the previous December, but most of the mandated changes could be deferred. What could not be deferred was the selection of a deputy accountable to me who could provide day-to-day leadership. As far as I was concerned, this was, at least initially, largely a matter of optics. Congress had mandated the transfer of these institutions from the DCI to the DNI to correct what it (and the Commissions) regarded as structure-based problems that gave CIA disproportionate—and largely unchecked—influence at the White House and in the policy community more generally. Some merely wanted to fix these problems; others wanted to punish the CIA. I was interested in performance, not punishment, but I considered it imperative to demonstrate that both of these key IC components were "under new management." In this as in other respects, symbolism was as important as substance and doing "something" was more important than what we decided to do.

Because I did not yet have a clear—or even a dim—understanding of the PDB process and, conversely, because I was confident that the NIC did not require immediate or fundamental changes, I decided to satisfy the demand for immediate action by engaging in a bit of Kabuki. Rather than making immediate and ill-considered structural or procedural changes, I announced with more fanfare than reality that the PDB was now a community product to which analysts from all IC agencies could contribute, and that I had exercised the DNI's prerogative to appoint the people who now headed the PDB and the NIC. In fact, as will be discussed further on, I retained the same CIA officer as head of the PDB and exaggerated the significance of the DDNI/A's role in selecting and supervising the work of the NIC by downplaying the fact that as NIC Chair I would be reporting to myself. The important point here is not that I pulled a fast one or got away with sleight of hand, but that doing "something" quickly bought relief from pressures to make major changes and bought time to consider, test, and secure buy-in for more significant moves.

Despite my rhetorical emphasis on transforming the PDB into a community product, at this stage I judged that it would be unwise and practically impossible to extricate the PDB from CIA structures in which it was embedded. We might do so eventually, but I was not going to risk breaking a process that worked and on which the President and other top national security officials depended. In other words, I opted for changing the sign on the door and deferring more substantive changes to a later date.[6]

The second category or bin of activities was for tasks directly related to analytic integrity and standards, many of which were enumerated in the IRTPA legislation and/or in the list of seventy WMD Commission recommendations accepted by the President on June 29, 2005.[7] What we had to do—the mandated reforms—was pretty straightforward, and I did not anticipate major opposition because most of the requirements, as I interpreted them, were essentially refinements of what we were already doing, were supposed to be doing, or should have been doing. Indeed, I saw that as a potential problem because individuals and agencies were likely to want to check the box without serious effort to determine what could and should be done better. But it was also easy to see that more could be done to determine which agencies were strong or weak on which topics, whether and why there was duplication of effort, how to take better advantage of distributed expertise and opportunities for collaboration and divisions of labor, and so forth.

At this point, I certainly did not yet know exactly what I wanted to achieve (beyond implementing the mandated reforms) or how to perform the diagnostic and missionary work required to accomplish the larger goals I was beginning to envision. It was also clear that we—the analysis directorate—needed much more information about the responsibilities and capabilities of each agency than then existed in any centralized repository. The paucity of information was in part a function of the distributed character of the Intelligence Community, but it was also a fact that agencies and individuals had greater incentives to hide than to reveal capabilities to other IC components. Components that had linguistic, technical, area studies, or other strengths in particular fields were wary of revealing those strengths because doing so might result in efforts to poach analysts for temporary or permanent assignments, or to impose additional work on units and people with the greatest expertise. If we were to make real and lasting progress toward greater efficiency, synergy, and collaboration, we had to address these problems. How was still to be determined.

Although it was clear that however we decided to implement mandated reforms in the context of a broader effort to transform the way analysis was done in the Intelligence Community the effort would have many interconnected and interdependent parts, it was not at all clear to me how to organize our efforts or what skills would be required to lead the effort. At a minimum, we would need administrative, pedagogic, technical, and hortatory skills organized as a team effort. Some of the component tasks, I judged, could best or only be achieved by people with intimate knowledge of the Intelligence Community. But the more I thought about the mandated reforms and training dimensions of the task, the more strongly I felt that it was critical to convince external critics and observers that "we got it" with respect to improving analysis if we were to garner the time and latitude needed to experiment and to implement transformational changes. There would have to be trade-offs. Naming an outsider to lead the implementation of mandated reforms would demonstrate seriousness of purpose, but at the cost of offending and possibly engendering resistance from analysts who didn't think they or the IC needed external assistance.

Optics and trade-offs aside, however, I realized that we had the first real opportunity in fifty years to transform rather than merely tinker with the way the Intelligence Community conducts analysis. I did not want to squander that opportunity and rather quickly concluded that I wanted an outsider with outstanding credentials for rigorous analytic tradecraft not only to appease external critics but, more important, to really push the Intelligence Community to adopt transformational behaviors. But the range of skill sets required and magnitude of what I was beginning to think of as a transformational agenda made it imperative to subdivide the overall undertaking into discrete but interconnected parts. What those subdivisions would entail and what type of person should head each part of the overall effort remained undetermined until I began to identify specific people that I wanted on the team.

After musing about how I would organize my directorate to perform the specific tasks in my portfolio, I began to consider ways to address two additional requirements that derived from the existing structure of the IC and the emerging structure of the ODNI. With regard to the former, it struck me during my final week in INR that I would be dealing with thousands of people in uniform with cultures and operating norms very different from those of civil service and Foreign Service analysts in the State Department. Two decades of working in a civilian agency had given me a reasonably good understanding of certain types of bureaucratic organizations and personnel systems, but more than three decades had elapsed since I was a junior enlisted man in the US Army.[8] If I was to succeed in this new venture, I needed to be able to understand and communicate with the people who perform analytic work in military-affiliated intelligence components.

I also needed to be able to connect with the world of law enforcement. The reform legislation had mandated a "national" effort to protect our country and our people that lowered the wall between intelligence and law enforcement and made Homeland Security, Coast Guard, FBI, and police forces at all levels part of "my" analytic universe.[9] The number and diversity of intelligence and analytic components had expanded far beyond the foreign intelligence community and the fifteen (soon to become sixteen) agencies subsumed under the ODNI. This created a wide spectrum of new challenges, from helping the FBI stand up a new analytic component to integrating the information and analytic efforts of the Homeland Security Department, the Drug Enforcement Agency, and some eighteen thousand state, local, and tribal police forces. I clearly needed people who understood and could connect to this component of national intelligence.

A few moments of cogitation persuaded me that I would not and should not want to be responsible for the "big" integration of intelligence and law enforcement, only the analytic part. But someone or some component of the ODNI would have to be responsible for the myriad challenges of linking intelligence and law enforcement capabilities. That line of thinking took me to the crude organization chart that Mike Hayden had shown me. I decided, not entirely accurately, that this must be one of the tasks of the otherwise inchoate "customer support" directorate. After experiencing a welcome feeling of relief that this was not in my portfolio, I realized that the partial overlap of responsibilities between analysis and customer support was replicated in the other directorates as well. For example, development of training programs for analysts overlapped with the responsibilities of the management directorate, and if analysis was to drive collection, I needed to devise mechanisms in coordination with the collection directorate to make that happen. Again, how to do so was yet to be determined.

As I write these paragraphs, I realize that they depict my thought process as more orderly than it was. In real time, thoughts, insights, possibilities, and potential problems tumbled over one another, and each "solution" triggered new questions. But by the time I moved administratively from State to the ODNI and physically from INR to the NIC office suite at CIA, I had formulated a first approximation plan for the analysis directorate.[10] That plan envisioned separate divisions for the PDB and NIC, a still-to-be-refined division to manage interaction with military and law enforcement personnel and components, and a still-to-be-determined number of divisions responsible for analytic tradecraft, analytic transformation, mapping and integrating analytic responsibilities and capabilities, and coordination between analysis and collection. Even before my ideas had crystallized to the point summarized here, however, I had begun to search for members of the team needed to execute the still-evolving tasks.

Building a Team and Building Support

MANDATES AND IDEAS ARE IMPORTANT, but people are more important to the success of any venture, or so I believed before recruiting members of the DDNI/A team and believe even more strongly after working with that team for four years. I knew instinctively and from experience that my ability to achieve the goals enumerated in the reform legislation and those I wanted to achieve in addition to what had been mandated would depend heavily on the abilities, personalities, and commitment of the people I selected (and persuaded) to help me. This confronted me with yet another "chicken and egg" dilemma. In order to recruit people with the skills required for collective success, I had to have at least a rudimentary notion of what I wanted them to do and how they would fit into a broader organizational structure and strategy for analytic reform. But I did not yet have an organization chart or detailed strategy with clearly identified roles and responsibilities. I needed good people to help develop the strategy and define the missions and responsibilities of key players, but I needed at least a tentative plan in order to identify requisite skills and induce good people to join me in an inherently uncertain, and in that sense risky, undertaking.

When I accepted John Negroponte's invitation to become his deputy for analysis, I understood (albeit imperfectly) that I was about to join a completely new and unformed organization. The directorate for analysis at this point consisted entirely of a box labeled "Director" and the two legacy institutions, the *President's Daily Brief* and the National Intelligence Council, that would henceforth report to me. Everything else was yet to be determined. This was the first time in my government career that I was required to build and staff an organization from the ground up. Although I had held a number of senior positions, in each case I had moved into a well-defined job with predecessors and personnel who could educate me on my new responsibilities and standard operating procedures, and provide a safety net to prevent me from making serious errors or overlooking critical tasks. This time there were many inside and outside the Intelligence Community who were eager to offer advice, some who wanted the Office of the Director of National Intelligence experiment to fail, and none who had actually performed the tasks I had agreed to undertake.

The character, caliber, expertise, and ideas of the people I selected for my senior staff would shape both the content and the outcome of the changes we undertook. However, to know what types of expertise I needed to recruit, I had to make at least tentative decisions on structural and organizational issues. More by serendipity than design, I dealt with the chicken-and-egg dilemma through an incremental process in which I talked to potential candidates with only a rough idea of what I was seeking or how I would use them. Explaining what I had in mind, in broad terms, and listening to their questions and comments helped clarify what I wanted to achieve and my initially inchoate thoughts on how to structure the directorate.

One of the questions I had considered briefly before embarking on the task of recruiting deputies and other senior staff was how to strike a balance between recruiting "really good people" with complementary skills and experience, regardless of individual quirks or foibles, and looking for "plays well with others" traits that would facilitate both team-building and interaction with counterparts in the ODNI and constituents across the community. Resolving this issue was relatively easy because I have a strong bias for competence and a high tolerance for quirky behavior, and recognized that it was my responsibility to forge and lead the ODDNI/A team. I decided to place the balance point far toward the "good people" end of the spectrum. De facto, my approach was to recruit "best available athletes" rather than "best players for specific positions." I say de facto because my original inclination was to move from structure to people. My approach changed as I began to explain how I defined the mission of the ODDNI/A to the people who had been recommended to me, volunteered to join my team, or were on my own preliminary list of potential colleagues. Those early discussions made it clear to me that it would be better to build

the new organization collaboratively and incrementally than to attempt
to forge a comprehensive strategy with detailed organization charts before
recruiting people.[1]

Although I did not yet know exactly how the PDB and NIC would
fit into the ODDNI/A organization chart or how the people who headed
them would fit into my leadership team, I was certain that the perceived
success or failure of both would be critical to assessments of the ODNI and
my own performance. Seen by very few people, all of whom were senior
policymakers, the PDB was widely considered to be the Intelligence Community's most important analytic product. "Getting it right" for the President was an obvious but high-bar requirement. To meet that requirement,
the publication and the process subsumed under the PDB rubric had to be
useful to and valued by the President. It was—and must be—tailored to
the needs and concerns of the President. When I assumed responsibility for
this process, President Bush had been in office for four years and the extant
version of the PDB had evolved in response to his changing requirements
and guidance. It was, in a very real sense, "his" PDB. Understanding that
constrained my ability to "reinvent" the way information was presented to
"Customer Number One."[2]

Although the PDB was often described as the IC's "flagship" analytic
product, the same terminology was also used for National Intelligence Estimates (NIEs) and other NIC products. Estimates had long been considered
important, but their imputed significance was magnified—even reified—by
the critique of IC performance and Congressional rhetoric centered on the
shortcomings of the flawed 2002 NIE on Iraq's weapons of mass destruction.[3] Like the PDB, NIC products were (and are) intrinsically important,
but they had also become a high-profile indicator of IC analytic capabilities.
To a significant degree, the IRTPA-mandated reforms were keyed to identified and perceived shortcomings in the much-studied Iraq weapons of mass
destruction estimate.[4] This meant, or so I judged, that executive branch customers, Congressional oversight committees, and the President's Intelligence
Advisory Board would use NIC products as litmus test indicators of whether
IC analytic performance had improved. Like the PDB, the NIC could not be
taken down for maintenance or reengineering. Any changes—reforms—had
to be made while meeting escalating demands for "community judgments"
on issues ranging from political and economic developments in Iraq and Afghanistan to the danger of homegrown terrorists to child soldiers in Africa
and drug trafficking from South America.

In the case of both the PDB and NIC, I recognized—or, more accurately, I judged—that I had to make changes quickly in order to deflect criticism and "help" from oversight bodies and attentive others. But I had to do so in a way that did not imperil the ability of either component to meet the continuing and critically important needs of its primary customers. A CIA colleague aptly compared the challenge to that of changing the wings on a 737 loaded with passengers and flying at thirty-thousand feet. To meet that challenge, I decided that I needed to recruit people with long experience and deep understanding of PDB and NIC functions and procedures. I recognized that recruiting such people might increase the likelihood that the people I selected would be defensive about existing procedures and reluctant to implement mandated and other reforms, but that risk seemed more than offset by the need to avoid "failure" resulting from inadequate understanding of how and why extant procedures were utilized.

The *President's Daily Brief*

Almost as soon as I began to think about the structure of my directorate, I decided that the PDB and NIC should each have the status of a division. These and other head-of-division positions ultimately were assigned the title of Assistant Deputy Director of National Intelligence for Analysis(ADDNI). Steve Kaplan, the career CIA officer who headed the legacy PDB team, assured me that he was willing to stay on until I had selected a replacement. I was very grateful for this assurance because it relieved pressure to appoint someone else to head a complex and extremely important activity about which I knew almost nothing because the PDB had always been an entirely CIA undertaking.[5] I interpreted his assurance as meaning that he did not want to remain in the position under the new structure but would continue until I had identified a replacement. At my request, he provided a list of potential successors. I also solicited names from other colleagues at CIA.

Interviewing candidates reinforced my conviction that it would be imprudent to risk disruption by going outside the apprenticeship process used by CIA to prepare people for PDB positions. I was still mulling the criteria I should use to choose from among those I had interviewed when I received a call from Kaplan in which he said, "I hope you realize that I really want this job." I explained that I had interpreted his earlier comments as meaning exactly the opposite and was delighted to learn of his willingness to stay on because I had been very impressed by what I had observed during my first week on the job. Steve became my first ADDNI for the PDB. We construed his reassignment from CIA to the ODNI as meeting the requirement to transfer that activity to the DNI.[6]

As I thought about "what to do about the PDB," I concluded that I had to balance two conflicting mandates and expectations. One was to address the high-profile demand to "fix" the PDB by improving the analytic tradecraft undergirding the articles it contained (part of the general mandate and rationale of intelligence reform) and to "make it a community product" that diminished CIA's hitherto near-monopoly ability to convey analytical judgments to the senior-most national security officials without having to acknowledge the existence of alternative assessments. The other mandate was to recognize that the PDB (as both product and process) had been shaped by President Bush's desires, demands, and evolving requirements. By the time I inherited responsibility for "his" PDB, the President had been "Customer Number One" for four years. Whatever else one thought about the PDB, it was tailored to his needs and expectations. He knew and had conveyed what he wanted.

Most of the demands and exhortations to make it into something different had been articulated by people who had never read a PDB, attended a briefing in which its contents were discussed, or shared the learning experiences and responsibilities of a President who had been on the job for more than one term. I was hesitant to depart very far from what the President said that he wanted and disinclined to accept guidance from people who knew even less about the PDB than I did. When thinking about how to move forward, I decided to interpret the mandate to make the PDB a community product to mean more than including articles written by analysts from outside CIA. That could be a long-range goal; in the near-term I could—and decided that I would—ensure that items destined for the PDB were reviewed by appropriate senior analysts in other agencies and that significant analytical differences were flagged to senior leaders as soon as they were identified.

The need to balance these demands and expectations suggested, and in my mind dictated, a three-part strategy. The most important part of the strategy was to maintain the type of coverage (range and mix of issues, depth and focus of analysis, and so on) that President Bush told us he wanted. Doing so did not amount to pandering or ducking our responsibility to "speak truth to power," as a few people maintained. Common sense and a few conversations confirmed the President's demand to receive bad news as well as good and to present our analysis as objectively as possible. His interests, needs, and preferences with respect to how intelligence was presented had evolved over time and the PDB reflected his preferences. Maintaining as much continuity as possible seemed to me both prudent and necessary.

The second part of the strategy was to adopt a "loud gongs and cymbals" approach to call attention to the "under new management" transfer of responsibility from the DCI to the DNI, and transformation of the PDB into a product reflecting and containing input from "all" components of the Intelligence Community. How we did this will be discussed further on. The point I want to make here is that while emphasizing (and maintaining) presentational continuity to those who received and relied on the PDB, I stressed—and overstated—the immediate significance of organizational and procedural changes that initially were more symbolic than real but acquired greater efficacy and importance over time.

The third part of the strategy focused on analytic tradecraft and had both instrumental and longer-term objectives. As is described more extensively in the chapter on analytic tradecraft, I decided to use my PDB authority to mandate immediate changes in the way analytic differences were identified and conveyed to senior officials, and in that sense to drive analytic transformation. These were important changes, and I included them in my "gongs and cymbals" presentations to external audiences and to the Intelligence Community. But I also took a longer-term perspective that assumed the quality and utility of the PDB would be enhanced as the overall quality of IC tradecraft and products improved. In other words, a key part of my strategy to improve the PDB was to improve the quality of analytic work in all IC components.

Characterizing the considerations noted above as elements of a strategy overstates the coherence of my thinking as I began the search for a deputy to oversee production and delivery (via a team of briefers) of the PDB. An obvious (to me) way to ensure the continuity required to meet the President's expectations was to retain the PDB team that was on the job on the day of transition from CIA to the ODNI but, as noted above, I had misinterpreted Steve Kaplan's statement of willingness to stay on temporarily as meaning that he did not want to be part of the new order. By the time he corrected my misinterpretation, the thinking summarized above had become more coherent. Accepting his offer to stay on would enable me to reassure PDB readers that the ODNI would maintain practices they had helped shape. As important, it reduced my concern that overseeing the PDB might demand so much of my own time that I could not tend to other high-priority tasks, and that unsuccessful management of the PDB transition would discredit the ODNI and fuel already-existing efforts to undermine the new structure that few in the IC had wanted.

Kaplan's agreement to stay on also relieved my concern that problems in the PDB transition would discredit me and degrade my ability to achieve other parts of my reform agenda. I hoped to leverage the PDB to enhance collaboration, demonstrate and capitalize on better tradecraft, and gain credibility to push contentious reforms. Being perceived to have screwed up one of the IC's flagship products would have had the opposite impact.

A second cluster of reasons for welcoming Kaplan's willingness to remain as my deputy for the PDB centered on his passion for the product and consummate professionalism. Despite warnings about the hypothetical possibility of sabotage, I had absolutely no concern that loyalty to CIA would tempt Steve to discredit the ODNI by countenancing actions that would degrade the PDB in the eyes of the President or other senior recipients. I viewed him as personally vested in the PDB and regarded this as ensuring against the very remote possibility of sabotage intended to reopen the decision to transfer the PDB to the ODNI. Although he and I never discussed the matter, I am confident that he shared my conviction that the PDB was far too important to the national security enterprise to allow it to be used as an instrument of bureaucratic warfare. Moreover, if the President or other senior recipients perceived the PDB to have become less useful, it would have severely undermined my efforts to restore confidence in Intelligence Community analysts and the viability of the ODNI. We had to get this one right, and that meant precluding any chance of screw-up. Concerns and warnings about whether CIA in general and Kaplan in particular would continue to give full support to the PDB proved utterly groundless. Both Steve and Director of Intelligence John Kringen did everything possible to ensure a smooth transition and continued support.

The final reason I was delighted to retain Steve was more subjective; I liked him and respected the breadth of his experience and expertise. His multiple assignments to the PDB staff had given him a difficult-to-equal ability to assess analytic products on all countries and issues. We had not worked together previously, and a few people complained that he was something of a curmudgeon with a difficult "bedside manner," but his positives far outweighed any negatives and my assessment was quickly vindicated by his performance as a team player.

As I reflect on the decision to retain Kaplan as majordomo of the PDB, I cannot remember whether we ever discussed the title he would have or his place in the still nascent structure of the ODDNI/A. I doubt that we did. I was certainly thinking about structure and filling out an organization chart, but the only conversations I recall about his role in the emerging organization focused on substance and how to manage the *President's Daily Brief.*

The National Intelligence Council

The National Intelligence Council involves more people and activities than the PDB, but changing accountability was accomplished in essentially the same way. The formal transfer of accountability was accomplished by naming me chairman, but the amount of time I could devote to the NIC was limited. As with the PDB, I—and, more important, the ODNI and entire national security establishment—needed a deputy to provide immediate guidance and oversight. Fortunately, I did not have to look far. David Gordon, who was acting chairman at the time of my appointment, was a NIC veteran who had also worked in academe, on the Hill, and in the NGO community. He was exactly the type of person I wanted for the job and, fortunately for me, he was already there and willing to stay on as my first ADDNI for the NIC.

My calculation with respect to the National Intelligence Council was different from that of the PDB. The 2002 National Intelligence Estimate on Iraq, a NIC product, had become the poster child for much that was wrong with intelligence analysis and the illustrative case used to justify many mandated tradecraft and procedural reforms.[7] Moving the NIC from the DCI to the DNI and my second-hat appointment as chairman served the symbolic purpose of establishing that the IC's premier analytic component was now under new management. I nevertheless felt compelled to think about the advantages and risks of replacing and retaining incumbent National Intelligence Officers (NIOs). I quickly dismissed the possibility of a wholesale housecleaning because whatever benefits doing so might have had as a demonstration of ODNI resolve to fix analysis would be more than offset by damage to morale and the costs of disrupting a very important part of the analytic enterprise. Moreover, I knew that such a move would be completely unwarranted and seen as such by analysts across the community.

For starters, I was guiltier of the sins manifest in the Iraq WMD estimate than were most of the NIOs. INR had dissented on some of the key findings but had signed on to most of them, and I was the one at the table for INR when the National Foreign Intelligence Board (later renamed the National Intelligence Board) approved the estimate. It would have been hypocritical to fire others for sins they had not committed. More important, I was very uncomfortable with the idea that analysts should be "held accountable" for their judgments and punished in some way for being wrong. There is an important difference between getting the wrong answer and using sloppy tradecraft to arrive at a judgment, regardless of whether the judgment proves to be correct or incorrect. Intelligence analysis is an uncertain business; officials turn to the Intelligence Community for help when information is scant, the developments in question are potentially consequential, and time is of the essence. I believed strongly that we could and must improve analytic rigor and the quality—by which I mean utility—of IC analytic products, but I also believed strongly that it would defeat the purpose of intelligence analysis to drive analysts and the process toward only "safe" judgments.

My concern was about the temptation to eschew judgments that could be proven wrong in favor of judgments enabling NIC or any analyst to cover their posterior by presenting a range of possibilities without probabilities or avoiding important questions on which information was scant or inconsistent. Neither "safe" course of action is helpful to policymakers. The Intelligence Community exists to make tough calls on consequential issues when information is inadequate and time is of the essence. Clarifying the limits of what is known and uncertainties regarding information and judgments is essential. It is also more useful to decision makers than analytic pablum or confident judgments about things irrelevant to the issues facing key customers.[8]

The decision not to pursue, or even consider, major restructuring of NIC or major changes in personnel was an easy one for reasons in addition to the one noted above.[9] First of all, I was—and still am—a great fan of the NIC and considered it to be one of the truly bright spots in the Intelligence Community. There was unquestionably room for improvement, and I had ideas about steps we might take. But the NIC was already closer to the mandated ideal of a fully integrated and collaborative analytical enterprise than was any other IC component. It could be better, but was already a concrete example that could be used to illustrate the modalities and efficacy of changes we needed to make across the community.[10]

The second additional reason was the need for stability in order to sustain already quite high levels of performance while introducing changes designed to improve tradecraft and support to decision makers. I knew that the NIC and its products, especially national intelligence estimates, would be subjected to particularly close scrutiny because the flawed Iraq WMD estimate had become "Exhibit A" in the case for intelligence reform. But I also knew from two decades of engagement with the NIC and from the fact that I had been the final INR reviewer of virtually every NIE produced since early 1994 that the vast majority of NIC products were far better than the one being held up as "typical" by critics.

Knowing—or at least believing—this to be the case, I was reluctant to risk temporary degradation of performance by introducing potentially disruptive change when the NIC was providing critical support related to the wars in Iraq and Afghanistan, the war on terror (as it was styled at the time), nuclear programs in Iran and North Korea, and many other front-burner issues.[11] Sustaining existing breadth of coverage and levels of performance was going to be difficult enough at a time when the NIC had to pick up responsibility for intelligence support to National Security Council meetings that previously had been provided by CIA.[12] This particular transfer of responsibilities was not mandated by the reform legislation, but Negroponte had decided that it should happen before naming me Chair of NIC. I understood why he wanted to do this and did not seek reconsideration of that decision. It was clear from the beginning, however, that implementation would impose an enormous burden on the NIC and certain NIOs. I confess to underestimating the magnitude and unpopularity of the additional burden. Indeed, at the time I saw it as a convenient vehicle for moving toward more cross-agency collaboration that tapped the best expertise available in the community.

Taken together, these considerations provided both an argument for basic continuity that I found persuasive and a rationale for retaining key people. Moreover, I knew all of the NIOs and many of their deputies and knew them to be competent professionals who knew their accounts and their peers in other agencies. Making changes for the sake of change would not result in a better stable of experts, but the same good people could produce better results if we developed procedures to address the process deficiencies that contributed to the systemic flaws criticized by the SSCI and WMD Commission reports.[13] One of those very good people was David Gordon, the acting chairman.

Since David was in that position, I began the search for a deputy to head NIC by looking at him rather than by developing a list of desirable qualifications. In other words, I began by asking, "What does he bring to the job and what could he contribute to the leadership team I hoped to build?" It did not take long to conclude that asking him to stay would give me far more than just the sense of stability outlined above. He had spent more of his career outside than inside the Intelligence Community but had served at CIA and the NIC long enough to have an insider's knowledge of the intelligence profession. His PhD (like Steve Kaplan's) gave him a credential useful when dealing with critics prone to disparage the academic preparation of IC analysts and,

more important to me, to understand and contribute to the quest for greater
analytic rigor that would be at the core of the transformation agenda. Finally,
like Steve Kaplan and me, he was a "global guy" who had worked on all parts
of the world and a wide spectrum of issues. There are not many such people
in the Intelligence Community, and I knew from my own experience how
valuable that perspective is to overseeing and evaluating the work of area and
functional specialists. David was an ideal candidate and, more important, he
was willing to remain on the job as my deputy for the NIC.

Analytic Tradecraft
Unlike the PDB and the NIC, the "bin" I had labeled "analytic tradecraft"
contained no legacy organizations or people. What it did contain was a mix-
ture of mandated tasks, vague notions about how to improve collaboration,
and intuitive understanding that whatever we undertook would have to include tradecraft standards and guidelines, securing buy-in and acceptance of
the standards, training in the use of newly mandated guidelines, mechanisms
to evaluate the utilization and efficacy of the standards, ways to evaluate and
diagnose performance, and ways to capture best practices and lessons learned.
It would also include a technical or "tools" dimension intended to enable
analysts to work smarter, collaborate at a distance, and facilitate the sharing
of information, along with mechanisms to collect information about analytic
skills, to evaluate the missions and priorities of IC components and production on specific topics, and to facilitate interaction between analysts and collectors. As I began to compile a first approximation list of tasks in this bin, I
became convinced that I probably needed more than one division and deputy.

After compiling an initial list of mandated tasks and necessary prerequisites for achieving them, I began to subdivide them into groups of similar or
inextricably linked component tasks with the goal of moving toward a more
refined binning exercise helpful to making decisions about organizational
structures and reporting lines. My plan was to move quickly from major tasks
to constituent tasks to aggregation of the constituent tasks into the missions
of particular divisions to construction of job requirements for candidates to
head each of the divisions to a search for people with the requisite skills and
experience. That would have been a logical way to proceed, but it probably
would have required more time than I judged to be available.

The sense of urgency that permeated my thinking about this and all other
dimensions of team-building and initial steps to transform analysis was driven
in part by perceived need to appease external overseers like Congressman

Hoekstra and to meet the expectations and demands of the new DNI and the White House.[14] Those external drivers were probably less important, however, than my own sense—conviction—that if we did not start quickly, we would squander a short-lived opportunity to initiate meaningful reform.

There is considerable inertia in every organization. In the federal (and other government) bureaucracies, inertia is particularly strong because it results from legislatively imposed constraints, low tolerance for risk and the high value of regularity and predictability, and the difficulty of winning approval for even modest departures from time-tested routines. At the start of every new administration there is a small window of opportunity to introduce change, but it closes quickly. The window might be a little wider and remain open a little longer because fixing the Intelligence Community was a high-profile mandate, but I was convinced that we had to act quickly—and effectively—or IC analysts and agencies would conclude that the ODNI was just the latest incarnation of "same ol,' same ol'" and that they could hunker down, wait out the period of heightened attention to reform, and generally ignore the new structure. I estimated that the window of opportunity for transformative change would remain open for only a few years.

Experience during my decades in Washington had taught me that time was always at a premium and action and results were more important than having a fully developed plan or strategy. The reality, as I had come to know it, is that time becomes compressed, logical sequences are squashed together, targets of opportunity arise, and immediate problems cannot wait for best possible arrangements to address them.[15] In this case, orderly process was trumped by pop-up opportunities in the form of three remarkable people.

Just days after I had accepted the DDNI/A position, I received a call from Andy Shepard. I knew Andy in three capacities (we had worked together briefly years earlier when I did work for CIA while still at Stanford, we sang in the same church choir, and we had interacted when he was assigned to the WMD Commission), but I seriously doubt that I would have sought him out if I had completed my logical construct of requirements. Andy wanted to discuss two subjects: his interest in coming to work for the ODNI, and his passion for transformational change of the way IC analysts worked. I would have seen Andy as soon as possible simply because he was a friend, but I was instantly eager to do so because IC analysts were not exactly clamoring to cast their lot with the new, untested, and unproven organization, and because his brief comments about transformational change came right at the time that I was wrestling with the challenges summarized above. A third reason was more tactical; I judged that his engagement with members of the WMD Commission could be a source of insight into their thinking about analytic reform and the criteria they would use to assess my progress and performance.[16]

Virtually our entire conversation focused on the rationale for a subset of WMD Commission recommendations and Andy's vision of existing impediments and attainable improvements with respect to the way analysts worked and interacted with one another and with collectors. I will discuss his ideas more fully in the chapter on analytic transformation; the point I want to make here is that his fortuitous arrival in my office was enormously helpful as I struggled to get my mind around the challenges of reforming the way analysis was done in the community. I decided on the spot to "hire" Andy even though I had only the dimmest notion of what I would do with him.[17] I could not even tell him what "box" on the nascent organization chart of the ODDNI/A he would occupy.

Lack of clarity about organizational structure and job titles was an obstacle to recruitment. The paucity of eager volunteers across the IC was an understandable manifestation of both a "stick with the devil you know" and a "chicken and egg" problem. High flyers eager for and anticipating upward mobility in the IC were reluctant to damage their chances by "defecting" to a new organization that might fail and take them down with it. Those willing to take a chance wanted a clearer picture of what they would be asked to do and how their role would fit into a broader organizational and mission structure than we were able to provide at the beginning. Recognition of this reality made me both grateful for and somewhat cautious about those who did volunteer.

The second pop-up opportunity was John Keefe. I did not know John; his name was forwarded to me by Lieutenant General (retired) Jim King, who was working with the ODNI transition team. About the only thing I remember from the conversation with King is that Keefe worked on the Hill. I do not recall him saying explicitly that John wanted a job in the ODNI, just that I might want to take a look at him. As I was soon to learn, John was working for Congresswoman Jane Harman on the House Permanent Select Committee on Intelligence (HPSCI) staff and had served as special assistant to Ambassador (and retired Admiral) Joe Prueher in Beijing at the time of the EP-3 incident in April 2001.[18]

His experience in Beijing and working the EP-3 incident provided a starting point for our conversation because I had worked on that from the Washington end.[19] During the conversation, I learned that John had aeronautical engineering degrees from Stanford and an impressive understanding of how Congress viewed the Intelligence Community. As in the case of Andy Shepard, I knew that I wanted John on my team even though I had almost no idea how I wanted to use him beyond a vague notion that his engineering background might be helpful as I addressed demands to strengthen IC analysis on science and technology, and that his knowledge of the Hill might help me with that important customer and critic.[20]

The third person I recruited to the ODDNI/A without a clear notion of how I would use him was Mike Wertheimer. Mike is a cryptologic mathematician with a PhD from the University of Pennsylvania who had worked for many years at NSA before leaving for the private sector. Wertheimer was recommended by Mike Hayden, who knew him well from his time as Director of NSA and thought I needed someone with Wertheimer's technical expertise to facilitate the linkup between analysis and collection envisioned by the still very crude ODNI organization chart. I understood neither the linkage envisioned nor why I needed a mathematician. I called Wertheimer because Hayden asked me to; Mike agreed to talk with me because Hayden asked him to. I suspect that we both thought the phone conversation would end our relationship and each could report to Hayden that we had spoken to one another.

But our talk was anything but pro forma. We quickly moved past the awkward "Why am I talking to you?" stage and began to discuss "big ideas" that I subsequently characterized as philosophies of analysis and the psychology of man-machine interaction. I cannot remember the details of our conversation, but I do remember clearly that it was intellectually stimulating and a lot of fun. I think I offered Mike the position of Chief of Technology with no idea what that would mean. I felt pretty good about my chances of recruiting him when my offer of lower pay and a longer commute for the chance to do something really exciting elicited a promise to think about it. He did, and I am very grateful that he decided to join the nascent team.

The conversations with Andy, John, and Mike were important to the incremental process of thinking through how to structure and organize the expanding number of items in my "analytic tradecraft" bin. Those conversations also convinced me that it was unnecessary—and probably counterproductive—to over-think the task or try to come up with a "perfect" plan for moving forward. As with Steve at the PDB and David at the NIC, I was confident that they had bought in to the idea of analytic transformation and would help to design and refine the effort in the course of implementation. It could be and would be a team effort.

Though I did not yet know exactly how I planned to use my target of opportunity additions, I felt confident that none of them had the interest or background to lead the more clearly defined tasks of setting standards, developing training programs, and designing evaluative criteria and procedures. I still had a very big hole in the area that was sure to be treated as a litmus test for ODNI performance, namely, the speed and efficacy with which we implemented the reforms mandated by the IRTPA and the White House. About a week into the process of standing up the ODDNI/A, I turned again to the task of developing a job description and list of desirable characteristics.

I began by revisiting the trade-offs between bringing in an outsider to demonstrate seriousness of purpose and recruiting an insider knowledgeable about how to get things done in the Intelligence Community. I quickly came to the obvious conclusion that I should think of a tandem arrangement with one person from the outside and one from the inside in order to capture the advantages of both and mitigate the disadvantages of either. That decision, albeit a tentative one, drove me toward a structure with a number of persons (I was thinking five to six; it turned out to be six) who would have the title of Assistant Deputy Director of National Intelligence for Analysis, and a number of deputies to my deputies. There was a piece of me that wanted to say, "Who cares what they are called?" but I had been in government long enough to know that titles matter, not just for reasons of ego but also because they are often tied to grade and salary and could make the difference when trying to recruit well-qualified people to work in the fledgling organization. Giving many people titles has a downside, however. It can fuel perceptions and criticism of "bureaucratic bloat." This was yet another case of contradiction between what might be a good idea for recruitment and effectiveness inside the community, and what might be a bad idea in terms of optics and oversight bodies.

I thought about this position in ways analogous to my earlier consideration of qualifications for the DDNI/A position, but this time I came down in favor of recruiting an outsider in order to demonstrate serious determination to improve analysis. Being an outsider would help, but garnering the kudos, time, and leeway that this might bring would be irrelevant if it did not also produce effective mechanisms to improve analytic tradecraft. I wanted—and needed—a rigorous and respected scholar with US Government experience and the ability to build a program virtually from scratch. The name that first came to mind was Joe Nye at Harvard, but I quickly dismissed the idea because he had already occupied more senior government positions. I was still thinking about possible names when I happened to read an article in *The Journal of American History* by my friend and Georgetown professor of diplomatic history Nancy Tucker.[21]

That I happened to read that article when I did is a matter of almost complete serendipity. She had sent the article to me a few days earlier, and I just happened to get to it after a day spent thinking about who I wanted to lead the effort to improve IC analysis. The rigorous analysis in that article and the fact that I had known Nancy for twenty-five years and had worked with her at the State Department when she was there on a Council on Foreign Relations fellowship sparked an aha moment. I doubted that she would be able to take leave from Georgetown or be willing to join me in the ODNI adventure, but decided to give her a call right away. To my great surprise and delight, she was interested and promised to confer with her husband (the historian Warren Cohen, another friend of many years) and her university department. The prospect of having Nancy at the top of one of the analytic tradecraft divisions prompted and enabled me to think more systematically about the tasks to be assigned to "her" directorate and the skill sets needed to complement her own.

A few days later, she was ready and able to accept and my thinking had gelled enough to offer her the position of deputy in charge of developing analytic standards with a concurrent second-hat position as ombudsman responsible for analytic integrity, a position mandated by the IRTPA legislation.[22] Everything else about the position was to be worked out later or on the fly, including who from inside the IC would serve as her deputy. It was at this point that I realized that I could and should leave most of the detailed planning about how to structure my divisions to the people I tapped to head them. That changed my task from "doing it all" to "making sure that my deputies (and others) understood my vision of what we needed to accomplish" and giving them wide latitude to refine or challenge my preliminary ideas and devise ways to achieve our objectives.

Although there was still a long way to go, I was making progress on the stand-up of my directorate and sat down with John Negroponte to give him an update. The conversation reaffirmed the leeway he had given me to design and staff my component of the ODNI, but it also prevented us—me—from making a damaging error. When I told John whom I had selected for the analytic standards position, I emphasized Nancy's academic standing and reputation as a tough-minded scholar. He replied, "You're kidding." I explained that, no, I wasn't kidding, I really thought she was the best person for the job and would demonstrate that we were serious about implementing the tradecraft reforms because of her reputation for scholarly rigor. This time he replied that he knew Nancy was a hard-ass because she was his wife's dissertation adviser. I did not know that but immediately saw the potential problem of a perceived conflict of interest. Fortunately, his wife, Diana, had already submitted her dissertation, so we needed to delay Nancy's appointment for only a few weeks.

Liaison

At some point when assigning tasks to bins and thinking about the skills needed to manage those tasks, I realized that the functions and what was required subdivided naturally into three categories: maintain and modify (the PDB and NIC), create and integrate (the various dimensions of analytic tradecraft and transformation), and engage (for example, with military and law enforcement agencies and personnel and with other components of the ODNI). The last category was even more diffuse than the second one, but I concluded rather quickly that focused effort would be needed to integrate law enforcement units and personnel into the analytic enterprise—terra incognita for me and for the IC as a whole—and to engage with military commands and intelligence units with structures, missions, and operating procedures different from anything I had encountered previously. I was also aware that what we did in the ODDNI/A would be done in the context of parallel, overlapping, and necessarily coordinated efforts to build and achieve multiple goals in other components of the ODNI. Coordination was imperative if we were to avoid duplication of effort and working at cross-purposes, but it was unlikely to occur spontaneously.

The initial focus of my concern about coordination and liaison stemmed from awareness of how important intelligence support was both to the active military conflicts in Iraq and Afghanistan and to detecting and disrupting terrorist plots. The need to ensure that nothing we undertook for the purpose of improving intelligence analysis had detrimental consequences for force protection, defeat of enemy combatants, or disruption of terrorist plots was an absolute constraint on what we did and how we did it. As with the PDB, it was essential not to "break" existing support mechanisms while attempting to improve them. Indeed, I thought it even more important to maintain high-quality intelligence support to warfighters and law enforcement officers than to the White House. Rightly or wrongly, I was less worried about making the President angry than about intelligence breakdowns that could endanger American lives.

Worrying about the problem was not going to solve it, and my own limited experience as a US Army linguist was not an adequate basis for identifying, let alone avoiding or ameliorating, actions detrimental to those on the front lines. That is why one of my first calls after accepting the DDNI/A position was to Under Secretary of Defense for Intelligence Steve Cambone. Steve and I had spent many hours together working on the administration's draft intelligence reform legislation. That experience had sensitized me to his (and Secretary Rumsfeld's) concerns, and I decided that the best place to go for help with this problem was to him.

Going to see Steve in his Pentagon office underscored the seriousness of what I had come to discuss because the office was in the portion of the building rebuilt after the 9/11 attack. Like any good bureaucratic player, I had told him why I wanted to see him so that he could think about a response before I arrived. He had done his homework. Almost immediately after initial pleasantries and joking about the challenges of the job I had accepted, Steve said, "I cannot give you a flag officer." I replied that was fine because I didn't want a flag officer. Flag officers come with an entourage and too much baggage. I wanted an O-6 (Colonel or Navy Captain).[23] Steve then said, "Good, I've got a Navy Captain for you. He's yours." I thanked him, took the papers he held out to me, and left after confirming that I had the necessary contact information.

A short time later, when I met Captain Ron Rice for the first time, I began by trying to discover why he was interested in the still ill-defined job and whether the number of unresolved matters and raggedy edges troubled him. Ron's to-the-point response was that he had been assigned to the position, would figure it out, and looked forward to working with me. I knew immediately that this was going to work and spent the rest of the time outlining the kinds of issues and relationships I wanted him to tackle. For starters, he needed to make an initial list of tasks, to prioritize them, and to figure out what he needed to do them. We would take it from there.

After approximately a week, serendipity and the step-by-step process I used to identify and catalog tasks and to match people to responsibilities seemed to have covered most of the first-order challenges we faced. Most, but not all. I still needed a way to ensure coordination within the ODNI. Others on the leadership team being assembled by the DNI, specifically Mary Margaret Graham, the Deputy DNI for Collection, and David Shedd, the career CIA officer who had become Negroponte's Chief of Staff, told me that I too needed a Chief of Staff to handle all the essential but non-sexy stuff that would otherwise land on my own desk. Since I was still operating out of my

INR office, I decided to discuss this with Paula Causey because her advice over twenty years had always been helpful. The conversation was brief. She knew me well enough to say, in effect, you will not want to do lots of the down-in-the-weeds stuff and you won't do it. But it has to be done. Ask Jan Karcz to be your Chief of Staff.

I knew Jan, but Paula knew him better than I because she had worked with him on projects undertaken by Mark Lowenthal as Assistant DCI for Analysis and Production. A retired Colonel who had worked in the IC for a number of years, Jan had experience and skills that I lacked and, more important, he had been recommended by Paula and was included in the staff that I had inherited from Lowenthal's now disbanded office. He had a great advantage in our initial conversation about the position because he actually knew what a Chief of Staff could do in and for an organization. I cannot remember whether we closed the deal immediately or if Jan wanted to think about it for a bit, but, happily for me, he came on board very quickly and hit the ground running.

Approximately two weeks after accepting the DDNI/A position, I had assembled members of my senior team, ensured stability at the PDB and NIC, and made significant progress toward identifying tasks and organizational subunits of the analysis directorate. In the process, I had acquired a much clearer understanding of what needed to be done and was developing preliminary ideas about how to do it. The critical next steps were to align people with responsibilities, prioritize objectives, and develop a strategy for moving forward.

Succession and Sustainment

Personnel turnover is an unavoidable attribute of life in any organization. Good people are promoted or offered new opportunities, persons on rotational assignments must return to their home agencies, people burn out or want new challenges, and other perfectly normal conditions arise that require recruitment of successors. Building an effective team is critically important and, having done so, I naturally hoped that it would remain intact for the duration of my tenure. But that was never a possibility. I knew from the start, for example, that Nancy Tucker's leave of absence from Georgetown would be time-limited, and that Sherry Hong, the staff assistant who followed me from the State Department, would move on in the next Foreign Service assignment cycle. Moreover, given the caliber of the people I had been able to recruit for our ambitious but uncertain journey, I knew from experience that other managers would attempt to "steal" them. The challenges of team-building would not and did not end in the first weeks of my new assignment.

Despite knowing that I would have to recruit successors at some point, I did not have to deal with that problem until it arose. That did not mean, however, that I could ignore it completely, and I did think about it when making early decisions. One way in which I thought about it was somewhat analogous to the way I thought about strategies and plans, namely, that I was unlikely to get everything completely right the first time. In fact, I think that I did assemble a near-perfect "dream team" in the spring of 2005. The point I want to make here is that I was able to avoid excessive concern about the compatibility of personalities and whether I had exactly the right skill sets for the still-evolving tasks of analytic transformation because I knew from experience that normal turnover of personnel would create opportunities to recalibrate and rebalance. Of course, I also knew that I had—but did not expect to exercise—the ability to remove or reassign any member of the team who proved to be ill-suited for the initial assignment.

The second way in which knowledge of future succession requirements entered into my initial thinking about what to do was by providing yet another incentive to begin fast and seek early successes. When recruiting members of the first team, the challenge was shaped by the fact that the organization was brand new and its missions only vaguely defined. It had no history or reputation. Relatively quickly, however, the ODDNI/A would begin to announce and implement decisions. If these initial efforts were deemed to be sensible and reasonably successful, it would be easier to re-cruit successors than if we appeared to over-reach, to address the "wrong" problems, or to have failed.

On the whole, things were going reasonably well when the time came to replace members of the core team. That meant, inter alia, that the choice of successors could be geared to ensure continuity and the sustainability of what we had launched rather than recruitment of people able to take us in a dif-ferent direction. I gave only fleeting consideration to playing a major role in the selection of successors because, by this time, I was juggling many other important balls and was ensnared in "in-box" and transformational responsi-bilities. Members of my team recognized this and, without much discussion, each departing teammate assumed primary responsibility for finding a succes-sor. No one knew better than they what was needed to sustain the activities they had shaped and initiated. I was both comfortable and relieved to give them the lead. This proved to be a wise decision.

Nancy Tucker was the first to depart and, after only a brief conversation, we agreed that her immediate replacement should also come from outside the

Intelligence Community. She recommended and recruited Temple University professor Richard Immerman, a diplomatic historian and past president of the Society for Historians of American Foreign Relations who had written about the role of the Intelligence Community in US foreign policy. I knew of Richard but had not met him until we had an introductory lunch in the CIA executive dining room. I learned then that he (like I) had studied with Walter LaFeber at Cornell. Nancy had recommended him very strongly, so I interpreted the lunch conversation not as a job interview but as an opportunity for me to persuade him to join us. Richard accepted and did a fantastic job executing projects that Nancy and others in the Analytic Integrity and Standards (AIS) directorate had begun and building on that foundation to deepen the process of analytic transformation.

Captain Ron Rice, who left the position when he retired from the Navy, also took the lead in identifying his relief. His choice, Air Force Colonel Jon Wohlman, hit the ground running and, like Ron, did an excellent job in a position that retained an ad hoc and fire extinguisher quality throughout my tenure but required constant attention to ill-defined interactions with law enforcement agencies, counterterrorism task forces, and military intelligence units. I would not have known what guidance to give Jon, but Ron understood what we collectively were trying to do, what problems he had encountered, and where to turn for advice and assistance. This position was the prime example of why it is imperative to delegate authority and responsibility to people who share the leader's vision, are prepared to make decisions, and know that the boss will support what they decide.

The final successor appointment that I will mention here is that of my Chief of Staff. As noted above, when I set out to recruit someone for this position, I had only the dimmest idea what the job would entail or even why I needed one. Jan understood what the job required and handled almost all routine interaction with other components of the ODNI on matters ranging from personnel problems to turf issues to compliance requirements. When Jan had an opportunity to take a more senior position, I urged him to accept because he deserved it and because I felt strongly that it would be deleterious for the DDNI/A position if I was perceived to have attempted to block opportunities for promotion. I wanted to make the ODDNI/A a place that good people would see as a stepping-stone, not a dead end. Jan, as had Nancy and Ron (and staff assistant Sherry Hong), took the lead in finding his replacement. Craig Gralley, a CIA analyst, proved to be as good in the position as Jan was. Indeed, they were both so good, and the delegation of responsibility so effective, that by the time I departed I still had only a dim understanding of what the Chief of Staff position did or required. I say this not to be facetious but to underscore the importance of delegating responsibility to and backing the decisions of people you trust.

Translating Ideas into Actions

WHILE I WAS STRUGGLING TO COMPREHEND the myriad tasks in my new portfolio, my colleagues and counterparts in the Office of the Director of National Intelligence were doing the same. By mid-June 2005, that is, just two months after John Negroponte was confirmed as the first Director of National Intelligence, each of the four deputies had disengaged from previous positions, assembled key members of their staffs, and begun to develop strategies to implement mandated and other changes. We had also begun to gel as a team. Nobody on the senior team had known all of the other members before we sat down together at an ODNI meeting, but there was a remarkable camaraderie from the start. Perhaps the reason was that each had had a "What have I done?" epiphany that included realization that we could not succeed individually unless we succeeded together; Negroponte's skill as a talent spotter and experienced builder of country teams in the embassies he led was also a factor.

Geography was not our friend during the initial months of the ODNI. Until Pat Kennedy secured a temporary home for some of us at Bolling Air Force Base (later renamed Joint Base Anacostia-Bolling), we were scattered hither and yon and came together only for weekly meetings that included both staff and members of the transition team. What I remember most about these meetings is the focus on speed, assignment of principal responsibility for implementing each of the IRTPA mandates and presidentially approved WMD Commission recommendations, and associated "Deputies Meetings" that we held before or after the larger gathering. Those participating were the four Deputy DNIs (Pat Kennedy, Management; Mary Margaret Graham, Collection; Lieutenant General Ron Burgess, Customer Outcomes; and me, Analysis) as well as DNI Chief of Staff David Shedd and his deputy, Mike Leiter.

We met in David's temporary office in the New Executive Office Building. The office was so small that it could accommodate only three chairs plus the one behind his desk. Mary Margaret always got a seat, and Mike always got to sit on a piece of furniture. The last arriving male deputy had to sit outside the doorway. It was so uncomfortable—often very hot—that we learned to deal with matters expeditiously, despite a lot of joking about newly discovered problems or inanities. The centerpieces of our discussions were brief summaries of what each was trying to do, what problems and possibilities each had discovered, and what each needed from the others or from the DNI. We learned from one another. The short-term priorities of each were modified to help others overcome specific obstacles or put in place a new capability, and we identified or designated people on our individual staffs to work with counterparts to accomplish specific objectives. The large meetings with the DNI and his principal deputy, Mike Hayden, focused on what we had to do and the need to demonstrate action and results quickly; our smaller meetings focused on how to do this.

The reason I begin this chapter on the development of a strategy and plans to implement change in the analytic arena in this way is to underscore the importance and impact of competing imperatives. One was the need to act quickly. All members of the senior team had been in the Beltway environment during the years before passage of intelligence reform legislation and perceived that the success of the ODNI, and therefore of each subcomponent of the ODNI, would be judged to a significant extent by how quickly we translated mandates into action and actions into results. To a considerable degree, the need to move out smartly trumped the utility of knowing exactly where we wanted to go. The competing imperative was to avoid mistakes that would jeopardize the provision of continuous intelligence support to the President, military commanders, and all other national security customers while reducing duplication, enhancing integration, and building for success over the long term. The discussions in our Deputies Meetings also underscored another contextual parameter: the strength and diversity of opposition to what we were charged to do. We were determined to succeed; some others were equally determined that we should fail.

The fact that so many strands of the reform garment were interwoven created many points of vulnerability for all of us because of the potential—probable—ripple effects of delay or derailment anywhere in the reform undertaking. For example, FBI reluctance and foot dragging when implementing changes initiated by the directorates for management or collection affected the ability of my directorate to implement analytic tradecraft reforms. This created incentives for each of us to build firewalls to protect our own responsibilities and actions, but doing so would come at the price of reduced long-term effectiveness and increased danger of short-term failure. We all recognized this and were determined to seek collective, not individual success.

The considerations summarized above and those outlined in previous chapters were very much on my mind as I prepared for the first meeting of my own senior staff.[1] I knew they expected me to present a game plan and individual assignments, but I wanted and needed their ideas about how best to proceed. With this in mind, I decided to focus on how we would try to do things rather than on precisely what we would do. Toward that end, I decided to begin by describing my primary objectives and how I thought we should proceed. After acknowledging the need for speed and necessity of integrating our own efforts and those of the other directorates, I articulated the following goals.

Restore Confidence

Restoring confidence in the Intelligence Community, first and foremost in the quality and utility of the analytic support we provided to the national security enterprise, was job one. Several considerations led me to make this my highest priority. One was professional pride and conviction that, despite our flaws, the Intelligence Community could—and usually did—provide the best informed, most objective, most timely, and most carefully tailored analytic support to USG decision makers. Day in and day out, we were and had to be better than any alternative sources of analytic input.[2] No individual or organization understood or could understand better than IC analysts what policymakers knew, wanted to know, and did not fully understand; what they were trying to accomplish; what they already believed to be the case; and when and how they wanted to receive information and insights. Decision makers could not stop making decisions because they had lost confidence in the IC, and they would continue to seek and receive input from other sources with more limited access to information and, often, agendas of their own. If we did not quickly regain their confidence, we would become an expensive irrelevance no matter how much our tradecraft improved.

A second consideration was that, unless we restored confidence in our work, it would be impossible to repair and bolster critical links between policymakers and the Intelligence Community, most of which were manifest in the relationship between analysts and the officials they supported. The more analysts know about the goals and concerns of the officials they support, the better they can focus their own analytic work, the work of analysts in other agencies, and efforts to collect additional information germane to the problem under study. For me, this was not just a matter of maintaining good relations between policymakers and analysts; it was a key factor in the ability of the US Government to protect Americans and advance American interests.

The third reason was morale. As noted previously, analysts across the community were tarred with the brush of criticism that might more appropriately have been directed at those most responsible for the flaws of the Iraq WMD estimate. Months of disparaging commentary on the Hill, in the media, and from insensitive friends and neighbors had taken a heavy toll, and I worried about the loss of experienced analysts at one end of the age spectrum and talented newcomers at the other. If we were to attract and retain the best and brightest our country has to offer, we had to improve our image and public confidence in the quality of our work and our people.[3]

The final reason for making this my highest priority was more tactical; I judged that the bundle of things we would have to do to restore confidence would also buy time and leeway to work the most difficult issues. If customers and critics thought we were doing better, they would not care very much about what we had done to improve. But if they judged we had not improved, they would be all over us for our failure to implement specific recommendations and reforms and impose more reporting requirements and procedural hurdles to "help" us a little more. This may sound cynical, but twenty years in Washington had convinced me that it was the case.

Improve the Quality of Analysis

I saw this as the most important requisite for restoring confidence. If we were going to be perceived as doing better work, we actually had to do better work. I thought of this as a two or possibly multistep challenge. Step one, demonstrating immediate improvement by adopting a limited number of visible changes, could be achieved quickly because I had the authority to mandate changes to the *President's Daily Brief* and National Intelligence Council products without having to seek Intelligence Community approval or preparation of formal directives. All that was required was John Negroponte's concurrence. The specific changes I had in mind were to circulate PDB drafts and drafts of NIC products such as briefing papers for National Security Council meetings to senior experts across the community with instructions to identify any factual errors or any analytical judgments with which they disagreed. If they had an analytical disagreement, they must indicate why. Flagging the existence of analytic differences clearly and early would send a useful cautionary signal to decision makers at the top of the bureaucratic totem pole. If they saw this as an improvement, the word was likely to spread downward.

I saw this as far more than a gimmick because it was also a model for agency products and a mechanism that forced dissenting analysts to be clear about why and how they disagreed with something colleagues had written. The process often produced dialog among analysts across agency boundaries, greater understanding of the subject, sourcing, or alternative ways to close information gaps that ultimately produced analysis that was clearer and more appropriately caveated. It was also instrumental in another way. Sharing draft assessments with information on the evidence used to support or challenge them was also a mechanism to enhance information sharing across agency boundaries. Since enhanced information sharing was both a priority objective of intelligence reform and a major demand of analysts, using PDB and NIC products in this way enabled the ODDNI/A to demonstrate progress on two important reform targets.

Improve Intelligence Community Analysis by Improving the Work of Every Agency and Analyst

I thought of the subhead title above as a bumper sticker way to encapsulate and communicate the approach I planned to follow, but it was also intended to signal that we did not plan to seek improvement through structural changes, movement of people, or changing the scope of work performed in individual agencies. Rather, we intended to begin at the individual analyst level by making it easier for every analyst to access information, identify and collaborate with colleagues in other agencies, learn and apply good analytic techniques, and have their work evaluated against a common set of standards. If analysts did better work, their agencies would regain confidence, find it easier to attract and retain good people, and enhance support to their primary customers and missions. If all agencies performed better, all work was evaluated against common standards, and all analysts were trained in the same tradecraft skills, it would be easier to work out divisions of labor and collaborative arrangements, and to reduce unnecessary duplication. The IC as a whole would perform better.[4]

Achieving these goals—and more—would not be easy, and I certainly needed ideas from my own team and anyone else able to contribute. Many details remained to be worked out, but I wanted to signal the approach we would use, the key message I wanted conveyed to analysts and managers across the IC, and that we intended to work with, not against, individual agencies and their senior managers. These admittedly vague but overarching objectives provided the initial focus for our efforts to determine precisely how to accomplish our initial objectives. This constituted our number one task over the next several months.

Operate as a Team

My confidence that the people I had selected would come together and function well as a team was based on more than arrogance about my own leadership abilities, although I confess that was a factor. I did not worry overly about the ability of good people to work effectively as a team because I had seen it happen many times during my years as an "intellectual entrepreneur" at Stanford and in the Bureau of Intelligence and Research front office. Indeed, some of my ideas regarding teams originated in or were reinforced by a study of teams in INR conducted by Harvard psychology professor Richard Hackman. Hackman, an expert on team dynamics, called me when I was the principal deputy in INR to say that he had been commissioned by the IC (I believe it was Assistant Director of Central Intelligence for Analysis and Production Mark Lowenthal) to examine the use of teams in different agencies. He complained that he was having difficulty gaining access to more than a small number of teams because agencies told him they did not have teams of the type they thought he was looking for. When I asked how many teams he wanted to interview in INR, he replied, how many do you have? I suggested we start with ten to twelve and take it from there. He said that would be more than he had interviewed in all other agencies combined.[5] I explained that my working definition of a team was a set of analysts who interacted informally but regularly because they had overlapping portfolios or shared interests in particular subjects. He questioned whether such groupings would qualify as a "team" but agreed to conduct the study.

After the interviews of INR analysts had been completed and the data analyzed, Hackman called me again. The gist of his report was that the situation in INR was unlike anything that he had found in his study of successful and unsuccessful teams. According to Hackman, INR violated all the rules for organizing effective teams. He noted, for example, that members of several groups I had described as teams denied that they actually were a team. In some groups, members said the team had no leader. In others, every member claimed to be the leader. Despite these and other confusing anomalies, he reported, with a degree of puzzlement, that INR had the most effective "teams" he had interviewed in the IC.[6]

Analytic teams will be discussed later in this book; the point I want to make here is that when recruiting deputies, I was influenced more by the experience and expertise of individuals than by consideration of how difficult or easy it would be to forge an effective team. My experience at Stanford and Hackman's findings when he studied teams in INR made me confident that having a clear and shared vision of what we wanted to achieve would be a more important determinant of success than the personalities of team members and formal divisions of responsibility.[7] But confidence is not a strategy.

During the weeks required to identify members of the team and work out the terms of their assignments to the ODNI, I had both the opportunity and the necessity to think more systematically about what had to be achieved, how to prioritize and accomplish myriad interconnected goals, and how best to utilize each member of the team.[8] Inevitably, Washington being the kind of town that it is, I began to be asked with increasing frequency to describe my strategy and implementation plan. Those asking wanted to know what I intended to do and, in many cases, to be reassured that the ODNI took seriously the proclaimed need to "fix" analysis in the Intelligence Community. To have stated that I did not yet have a plan would have been untenable and would have subjected me (and my deputies) to even greater pressure and "help" from well-intentioned or self-serving individuals and firms with ready-made solutions to any and all problems.[9] At this point, I did have elements of a strategy but was reluctant to describe it for both procedural and tactical reasons.

After thinking about the tasks in my portfolio for three or four weeks and listening to what my interlocutors and I said about specific dimensions of analysis and reform during the recruitment of my leadership team, I was beginning to have a reasonably coherent vision of what I wanted to achieve and possible ways to package and implement reforms. But I was also convinced that the ODDNI/A implementation plan would be more successful if it was developed incrementally as a team effort than if it was presented as or perceived to be "my" plan. The downside of an incremental approach was that it would fail to satisfy expectations and the political imperative to act quickly.

The challenges of building a team while building an organization and developing a strategy and detailed plans to transform analysis might be compared to hiring contractors to build a house while designing a building that incorporates features desired by several members of the family. The intelligence reform legislation, presidential directive, and continuing responsibilities of the PDB and NIC specified many of the features that had to be incorporated into any plan but provided little guidance on how to do so. The skills, experience, and ideas of those recruited to my leadership team constituted a diverse toolbox of possible approaches and actions, but did not mandate how best to assign roles and responsibilities or how to align responsibilities and organizational subdivisions. I once defined the challenge as a three-dimensional chicken-and-egg problem or a pyramidal Rubik's cube.

Rather than spend time agonizing over structural issues, detailed implementation plans, or precise delimitation of authorities and responsibilities, we made a de facto decision to begin by identifying and tackling specific tasks and components of what would eventually become an integrated strategy with clearer divisions of labor. A less elegant way to put it is that we began with some big ideas and boxes of mandated tasks and made it up as we went along. We had overarching ideas, but no master plan.

Organizing Themes and Goals

WHEN JOHN NEGROPONTE offered me the chance to become the first Deputy Director of National Intelligence for Analysis, I quickly realized that my decision to accept or reject the offer would be determined by my assessment of what might be possible. As I framed the analytic question, it had two components. One centered on the extent to which Negroponte and the Office of the Director of National Intelligence would allow me to pursue big, transformational changes in the way analysis was done in the Intelligence Community or limit my writ to minimalist implementation of mandated reforms. The second component was my assessment of whether I had the will, skill, and resources to overcome resistance from within the community. Even though we had not really discussed the issue in these terms, I was reasonably confident that Negroponte had not accepted the DNI position in order to play "small ball" and that his response, had I asked him, would have been "go for it." I was less confident that he, the unproven ODNI, or I could overcome inertia, resistance, and animosity toward change and the DNI from within the IC. In the end, I decided to accept the challenge of attempting something big but was acutely aware of the need to proceed in ways designed to limit hostility and production of unhelpful antibodies in the Intelligence Community.

In addition to external pressures to begin implementing mandated reforms, I was under self-imposed pressure to develop an initial strategy or approach that would ensure performance of continuing analytic responsibilities newly assigned to the ODNI (the *President's Daily Brief* and National Intelligence

Council products) and remaining in each IC component while facilitating implementation of mandated reforms. Other initial goals included adopting measures that would demonstrate improved analytic tradecraft and rebuild confidence in IC analysis; soliciting ideas and obtaining buy-in from analysts and analytic components; and beginning to collect information necessary to enhance collaboration, synergy, and efficiency. My goal was to develop a first draft or concept that I could use with my staff and to explain my approach to analysts across the community. The key elements in this early formulation included the following.

Reassuring Analysts and Seeking Their Support

My years in the Intelligence Community and understanding of human nature convinced me that it would be prudent to make "parish calls" to each of the analytic agencies or components. Making the calls would reduce the time available to develop plans, draw organization charts, and oversee analytic products, but I judged it essential to do so for symbolic and instrumental reasons. I am a firm believer in the virtues of "management by walking around." I calculated that attending town-hall-like meetings with junior and senior analysts to outline my vision, priorities, and approach to analytic reform, and to solicit their questions, concerns, and suggestions, would provide valuable input to me and demonstrate respect and appreciation for the people and missions of each component.

Specific goals for these early meetings included direct, unfiltered communication of information about what I was trying to do, DDNI/A priorities, and how I intended to implement mandated reforms and changes I judged necessary to make intelligence analysis even better, and to respond to any questions or concerns people wanted to raise. I also wanted to hear their ideas with regard to what could be done better or more efficiently, and to identify impediments to doing their jobs as well as they thought they could. In other words, I wanted both ideas and buy-in for what we were trying to accomplish.

In these agency town meetings, I wanted to make clear that what I was outlining for them was a work in progress, not a fully developed or immutable plan. If there was a better way to improve analysis, we should adopt it. If something we introduced did not work or seemed counterproductive, we wanted to know about it so we could try something else. I invited everyone to contact me directly, and introduced Ron Rice, the Navy Captain who had become my Deputy for Community Support, and identified him as another go-to person.

After the second or third parish call, I hit upon another way to regularize interaction between analytic components and the ODDNI/A. Before passage of the Intelligence Reform and Terrorism Prevention Act, Assistant Director of Central Intelligence Mark Lowenthal had established the Intelligence Analysis and Production Board (IAPB) to facilitate communication with and among components. I decided to reconstitute the IAPB as a "Board of Directors" for analysis through which I (and thus the ODDNI/A) would communicate and solicit information, and through which the components could communicate with all counterparts at the same time. I viewed this as more communication vehicle and integrative mechanism than as a body that would provide oversight to my directorate (which was formally accountable only to the DNI), but over time it became a useful source of ideas and feedback.

A second goal of my parish call message was to ease concern that integration of the analytic enterprise would entail major structural change or the reassignment of functions, missions, and personnel to other components of the Intelligence Community. Even if I had thought it necessary or desirable to "streamline" or reorganize the analytic enterprise, which I did not, the experience of participating in the meetings to draft an administration intelligence reform bill had underscored my conviction that it would be monumentally foolish to antagonize every analytic component and their parent agencies by attempting structural changes that were sure to be resisted. Picking a fight that I did not need and could not win would jeopardize my ability to make other, more meaningful changes. We could improve analytic performance without changing the internal structure or primary missions of the analytic components. This did not mean that I was willing to live with unnecessary duplication of effort or to countenance poor performance on particular subjects. I wasn't. But, as will be described further on, I thought there were better ways to address those problems.

I do not know what percentage of those attending the town meetings appreciated the fact that I had "shown up" early in the process to answer their questions and solicit their input. What I do know is that these exchanges sensitized me to both individual and institutional concerns and helped me to obtain input to and buy-in for the reform process. "Showing up" and my responses to questions from the workforce certainly did not alleviate all skepticism and concern about intelligence reform, but I am confident that doubts and resistance would have been greater if I had attempted to formulate and implement analytic reform without interacting with the workforce. I explained that I wanted these exchanges, and follow-on meetings with agency managers, to be part of a continuing and incremental process intended to make "everything" better without making anything worse. At least some of the analysts attending believed me. I continued to receive unsolicited suggestions from across the community until the end of my tenure.

Improving IC Performance: A Building Block Approach

The first several times that I used the expression in the title above to summarize a principal goal and strategy of intelligence reform my primary objective was to address and alleviate concerns that the ODNI intended to consolidate analytic components, eliminate programs, and transfer funds and analysts from poorer performers to better-performing or "more important" agencies. That was never my intention, and I do not believe that any of my ODNI senior colleagues considered it to be a viable or desirable way to enhance Intelligence Community performance. But the fact that such concerns existed was a manifestation of widespread uncertainty and worry about how reform would affect specific missions, agencies, and career prospects.

As I prepared for my initial town meetings, I judged it imperative to address these concerns immediately even though I did not yet have a clear vision of what analytic reform should encompass or how to achieve mandated and desirable objectives. In theory, it might have been better to defer the parish calls and first-cut explanations of what I hoped to achieve until I had a clearer idea of where I wanted to go and how to get there. However, I did not know how long that would take and was convinced that delay would exacerbate uncertainty and concerns about the future. As was the case with many other decisions that I had to make, I decided that speed and an incremental approach were preferable to an almost certainly vain attempt to get it completely right the first time.

By the time we scheduled the first parish call, I had already decided to eschew major organizational changes because of the near-certainty that they would be resisted (probably successfully) by agency heads and the cabinet secretaries to whom they reported. Even though I had no doubt that retaining existing organizational arrangements would evoke criticism from those who decried alleged duplication and inefficiency, I judged that this was a fight I did not need and could not win, and it would make it more difficult to achieve more important objectives. As important, I judged that even if I did manage to make structural changes, doing so would not automatically improve the quality and utility of analytic support to policymakers, military commanders, and the law enforcement community.

Having decided against making organizational changes that would be difficult to achieve and risk at least temporary degradation of IC support to critical
missions, it was easy as well as appropriate to reassure the analytic community
that such changes were not being considered. A separate but related concern
was the possibility that missions and people might be reassigned to different
agencies. Random conversations with analysts and managers suggested that
concerns about the reassignment of missions and personnel were both professional (this mission is critical to the security of our nation) and personal (I do
not want to move or lengthen my commute). Even though over the longer
term it might make sense to reassign missions and people, I judged that doing
so right away would degrade performance, worsen morale, and require expen-
diture of more bureaucratic and personal capital than I was willing to spend.

Providing reassurance on these points was intended to improve morale
and secure buy-in for the changes that I did intend to make. However, it did
not ensure better performance. That really was a priority objective, but at this
point I had only a dim idea how to achieve it. When I began to hold town
meetings, the characterization of a yet-to-be-developed strategy—improve IC
performance by improving the performance of all agencies and analysts—was
little more than a slogan. It sounded good and was generally well received by
analysts, but it was almost completely devoid of substance. In other words, it
was not yet a summary characterization of measures in a carefully constructed
strategy. But it did serve as a prod and framework for identifying steps required to achieve the goal of improving individual and agency performance.
Identifying possible and requisite steps became a priority task and defining
factor as our leadership team considered how to organize the Office of the
Deputy Director of National Intelligence for Analysis and what to tackle first.

Think Big, Start Small, Fail Cheap, Fix Fast

THE INTELLIGENCE REFORM and Terrorism Prevention Act and President Bush's directive accepting most of the recommendations proposed by the Commission on the Intelligence Capabilities of the United States Regarding Weapons of Mass Destruction mandated a number of changes affecting analysis in the Intelligence Community. Most of these changes were clearly within the purview of ODDNI/A responsibilities, but the IRTPA and the directive allowed considerable latitude for deciding how to achieve or implement them. I have no idea whether leaving much to the discretion of the DNI was deliberate or a function of the way in which the legislation was cobbled together but suspect that it was mainly the latter. Regardless, it gave me welcome leeway to develop an implementation plan.[1]

While I waited for members of my leadership team to disengage from their previous positions and move to our temporary quarters in the CIA headquarters building, I thought a lot about what I wanted to accomplish and how we—the leadership team—should use the unprecedented opportunity to pursue transformational change. It did not take long to decide that simply implementing the many mandated reforms would be a managerial challenge but would squander the opportunity to pursue more ambitious goals. The impetus to "think big" came from many sources. Though I would like to say that I already had reasonably well-formed ideas about what a transformed analytic community should look like, that was not the case. Indeed, my thinking about this challenge was stimulated far more by the realization that we had an opportunity than by preexisting notions about how to use it.

More important stimulation came from the informal discussions among senior analytic managers before passage of the IRTPA in December 2004, and my conversations with candidates for my senior leadership team. There were more—and more exciting—ideas floating around than were captured by the mandated reforms. As important, I realized that my new team would be a rich source of ideas and was already thinking bigger than just implementing assigned reforms, and that there were several like-minded senior leaders in IC analytic units. In other words, the rare if not unique opportunity to attempt fundamental change was a function of more than just the leeway inherent in the IRTPA and presidential mandate and the latitude Negroponte seemed prepared to give me. Leeway gave us the chance to try. Favorable circumstances created a real possibility that we would succeed. It was worth taking a shot.

Although I desired and expected that my new team and those who joined us in the weeks ahead would contribute ideas of their own and that our strategy and plans would evolve incrementally as we discovered new possibilities and realized that particular goals could not be achieved without first addressing or creating essential prerequisites, I recognized that I had to provide an initial framework. Shaping factors for that framework included the need to implement mandated reforms; recognition that the ODNI was a new, unproven, and for many in the IC unwanted and unnecessary layer of bureaucracy; my desire to minimize opposition and resistance to any changes we sought to make; and strong personal conviction that the best way to improve IC analytic performance was to facilitate collaboration among analysts across the community.[2]

Because I was asked with increasing frequency just what I planned to do and because I had begun to organize ideas for the initial meetings with my new staff, I began to compose an "elevator speech" outlining key themes and constraints.[3] Doing so forced and enabled me to develop a logical flow and to identify missing pieces that had to be addressed. Early versions of this speech incorporated both general goals and the approach I hoped to use.[4] I constructed it as I did with several audiences in mind: colleagues in other ODNI directorates, oversight groups on the Hill and in the executive branch, and media and think tank people who follow intelligence issues; my own deputies; and IC analysts.

ODNI colleagues were an important audience because what each of us did within the purview of our own directorates had implications for the other directorates, and what we did together had to be reasonably well integrated if we were to succeed. This was also an important audience (as I was for them) because we all had similar startup challenges and were eager to learn and borrow from one another. An early indicator that communication within the ODNI was working was the statement at a senior staff meeting by Mary Margaret Graham, the first Deputy DNI for Collection, in which she reported on a conversation on the Hill in which she was asked about what was happening in the analysis directorate. She looked at me, smiled broadly, and said, "I channeled you and they were happy."

My years in Washington had taught me that it is usually far better to tell Hill staffers and sensible reporters what you are doing and why you are doing it than to ignore or deliberately shut them out. They might not like what you tell them, but I think it far better to have them reacting to your version of events than to what they have imagined or heard from someone else. Moreover, I have usually found it useful to hear the questions and concerns of informed outsiders because they reveal where I have been unclear or have failed to consider something that I should have. An additional reason for sharing information with these groups is that it builds trust and confidence far more effectively than if one is perceived as attempting to keep them out of the loop. I wanted these people to understand what we were trying to do because they could explain it to others. I knew that would help me. Even if they did not say positive things, it would be helpful if they said fewer negative things or did not speculate about our goals and approach.[5] Whether it was the fact that we shared information in this way or because what we had to say was well received (or both), my directorate and what we did received less criticism and more praise than other actors and actions in the reform drama.

My deputies were a very different type of audience. They needed and expected me to provide guidance with respect to overarching goals and what specifically I wanted them to do. But I needed their input and ideas on what we should strive for, how to get there, and how to structure our directorate and assign responsibilities in order to achieve specific and overarching objectives. I worried that if I presented a framework and goals that were too detailed, it would stifle initiative and enthusiasm. Conversely, if what I told them was too vague, it might persuade them that the boss didn't have a clue or mislead them into making proposals inconsistent with what I thought was necessary and possible within the constraints of life inside the Beltway.

Intelligence Community analysts and the organizations in which they served were ultimately the most important audience. I needed their cooperation in order to do anything. I needed their enthusiasm and support in order to succeed. Winning their acceptance, and eventually support, could not be taken for granted. As a group, they had been excoriated and demeaned for more than a year. The ODNI had been established explicitly, albeit not exclusively, to fix shortcomings in analytic tradecraft. The ODNI epitomized the negative implications of "I'm from the government and I'm here to help you." There was very little enthusiasm for the new organization, much skepticism that it would or could do anything to address what analysts considered to be the most serious impediments to better analytic work, and considerable worry that mandated changes would make it harder for them to do their job and would jeopardize their ability to support key missions and customers. At best, this was a skeptical audience. At worst, it was hostile.

Framework and Organizing Principles

The starting point for my elevator speech and framework was a clear statement that I did not intend to seek any changes to the organizational structure of the Intelligence Community. Beginning in this way was intended to defuse or preempt concern about the way the ODNI in general and the ODDNI/A in particular would attempt to reduce duplication, enhance integration and information sharing, and appease critics of the IC's risible organization charts. A related, and perhaps greater concern was that responsibilities and personnel would be moved from one agency to another as part of the reform process.[6] In addition to wanting to relieve at least one source of anxiety in the analytic workforce, I wanted to rule out attempts to change the organization for three pragmatic reasons.

Reason number one was that it was unnecessary. The goal of reform, as I chose to define it, was to improve the quality of intelligence analysis support to national security decision makers, not to tidy up organization charts. To accomplish my goal required better tradecraft, improved sharing of information, and more extensive and effective collaboration across agency boundaries. We could achieve these intermediate or instrumental goals and the ultimate objective of better analysis without changing the structure or moving large numbers of people.

The second reason was that such an attempt would be opposed, accurately, as unnecessarily and dangerously disruptive. As chaotic as IC organization appears to outsiders—and many insiders—it does have an underlying logic that links each of the analytic units to particular missions and customers. Analysts are recruited and expertise is nurtured to provide tailored and timely intelligence to particular customers and missions. To be most useful, intelligence support must be tailored to the needs of specific missions and requirements. One-size-fits-all intelligence does not fit anyone. No one wanted or would tolerate "reform" initiatives likely to disrupt or degrade the flow of intelligence to warfighters, counterterror operations, counterproliferation work, or myriad other high-profile activities.

Third, this was a fight I was sure to lose. With the exception of CIA, all analytic components of the IC are subordinate to cabinet secretaries who understandably regard them as "their" intelligence units. They are funded through department budgets, accountable and responsible to the head of the department, and in many cases integral to the performance of departmental missions. Even if I had been inclined to seek structural change before inter-acting with counterparts from across the IC during deliberations to craft the administration's intelligence reform bill, which I was not, I would have been dissuaded by the vehemence with which we all defended our agency preroga-tives. In addition, I was quite certain that DNI Negroponte was not going to jeopardize achievement of other ODNI goals by allowing me to pick a fight we could not win.

The flip side of my message renouncing intent to seek structural change was a clear statement that I did intend to seek more, deeper, and more effec-tive integration and collaboration. Analytic units would remain where they were on organization charts, and analysts would remain in their home orga-nizations, but they would be expected and enabled to work with colleagues and counterparts outside the home unit. But collaboration was not going to happen by fiat. Recognizing that we would need to lower barriers, facilitate the sharing of information, and do many other things to achieve desired levels and forms of integration and collaboration opened our eyes to the need for a host of additional, nonmandated reforms (discussed further on).

Having ruled out pursuit of organizational changes, I turned to positive portions of my emerging agenda, declaring that restoring confidence in IC analysis was my highest and most urgent priority.[7] We would do that, in part, by demonstrating marked improvement in the quality of analytic products. Before discussing how we would do that, I sketched out the approach (calling it a strategy at this point would be an exaggeration) I intended to use. The essence of that approach, as stated earlier, was to improve Intelligence Com-munity support to policymakers by improving the quality of analytic prod-ucts, and that we would improve the quality and utility of analytic products by improving the performance of every analytic component. That would be achieved by providing more information and assistance to analytic managers,

and by improving the performance of every analyst. Implementing the reforms mandated by the IRTPA and the President would help improve the
performance of all analysts. Nevertheless, there were many other things that
we could and would undertake, including training in the use of good analytic
techniques, easier access to information and experts in and outside the Intelligence Community, and greater emphasis on collaboration.

After I provided this encapsulated summary of the approach I wanted
to use, members of my senior team began to pose questions and volunteer
suggestions. I do not recall any objections or challenges to the approach,
but whether that was because everyone agreed with it, needed time to digest
what I had said before commenting, or interpreted my words as holy writ
because I was the boss, we never revisited the question of whether this really
was the best way to proceed. The virtue of instant acceptance was that we
were able to move quickly to questions about next steps and implementation. The downside is that we did not consider alternatives or search for
a better approach. In retrospect, I'm sure that I was more pleased by the
prospect of being able to move out smartly (the need for speed) than worried about roads not taken.

The focus on "How can we do this?" rather than on "Is there a better
way to do this?" was consistent with and indicative of the *modus operandi*
that I had used many times before. That approach is to pull together a
first-approximation solution to a particular set of problems, see what happens during implementation, and refine the approach, strategy, or plan
in response to discoveries and feedback. I had confidence that we would
develop a more comprehensive, better-integrated, and more effective plan
of action in an incremental fashion. I was also quite certain that we were
unlikely to devise a "perfect" plan on the first try no matter how long we
deliberated or how many experts we consulted. My team quickly bought
in to this approach, and it was only a short time before Mike Wertheimer
pithily reduced it to a bumper-sticker-sized slogan: "Think big, start small,
fail cheap, fix fast."

Getting Organized

Using a process that began immediately and continued throughout my tenure as DDNI/A, we turned to the task of identifying obstacles and requisites
to improving analytic performance in the way outlined above. Specific steps
and objectives will be discussed later; the point I want to make here is that
the internal structure of the analysis directorate and the portfolios of each

member of the team derived from deliberations about what needed to be done. In other words, rather than fitting tasks into predetermined bins, we began by identifying what needed to be done, and grouped similar and interdependent tasks. Over time, this process enabled us to group similar and tightly linked tasks and to assign them to particular deputies. This process ultimately defined the portfolios and principal responsibilities of each component of the ODDNI/A. Sometimes the assignment of tasks to particular deputies was an obvious no-brainer, but often the task could logically have been assigned to more than one bin or deputy. That was usually a pretty good indication that we needed to establish working groups or special purpose teams composed of staff from multiple divisions.

Staffing each of the subcomponents of the directorate proceeded in tandem with the identification and assignment of tasks. Although I do not remember saying so explicitly, my deputies quickly realized that neither they nor I were going to build a bureaucratic empire. Even before the ODNI began to be hammered for "bureaucratic bloat," which happened almost immediately because some Members and staff apparently forgot how many functions and people the IRTPA had transferred from the DCI to the ODDNI, I had decided that I wanted my directorate to be as lean as possible.[8] My years in INR reinforced a long-standing preference for working with fewer, better-qualified specialists instead of attempting to human wave problems with hordes of lesser-qualified people. Beyond this personal predilection, which was reinforced by the first complaints from the Hill about empire-building and overstaffing, I believed that we were more likely to develop workable solutions to complex, interconnected problems if integration occurred in a few smart heads than if we tried to coordinate multiple pieces of a bureaucracy.[9]

Very quickly, certainly within a week or two of convening for the first time as the senior staff of the ODDNI/A, the nature of our discussions changed from one in which I dominated the conversation by enumerating my own goals and thoughts about achieving them and responding to questions from others, to one in which we began to function as a team with everyone contributing ideas. This evolved into a continuous incremental process in which overarching objectives were clarified and prioritized, requisite instrumental goals and conditions were identified, specific responsibilities were assumed or assigned, and discoveries made during the course of implementation triggered modifications. After a few weeks, this process gave birth to the initial structure and divisions of labor within the analysis directorate.

Ideas and feedback flowed into this process from three sources. One was internal to the directorate. As each of my deputies and Chief of Staff Jan Karcz developed and refined their responsibilities and recruited people with the expertise needed to perform those responsibilities, they discovered new opportunities and requirements, for themselves and for the directorate as a whole. What happened more than vindicated my confidence that I had recruited the right people and that their individual and collective commitment to transform as well as to improve analysis would generate more ideas and workable approaches than any off-the-shelf reform document.[10] The ideas generated in this process were both creative and pragmatic, combining lofty objectives and a pragmatic approach shaped by judgments about what could be achieved under current conditions and what could both produce short-term improvement and lay a foundation for transformational change.[11]

The second source of ideas was the ODNI. Daily meetings of the four Deputy DNIs and regular interchange among our staffs facilitated the exchange of ideas, information, and experience-based lessons. Illustrative examples include exchanges on what collectors wanted and needed from analysts in order to target coverage, assess sources, and adjust collection to address pop-up requirements, and those on changes needed to IT systems and security regulations if we were to enhance collaboration across agency boundaries. This interaction enhanced coherence and the efficacy of the steps we took. Sadly, but predictably, the ease and value of cooperation among ODNI directorates decreased as staffs became larger and more bureaucratic.[12]

The third source of ideas was input from analysts and analytic components of the Intelligence Community. I began making parish calls even before all members of my team arrived on the job, and some who attended these meetings responded to my call for ideas and invitation to ask questions. The number was small, and many reiterated concerns or suggestions that had been raised previously, but others were truly new, at least to us. Whether novel or familiar, I (actually my extremely capable staff assistants) tried to keep track of such input and to refer to it in subsequent town meetings and when describing what we were doing to members of our oversight bodies. My reasons for doing so were partly tactical, that is, to score points for the effort to be inclusive and to demonstrate to analysts that we were trying to address problems they considered important. But this was more than just a device to win approval and help secure buy-in. It was also a way to identify what analysts thought would have the biggest impact on their ability to perform at a higher level. Examples of tasks added to our "to do" list as a result of such input include reducing or eliminating restrictions that limited the ability of analysts to access databases and share information with colleagues who had the same security clearances, and procedures (rules) that empowered collectors to determine which analysts "needed" access to specific reports.[13]

Requisites of Greater Integration and More Effective Collaboration

Postmortems on the 9/11 attacks and the flawed National Intelligence Estimate on Saddam Hussein's WMD capabilities identified a plethora of structural and procedural problems in the national security establishment, but fixing "everything" was a bridge too far for Congress and the administration.[14] In the midst of wars in Iraq and Afghanistan and high public anxiety about the danger of additional terrorist attacks—fueled by statements out of Washington—the desire to find quick-fix solutions was understandable, and probably unavoidable. Pundits and politicians quickly downsized the task by focusing on the Intelligence Community and barriers to information sharing and collaboration across agency boundaries.[15] Lowering the barriers to integration and enhancing collaboration became the centerpiece of the 2004 intelligence reform legislation and a principal rationale for creation of the Office of the Director of National Intelligence.[16]

Although much commentary and the reform legislation decried the "stovepiped" character of the Intelligence Community and championed removal of legal and bureaucratic impediments to information sharing, it provided little concrete guidance on how to achieve those objectives. Declaring goals is a useful, even necessary step toward actually achieving them, but it is far from sufficient. My team and I understood that we would be judged in part by our success in better integrating the disparate components of the Intelligence Community and lowering barriers to collaboration. Achieving the desired outcome required a multifaceted strategy. We also recognized that improved information sharing and greater collaboration were instrumental objectives; the ultimate goal was to produce more useful and more accurate analytical support to policymakers.

Prioritizing our objectives in this way prompted us to accord higher priority to identifying and satisfying the critical requisites for collaboration than to reducing or removing a predetermined set of obstacles. Choosing this approach entailed an element of risk because demonstrating improved performance would be more challenging and subjective than preparing a list of obstacles and metrics to demonstrate progress toward better integration. But proceeding as we did enabled us to address impediments in the course of building what we judged to be a more integrated and effective approach to collaboration. Rather than tackling "all" of the previously identified obstacles without clear understanding of which were most or least significant to the task we had undertaken and running the risk that even eliminating all of them might not achieve the desired level of collaboration and enhanced utility, we made pragmatic judgments about what would produce the biggest payoff.

Determining what to do and how to do it was an incremental and sometimes messy process that unfolded as we stood up the leadership team, assigned responsibilities to each of the divisions, and began to receive input from constituent agencies. The description of decisions and actions that follows suggests greater coherence than was actually the case. What we attempted acquired coherence as we went along, but this was more the result of feedback and adjustment than the quality of an initial blueprint. The guiding logic of what we did can be summarized as follows:

- Priority number one was to restore confidence in the Intelligence Community, its analysts, and analytic products.
- The key to restoring confidence was to enhance the perceived quality of analytic support to national security decision makers. Analytic products and other forms of support not only had to be better, they had to be shown to be better by applying analytic metrics and perceived as better by national security policymakers.
- The most important requisites of enhanced analysis were better analytic tradecraft and more productive collaboration among analysts within and across agency boundaries.
- The most urgent task of the ODDNI/A was to create the conditions that would facilitate achievement of the other priority goals.

Over time—time measured in weeks and months—we compiled a list of requisite conditions and grouped them into linked and partially overlapping categories. Almost from the beginning, we saw the elements in each category as integral and instrumental parts of a transformational agenda. Keeping our eyes on the ultimate goal of producing better analytic support and the intermediate goal of making collaboration more common and more effective narrowed and focused the scope of what we attempted in each of the divisions. For example, the options we considered to meet mandated requirements to assess the performance of individual analysts and agencies were constrained by the need to make them compatible with new tradecraft directives, the content of training programs, and measures to enhance information sharing.

We might have adopted an approach that deliberately or accidentally produced discontinuities such that what was done in one bin or arena was more rigorous, innovative, or "advanced" than what was done in others in the hope that the most "advanced" would inspire or compel the less advanced to improve. I briefly considered doing that but soon decided that moving in tandem would be more coherent and ultimately more effective than encouraging each division and arena to move as far and as fast as it could. In effect, this was a decision to build collaboration by subordinating competition to demonstrate component success to the larger goal of enhancing overall performance. It made progress in the slowest-moving component the pacing element for analytic transformation, but it also helped to minimize the disruptive effects of change and the danger of systemic failure. Though we might aspire—and some of our external critics might demand—to change "everything," meeting the ongoing responsibilities of the Intelligence Community required that we do so without breaking anything.

Taking Stock

ONE OF THE FIRST DISCOVERIES we made as we set out to develop a strategy to enhance the quality and utility of analytic products was how little we knew about the base condition of the Intelligence Community and its component agencies. I had been in and around the IC for a long time, as had most of my deputies, but our understanding of matters critical to determining what to preserve, what to change, and how to pursue changes we thought necessary was extremely limited. I knew a great deal about the Bureau of Intelligence and Research and a fair amount about the National Intelligence Council, but distressingly little about other components. Much the same, *mutatis mutandis*, was true of my deputies and my counterparts in other directorates of the ODNI. Moreover, much of what we thought we knew was wrong or more accurately described as urban myth, caricatures, or deliberately misleading.[1]

The list of basic but critically important questions to which we were unable to obtain reliable answers included the following:

- How many analysts are there in the IC?
- What are their areas of expertise?
- What does each analyst work on and how long have they worked on those topics?
- Where do they work and whom do they work for?
- How many people work on a given topic and where are they located?

- What intelligence problems are addressed by each agency and what topics do they not address?
- Which agencies produce the best work on particular topics and what criteria are used to determine quality?

There were many reasons for the paucity and unreliability of such basic data. For example, obtaining reliable information on the number of analysts was complicated by disagreement about which positions or individuals should be classified as "analysts," budgetary conventions that aggregated "analysts" and the clerical and other staff assigned to support them, counterintelligence considerations that sought to obscure magnitude of interest and effort on particular subjects, and bureaucratic conventions that used current assignment rather than experience as the principal criterion for determining how many "experts" worked on a given topic. Other reasons the data were problematic include the desire of managers to "hide" their best experts so they would not be conscripted to staff a special team or project, and the fact that such data as were collected were often for a specific purpose (such as to answer a question from the Hill or to demonstrate ramped-up effort to address the topic du jour) and could not be aggregated to produce a snapshot of what analysts were working on at a particular point in time.

We needed to know more about the existing state of the IC analytic community in order to develop a strategy and implementation plan but were reluctant to launch the ODDNI/A by demanding data that we knew would be cumbersome to collect. Perhaps I was inaccurately projecting my own feelings onto the presumed attitudes of other managers, but I was afraid that issuing a call for data without first explaining to and, hopefully, obtaining buy-in from agency analytic managers would cause them to view the ODDNI/A as a new incarnation of the old Community Management Staff (CMS). During my many years in the INR front office, I hated to receive data calls from CMS because they were almost always difficult to answer and never connected to anything that helped the Bureau or me to do our jobs. Although I probably shouldn't admit it, my guidance often was "make something up." I suspect that I was not the only one who did so. Now I needed accurate input.

Reflecting upon my own past responses to CMS data calls, I decided that the only way to obtain the information I needed to pave the way for enhanced collaboration was to explain to other managers why I needed the information and how I thought having it would help them to align missions and capabilities, take advantage of capabilities elsewhere in the Intelligence Community, and make better-informed recruitment and other management decisions. Under normal circumstances, such an appeal to self-interest would have been received with the same degree of skepticism as any "I'm from the government and I'm here to help you" pitch. That is to say, my motives would have been suspect and the people whose cooperation I needed would have blown me off. But that didn't happen.

The reason it did not happen, I'm convinced, was that the informal discussions several of us began having during the months before the stand-up of the ODNI had produced a level of mutual trust and shared commitment that worked to my advantage. At minimum, key members of the informal grouping that I subsequently formalized as the Analysis and Production Board were willing to give me benefit of the doubt and endorse the data-collection exercise. In the event, securing agreement to provide data proved easier than actually doing so.

Mapping Who Does What

One component of the effort to determine baseline conditions in the Intelligence Community was to enhance understanding of what each agency did—the subjects they covered, how many analysts were assigned to each subject, and so on—and whom they considered their most important customers. Brief conversations with members of my leadership team and a few IC managers made clear that the utility of the information we obtained would be a function of what we asked and how well recipients of the questionnaire understood what we were trying to do. At the suggestion of John Kringen, Director of Intelligence at CIA, we decided to pilot the effort by asking for information about work on Iraq.[2] The initial results told us more about the importance of asking the right questions than about the state of analytic work on Iraq.

Our first attempt to elicit information asked broad questions and implicitly invited each respondent to interpret the questions in ways appropriate to their agency. That did not work. Some responses were more detailed than others, but what we learned from this iteration was, essentially, that all agencies worked on Iraq, that most worked on most or all of the subtopics we listed (such as military, economic, political, societal, terrorism), and that most analysts worked on multiple subtopics because the topics were interconnected. The results did not give us the data we needed, but they did provide a valuable insight that underscored the potential for gains from specialization, collaboration, and willingness to utilize work produced by colleagues in other IC components. The important insight was that regardless of primary customers and mission, most agencies attempted to provide "comprehensive" coverage of many topics, especially high-profile topics, because customers asked for it. More important, they worked on topics and subtopics that were outside their areas of greatest competence because they did not know where to turn for help, knew that they could request but not be assured of obtaining input from other agencies, and did not have confidence that what they received from colleagues in other agencies would be as good as what they were able to produce themselves. These were fixable and had-to-be-fixed problems.[3]

Although it was frustrating to discover how difficult it was to obtain essential and, one might have thought, pretty basic information about the coverage and magnitude of effort agencies devoted to the many topics of interest to the national security enterprise, the experience of trying to obtain reasonably accurate information also had a number of amusing aspects. For example, when trying to resolve a discrepancy between the number of analysts working on Iraq provided by the CIA's Directorate of Intelligence and the total of the subtopic analysts provided by the unit responsible for Iraq, I went to speak with unit chief Andy Liepman. Andy was a long-time friend who understood and was supportive of what we were trying to do. I anticipated that he would resolve the discrepancy by telling me that his numbers had not included a special subunit. That is not what happened. Instead, he asked, "Where the hell did you get the other (larger) number? I have nowhere near that many people." He was surprised and puzzled when I told them the number had come from his own front office. When we looked into the matter more closely, we discovered that a number of people who had been assigned to the Iraq unit were left on the rolls after being reassigned on temporary duty to Iraq or an interagency task force. There was nothing untoward about what had happened. The analysts in question continued to be assigned to their former unit for bureaucratic convenience because it was easier (and cheaper) to do that than to move them on organization charts while on a short-term assignment. Among other consequences, this incident sensitized us to the likelihood that many of the numbers we were collecting were, at best, reasonable approximations of reality good enough for our purposes but too imprecise to be used for budgets, recruiting, and other purposes.

Two more iterations were required to "get the questions right" and to educate ourselves, agency managers, and the administrative staff providing the data to a point at which we all thought we were examining the same questions. When we reached that point, we were able to construct a snap-shot of work on Iraq in each agency and the IC as a whole. The snapshot provided valuable information on the dimensions of the "Iraq problem set" being worked in each agency and the approximate number of people work-ing primarily on each of several specified subtopics. Among other insights, the snapshots helped to identify gaps and weak spots in coverage, apparent duplications of effort, and potential opportunities for divisions of labor and collaboration.

Having refined the process with our Iraq pilot, we used what we had learned to map dozens of additional national security topics. Several months were required to acquire and interpret the resultant data. When we were finished, we had a relatively comprehensive and reasonably accurate baseline understanding of agency priorities and magnitudes of effort. The snapshots were helpful, but they alone did not provide information on the expertise or experience of the analysts working specific accounts, or the quality of the products they produced. We had to go after that information in a different way (see further on). Even though the snapshots of individual agencies and the Intelligence Community as a whole were building-block inputs, we shared them with all agency senior analytic managers so they would continue to feel that they were part of the process and, more important, to provide information about the work being done on specific topics by colleagues in other agencies. As noted, one of the reasons agencies elected to do independent work on certain topics, even if they lacked expertise on those topics, was because they did not know where to turn for assistance. Sharing the snapshots did not tell them anything about the quality of products produced elsewhere or ensure that requests for assistance would be honored. However, it did provide a starting point or, in many cases, a number of potential starting points.

Mapping the Analytic Workforce

Although the paucity and problematic character of information about what IC component agencies did was one of the impediments to collaboration, it was not the most important. Rightly or wrongly, I considered collaboration to be primarily a relationship among people, not organizations.[4] Prerequisites for collaboration between or among people include knowledge that the potential partner exists, where he or she works, how to contact one another, the tech-nical and legal ability to exchange information, understanding of the other's expertise and perspective, and confidence that the prospective collaborator adheres to high standards of analytic tradecraft. In order to meet some of these requisites, we needed a much clearer understanding of the IC analytic community than could be gleaned from organization charts and statistics on the number of analysts assigned to particular topics.

I was not the first to seek better information on IC analytic capabilities. John Gannon, who was Chair of the National Intelligence Council from 1997 to 2001, attempted to build a database of analytic expertise that would enable the NIC and others in the IC to identify and contact analysts with knowledge of specific places, programs, or problems. I thought it was a great idea at the time and was dismayed when his efforts were thwarted by security mavens. They worried that compiling such a database, which John called the Analytic Resources Catalog or ARC, would (if compromised) make it easy for bad guys to assess IC capabilities and target individual analysts or agencies.

Mark Lowenthal renewed the effort to make the ARC a useful management tool when he served as Assistant Director of Central Intelligence for Analysis and Production and Vice Chair of NIC (2002–2005). But he, too, made only modest headway, albeit for a somewhat different reason than had thwarted Gannon. Lowenthal obtained greater support for the existence of such a database by arguing that it would provide a way for the DCI and other IC managers to quickly identify and coopt analysts with skills needed for a task force, emergency deployment, or other special undertaking. For understandable reasons, managers were reluctant to put the names of their analysts on a de facto "free agent list" from which others could recruit or reassign, and many analysts were reluctant to make themselves liable to possible involuntary reassignment.[5]

When I assumed the position of DDNI/A, I inherited the ARC prototype and the staff that had worked on the project for Mark Lowenthal. The technical capabilities of the database had been enhanced, but the project went into limbo during the transition from DCI to DNI. This gave me a tool, developers eager to demonstrate what it could do, and advocates hoping the ODNI would make inclusion in the database mandatory for all analysts. I was eager to take advantage of these fortuitous circumstances but had no idea what DNI authorities might be relevant.

Having come of age in the 1960s, I instinctively rebelled against the idea of using some unspecified authority to compel registration in the ARC. More important, I quickly decided that coerced participation would be counterproductive because I wanted analysts to view the ARC as a beneficial tool, not as something imposed by a new layer of bureaucracy. One of my key goals was to improve the quality of analytic products by making collaboration easier and more efficacious. I judged that this could better be achieved if it was something that analysts wanted to do because they found it valuable than if it was something they were forced to do. Indeed, using the word "collaboration" instead of "coordination" or "cooperation" was a deliberate choice because I wanted to emphasize that what we had in mind was something very different from the forced or mechanical coordination of products that was widely despised by analysts across the community.[6]

Although I was reasonably clear in my own mind about why the ARC was critical to the success of my still-evolving vision of a more integrated and impactful community of analysts, I recognized that simply rehearsing those reasons was unlikely to persuade analysts that registering would be useful to them. When thinking about how to make that case—how to make analysts want to be in and use the ARC—I drew upon what we were learning about IC demographics as part of our effort to develop a baseline for change. Early conversations with my own senior team and agency analytic managers indicated they shared my subjective impressions about the age distribution of our workforce. We thought we had a significant but rapidly aging baby boomer contingent, a great many young analysts, and relatively few middle-aged mid-career people. We all saw this as a problem and therefore set out to assemble real data.

For purposes of workforce planning, we wanted and needed to know the age distribution of analysts in individual agencies and the IC as a whole. One might think that would be relatively easy information to obtain—but only if one had never worked in a government bureaucracy. Privacy rules and non-discrimination regulations made it difficult to obtain the information directly, so we decided to use years of government service as a proxy indicator. The results confirmed what we suspected. The age distribution looked like the letter "J." The short leg represented our aging and rapidly eligible-to-retire baby boomer experts; the long leg represented the more than 50 percent of the analytic workforce that had joined the Intelligence Community after 9/11. The "U"-shaped trough in the middle—representing the middle-grade, mid-career, NCO-like cohort—was the result of "right sizing," "downsizing," and hiring freezes during the Clinton administration. Among other challenges, this demographic profile meant that we had to factor into our plans the need to persuade aging baby boomers to defer retirement, the paucity of middle managers able to supervise and train much less experienced "newbies," and a large majority of recruits who would move into middle-management positions and responsibilities far more quickly (and in many cases with less mentorship) than had been the case previously.

I will have more to say later about the implications of J-curve demographics, but here I want to focus on its relevance to the Analytic Resources Catalog and to the arguments we developed to entice analysts to register. The arguments were not contrived for purposes of persuasion; they had the additional virtue of being true. For example, analysts quickly understood that the demographic curve was also a J-curve of expertise and that being able to identify and locate people with more experience than they had would make it easier and safer (in the sense of increasing the likelihood of avoiding errors) to make judgments on complex and consequential matters. They also recognized the advantages of being able to connect to experts on topics in their own portfolio who happened to work in other parts of the Intelligence Community.

Anticipating questions about criteria for listing expertise, I explained that expertise was not the same as current assignment. Indeed, because most IC agencies reassigned people every two to three years (or sooner), it was often the case that individual analysts knew more about the subjects covered in their previous job than about those in their current portfolios. I had gained this insight several years earlier when I realized that analysts in INR continued to confer with analysts in other agencies who had moved on to new responsibilities because former counterparts generally forgot what they knew about past assignments less rapidly than they acquired expertise in new ones.[7] However, current assignment was an important data point because it would help people to find partners. We also wanted to know what each individual considered his or her own areas of greatest expertise.

We tried to make clear that the ARC—we—did not care where or how analysts had acquired knowledge of a language, country, transnational issue, or technical subject. The ARC would treat all sources of expertise, whether acquired in graduate school, in the Peace Corps or military service, or from previous assignments in the Intelligence Community, as equally valuable. We decided to forgo tests or demands for documentation in favor of letting individuals declare their own levels of expertise. This, of course, entailed risk that some would overstate their qualifications and others would be too modest. Our operating premise was that the truth would come out in the wash. Our immediate goal was to enable analysts to find and work with one another. If in doing so they demonstrated that they had overstated their qualifications, that would become part of their reputation. In effect we envisioned a "Yelp-like" process of evaluation and reputation building.[8] Conversely, if increased interaction with colleagues across the IC indicated that they had valuable expertise and insights, that would become known to a wider circle of analysts. Those who were good would gain recognition, and more IC products would benefit from their contributions.

Persuading individual analysts that enrollment in the ARC would benefit them personally and improve the quality of analytic support to the national security enterprise was only one of the challenges we had to address in order to make the ARC a useful tool. Another was the opposition of counterintelligence (CI) officials (affectionately, or not so affectionately referred to as "Security Nazis") that had frustrated John Gannon's efforts. The intelligence reform legislation did not give me greater authority on this matter than Gannon had possessed, but it did give me an additional and ultimately compelling argument. The IRTPA had transferred responsibility for the *President's Daily Brief* to the DNI and mandated that it include input and insights from across the Intelligence Community. DNI John Negroponte had delegated that responsibility to me. I was able to argue successfully that to meet that responsibility, I had to be able to identify and utilize the best analysts in the community regardless of where they were assigned or how they had acquired their expertise. We still had to overcome some technical and regulatory obstacles, but creating and populating the ARC database was a necessary first step.

We also had to overcome the reluctance of individuals and analytic managers to post their skills in a database that might—or as stated when Mark Lowenthal tried to invigorate it, would—be used to reassign analysts to meet IC requirements. I think Mark made the argument as he did, at least in part, to overcome CI objections. However, the effect of doing so was to discourage rather than encourage registration. I was able, happy, and obliged to address this concern head on. It had to be addressed because of concerns engendered by the provisions of the IRTPA that empowered the DNI to transfer funds and personnel to "higher priority intelligence activities."[9] Uncertainty about the intentions of the DNI and imperfect understanding of convoluted legislative language was a general problem. The specific manifestation of the problem that I had to address was concern among analysts and managers that we could and would restructure the IC and move large numbers of functions and people to tidy up organization charts and demonstrate that a new team was now in charge. This concern was expressed less as a fear of change than as an understandable concern that disruptive change would impede performance of mission.

The ODNI leadership team was acutely aware of the need to minimize threats to current performance of mission while attempting to enhance future performance, and it never intended to make major structural changes or transfers of people and portfolios. Knowing that was the case was not good enough. We had to communicate the message to the workforce without at the same time conveying a sense that we envisioned business as usual under a new layer of bureaucracy. My responsibility was to reassure IC analysts that we were determined to avoid disruption that would endanger performance and envisioned no immediate reassignments of missions or personnel beyond those mandated by the intelligence reform legislation. I attempted to provide reassurance by describing what we intended to do and how we would attempt to do it.[10]

Use of the "I" word in the preceding sentence is deliberate but requires explanation. On this and many other issues, my natural inclination and initial declared approach was to downplay my own role in favor of establishing an institutional persona for the Deputy Director of National Intelligence for Analysis. My determination to emphasize the position rather than the person was strengthened by gratifying comments from colleagues and others who referenced my reputation and the confidence it inspired that reforms to IC analysis would be well considered and constructive. Ego gratification is pleasant, but I viewed it as self-indulgent and antithetical to the building of institutions and mechanisms that would outlast my tenure. I eventually, albeit reluctantly, yielded to the arguments of my senior team that persuaded me that promises from the DDNI/A would be heavily discounted if not dismissed, and that if I really wanted to develop trust, inspire confidence, and win cooperation, I had to put myself and my reputation front and center in everything that we did. As one of my team phrased it, analysts would believe something because I said it, not because it was the policy or position of the DDNI for analysis.

Writing this more than a decade later still makes me uncomfortable, but I spent enough time in Washington to recognize that my colleagues were correct. Two observations or assertions were particularly important in changing my mind on this issue. One was from John Keefe, my Deputy for Analytic Mission Management (explained further on), former Hill staffer, and the member of our team with the most acute political instincts. After one of many exchanges on the best way to present our plans to the community, John said, "I cannot get anywhere when I try to enlist support for the goals and approach of the DDNI for Analysis because nobody knows what that is and few have any respect for the title. But when I say that I'm Tom Fingar's deputy and describing what Fingar thinks we need to do, it carries enormously greater weight and much greater effect."

I recognized that "my" reputation was enhanced by the fact that I held the concurrent and well-regarded position of Chair of the National Intelligence Council, and that I was able to bask in the reflected glow of INR's generally stellar reputation, but had to acknowledge that John had a point. The second reinforcing comment came from Maura Harty, a long-serving and highly regarded Assistant Secretary of State with whom I had worked for many years. In a chance encounter during a visit to the State Department early in my tenure as DDNI/A, we chatted about my new job and its challenges. Maura interjected, in effect, "You know, I hope, that you have a reputation to die for in this town. Use it to get things done and to build support for what you think needs to be done." I write this not, I hope, to brag about what others have said, but to underscore two important lessons. One is that everyone acquires a reputation in the course of his or her career. That reputation can be an asset or a liability; in either case, it often becomes self-reinforcing. Those with a good reputation receive more opportunities. This reinforces the view that they are trustworthy, competent, and so on. Those with a bad or limited reputation get fewer opportunities, and the bar for assessing performance is sometimes higher than it would be for someone with a better reputation. The second lesson is that in Washington, and probably other settings, a positive reputation can be a tremendous asset when trying to gain a hearing, win support, or in other ways influence developments.

The message we crafted to encourage registration in the ARC derived from our broader vision for analysis in the IC. As described earlier, the vision and the method were summarized as *Improving the quality of IC support to the national security enterprise by improving the performance of all component organizations by improving the performance and effectiveness of all IC analysts.* This was more than a slogan; it was the guiding principle undergirding most of the reforms we adopted or initiated. Training and tradecraft mandates contributed to this effort, but we were able to explain, persuasively in most cases, that we could not achieve our goals if we pillaged some components of the community in order to bolster the performance of others. Facilitating collaboration by building and using the ARC would help individuals to do better by linking up with more experienced analysts and/or with experts who had complementary knowledge and experience.

As pieces of our strategy came together, the Analytic Resources Catalog assumed an even more important role. So important, in fact, that I decided to supplement the inducements summarized earlier by utilizing leverage resulting from my concurrent positions as Chair of NIC and ODNI official responsible for the PDB. Judging that most analysts would be eager to write for the PDB or NIC and to be part of teams sent to brief select products on the Hill and to senior officials in the executive branch, I announced that registration in the ARC was a requisite for all three opportunities. The way in which I presented this requirement was to note that the ARC would be the authoritative database on analyst expertise. Any analyst not represented in the ARC would be assumed to lack expertise on anything because registration was to be at the initiative of individual analysts and/or their managers. Absence from the ARC database would be interpreted to mean that neither the individual nor his or her manager considered that person to be worthy of writing for the President and other senior officials or of representing their agency or the IC in briefings to policymakers. This was obviously an exaggerated position, but analysts understood its intent and implications.

I had been presenting regular updates on the ARC and many other ODDNI/A projects during the daily meeting of ODNI deputies both to keep others informed and as part of our ongoing effort to identify opportunities for synergy and steps that other directorates could take that would help me or another deputy to achieve his or her goals. Deputy for Management Pat Kennedy clearly took on board what I had been saying about the ARC because he added yet another incentive for managers to enroll their analysts. At one of our first meetings with the heads of all IC components, he added a coda to my pitch on the importance of including all analysts in the ARC. When I finished speaking, Pat said, "One more thing. Any analyst not included in Fingar's database is not in a funded position. We are going to reconcile budget and staffing numbers to the list of analysts in the ARC." I honestly do not know if Pat could have or actually attempted to do that but those in the room clearly got the message. Within less than a week, a great many names were added to the database.

The reinvigorated push for the ARC triggered questions from my staff and agency analytic managers that underscored, yet again, the depth of entrenched ways of thinking and the magnitude of reform challenges. Many of the questions amounted to some variant of "Who is an analyst?" I had not given much thought to this question before embarking on the quest to build a database of analytic expertise. To the extent that I had thought about it, I assumed that once analytic managers understood why we wanted to create a comprehensive repository of expertise and how we intended to use it, they would know which of their subordinates should be included and would see the advantages of erring on the side of including "everyone" with substantive expertise rather than risk excluding experts because of their job titles. My immediate, and probably flippant and unhelpful response was, "Anyone who thinks they have substantive expertise or whose boss thinks has expertise."[11]

Rejoinder questions reflected bureaucratic difficulty in applying this criterion. One set of such questions centered on the "class distinction" between "all source" and "single INT" (for example, signals intelligence or imagery intelligence) analysts and amounted to a question about which agencies were eligible to add analysts to the ARC. Hoary tradition if not formal statutes classified only CIA, DIA (Defense Intelligence Agency), and INR as all-source agencies. All-source (white collar) analysts provided direct support to national security policymakers and, in theory, had access to all forms of intelligence. Single INT (blue collar) analysts processed and provided signals intelligence, imagery-derived intelligence, and other types of information to the all-source analysts who would integrate and interpret their inputs.[12]

I do not know whether this distinction ever made sense in theory or practice, but it was clearly inaccurate and counterproductive in the twenty-first century. Imagery analysts needed human intelligence (HUMINT) and signals intelligence (SIGINT) to understand what they were looking at. Without other kinds of information, the photo of a crate on a flatcar is only that. One needs other information to determine what might be in the box, where it came from and where it might be headed, whether it is a licit or illicit transaction, and so on. The ARC-triggered questions alerted us to the importance of identifying and addressing impediments to giving all IC analysts access to all of the information needed to do their jobs properly.[13]

I listened to the arguments, which amounted to little more than assertions of "that is the way we have always done it," but declared *ex cathedra* that all agencies were eligible to add names to the ARC. That, of course, triggered another round of questions seeking further guidance on eligibility criteria. Thus, for example, "If analysts in single INT agencies can be listed in the ARC, what criteria should be used to distinguish analysts from collectors?" This was another variant of the "Who is an analyst?" question, and I confess to becoming impatient with bureaucratic thinking that seemed more interested in excluding categories of people than in capturing as much expertise as possible. I'm sure my impatience showed and probably upset some of my colleagues when I cut off further discussion and declared that expertise is a function of what people know, not job title or position on an organization chart. "Collectors" often know a great deal about the subjects they work on, and if they could contribute to the analytic mission of reducing uncertainty about complex and consequential developments, I wanted their help. Effectively ignoring Pat Kennedy's statement about a relationship between enrollment in the ARC and assignment to a funded position, I declared that enrollment in the ARC was open to everyone working in the IC who believed he or she had substantive expertise on matters germane to national security.[14]

Mapping Analytic Products

A third missing component necessary to establish a baseline assessment of IC analytic activity was a comprehensive database of analytic products. I was dismayed, but not surprised, to discover that there was no readily available answer to the question, "What analytic products does the Intelligence Community produce?" There was no easy way to discover which agency wrote on which topics, the degree of overlap or disagreement in the products of different agencies, which agencies produced the best or worst work on particular topics, whether one agency did or could have used analyses produced elsewhere in the IC to satisfy the requirements of its primary customers, or any of many other basic questions.

As in the mapping exercise to give us a clearer and more comprehensive picture of "what agencies do" and "what analysts know," we began with a data-collection exercise to tell us "what agencies produce." One of my first "directives" was that henceforth all agencies should send "me" one copy of every analytic product they disseminated. Someone in the group immediately asked if I really wanted to see everything that was disseminated. I clarified that I meant what I said metaphorically. What I desired was to have one copy of every analytic product sent to a single database. At the time, I did not know exactly how I would use this information, but I was quite sure that having it would facilitate making the evaluations needed to provide mandated reports to the Congress, evaluation of strengths and weaknesses within and across agencies, and evaluation of the amount and nature of duplication and coverage gaps.

Characterizing this instruction as a "directive" is something of a misnomer because I do not recall that this instruction to the few members of the ODDNI/A team on board at the time was ever translated into a written instruction and was never fully implemented. However, the intended process did result in collection of products from all agencies that were used to perform selective evaluations of analytic tradecraft and to respond to queries about the number and types of analytic products produced by all IC components on specific subjects. In the event, the database in question eventually was assigned to ODDNI/A/Analytic Mission Management and the contents of that database were used by ODDNI/A/Analytic Integrity and Standards to evaluate analytic products.

The predicable response to my instruction to send a copy of all products to the newly created database was an immediate request for clarification of the meaning of "all." I write this not to mock my colleagues, but to make the point that the question was neither unreasonable nor unexpected. If the IC had ever had community-wide guidelines defining what constituted an analytic "product," they had fallen into disuse. Each agency produced a variety of written products, briefing slides, and oral presentations tailored to the needs and preferences of their customers. It was reasonable to ask which of these were to be sent to the database.

The puckish part of me was momentarily tempted to respond, "All means all," but I recognized that the question identified yet another need and opportunity to bring analytic managers into the discussion. Doing so, I judged, would enhance our collective understanding of what was being produced; why different formats were used; and which vehicles were considered to be "community" products, "agency" products, or the products of subordinate units or individual analysts. It also provided an opportunity to build common understanding of and secure buy-in for what we were trying to accomplish. I envisioned this as an informal process and seem to remember kicking off the discussion but, as in most cases, left it to my deputies to develop and execute the means to achieve the specific objective.

The approach summarized in the previous paragraph was an early example of what became a deliberate and, I believe, effective part of my and my team's management style. Key elements of the approach were as follows:

- Aspire to build a more integrated analytic community by persuading constituent elements, managers, and other personnel that their own performance would be better if they worked with IC counterparts than if they treated collaborative undertakings as competing with and detrimental to what they could do on their own.
- Persuade component elements that we (the ODDNI/A) were serious about improving IC performance by improving the performance of every agency and analyst and would do all we could to preclude invidious and demeaning comparisons.
- Err on the side of transparency. Tell others what we were trying to do and why we chose the methods that we did. Explain and seek

feedback before acting and be prepared to admit errors and make course corrections quickly.

- Use ODDNI/A senior staff meetings to try out ideas, obtain feedback, and develop common understanding of what we were trying to do, and leave it to deputies and staff to operationalize and implement broad—strategic—decisions. I saw this as roughly analogous to providing what the military refers to as "commander's intent."
- When possible, eschew formal directives or guidance in favor of explaining goals, listening to feedback and suggestions, and allowing wide latitude for deputies and agency managers to decide how they should work to achieve those goals.[15]

The approach summarized above evolved fairly quickly but was still very nascent during the baselining stage of analytic transformation. The need to respond to questions about the product database helped—forced—me to think about "how" issues (such as how we would secure understanding and buy-in, and how we would use the data we obtained), and played a major role in shaping the way we handled many subsequent matters. The starting points of my own thinking about the database were three: that if we were going to operate the Intelligence Community as an integrated entity, we needed a single repository of products; that the database and what we did with it could be a useful management tool for agency leaders as well as for the ODDNI/A; and that it would facilitate preparation of the evaluative reports required by the IRTPA legislation (for example, on how well analytic products conformed to tradecraft standards).[16] Articulating these rather simple—even simplistic—reasons underscored the importance of thinking through and explaining how we intended to do this.

My initial answers to questions about how we would use the database were pretty vague and amounted to little more than stating that we intended to make it a tool useful for analytic managers and that we would not use it for invidious comparison or disparagement of agencies or individuals. In essence, I was saying, "Trust me." By and large, I think that they did. The driver that moved us toward more precise answers was the looming requirement to prepare the legislatively mandated report. Nancy Tucker, my first Deputy for Analytic Integrity and Standards (AIS) and concurrently Analytic Ombudsman, took the lead in developing mechanisms and criteria to meet the reporting requirements. Doing so raised a number of issues at the heart of agency concerns about how we might use the database and evaluations of performance.

The incremental and multifaceted character of this undertaking makes it difficult to describe in linear fashion. The product database provided the obvious source from which to draw the products to be evaluated, but there was no reasonable way to examine more than a tiny subset. Quick assessment of the number of products involved and judgments about the size of the evaluation staff we intended to form and the number of products each member and the team as a whole could examine persuaded Nancy that we could do and defend evaluation of all products written on three subjects. The criteria we established to select items for review were that the subjects should be "important," represent a mix of country or regional topics and transnational issues, and include products from all or most agencies. In keeping with the spirit of transparency, we informed agencies how we intended to proceed and what topics had been selected for review. We recognized that there was a small danger that agencies might give special care to the preparation of products on the topics to be reviewed but judged it more important to explicate exactly what we were doing than to mitigate the danger of distortion by keeping colleagues in the dark. Besides, most of the products to be examined were already in the database, and the percentage of new additions from any agency would be limited by the time remaining before review.

A second element in the process was to establish the criteria to be used when making the evaluations. This was relatively easy to do because reasonably clear criteria had been enumerated in the IRTPA legislation.[17] That being the case, it seemed prudent to base our report to the Congress on the criteria it had specified. Moreover, and more important, we agreed on the importance of the criteria and eventually incorporated them into formal tradecraft standards and training materials.[18] Although it took two years to produce the formal *Intelligence Community Directive: Analytic Standards*, we began to apply the standards almost immediately to evaluate published reports.[19]

The summary above obscures how difficult it was to translate broad goals and legislative mandates into effective metrics and evaluative procedures. As in most other areas of reform discussed in this volume, the difficult heavy lifting in this regard was undertaken by the staffs selected by my deputies, in this case, Nancy Tucker and her principal deputy, Becky Strode. Specific "implementation" requirements included development of workable and meaningful metrics, training the experienced analysts (detailees from within the IC and contract analysts) who would do the evaluations on how to apply those metrics, and explaining the process and training people in each of the IC components.

Even before the teams assigned to review the selection of analytic products had completed their work, we faced the question of how we would report the results to the Congress. The legislation required submission of a report but did not specify its structure. We determined that there were essentially two options, namely, to report on the performance of the IC as a whole or to report the performance of individual agencies. We decided to report on the IC as a whole and justified doing so on grounds that information sharing and integration of the Intelligence Community were among the principal reasons for undertaking reform. That was a real reason, but the more important one, as far as I was concerned, was that I judged it would be counterproductive to my integration and collaboration agenda to provide information in a way that facilitated invidious comparisons. We made this decision early on and communicated it to the Analysis and Production Board. We maintained this position throughout my tenure.

The first report to Congress established a baseline against which to compare the results of future evaluations. This turned out to be a tricky and somewhat subjective undertaking because examining different topics each year (which we thought it important to do to gain greater understanding of relative and absolute strengths and weaknesses) created inherent apples-and-oranges comparison problems. An additional methodological challenge was to ascertain and depict how much of assessed improvement or deterioration was a function of changes in one or two agencies that produced disproportionate shares of the work on a given topic. In the end, we—or at least I—decided not to worry about these problems because the Hill accepted our bottom-line judgments about improved performance.[20]

Although we did not report on the performance of individual agencies, we—the ODDNI/A—paid close attention to what we learned about each component. We wanted—needed—to know which producers were strong and which weak so that we could explore the reasons why, enlist good performers to mentor or assist younger or weaker ones, work with the poorer performers to understand why, and provide additional training or other support. We also wanted to discern and understand patterns of performance, for example, why a particular agency seemed to do better or worse on some topics than on others.

We needed to know such things in order to provide useful assistance to analytic managers and to achieve the goal of improving individual and overall performance. But we were not the only ones. Analytic managers needed detailed information on the performance of their analysts, but they did not need information on the performance of other units. We structured the process to provide complete transparency on a given unit to the head of that unit but to no one else outside of the ODDNI/A. Agency analytic managers needed to understand how well (or badly) they were doing as measured by the common tradecraft standards. They did not need to know how their people compared to other IC components. I was determined not to fuel the legacy practice of building component morale by disparaging IC colleagues.

As we began to accumulate evaluation data, we gained greater appreciation for its utility as a management tool. Feedback from analytic managers deepened this appreciation. Within a matter of months, a database and evaluation process that was initially viewed with skepticism and fear began to be seen as a valuable diagnostic tool. After receiving our initial evaluations, several agencies asked for voluntary review of other products they had produced.[21] We were eager to do so, within the limits of staff capability. After a few years, analytic managers began to ask for help to establish in-house evaluation units to review a larger percentage of their products and to use the findings to identify systemic and individual strengths and weaknesses. The venues for exchanges on the utility of structured evaluations varied, but we made a point of talking about them in meetings of the Analysis and Production Board so that all could learn from the experience and observations of peers. When it became apparent that almost all agencies wanted to have evaluation units but most did not have the staff or budgets to support them, I made the establishment of an evaluation unit mandatory and offered to fund them. The offer was readily accepted. I regarded this as an important milestone in the ODDNI/A's perceived transition from meddlesome mother-in-law to helpful partner.

The progression from mandatory evaluations to voluntary reviews of products selected by analytic managers to establishment of in-house evaluation teams or units in several agencies occurred slowly but proved to be a relatively low-cost, high-payoff way to improve performance. A natural next step taken by many agencies was to incorporate tradecraft evaluations into their normal production cycles. The objective was to identify and fix flaws before products were disseminated. Customer demands for timely input and the pace of developments sometimes made it impractical to delay delivery to double-check tradecraft, but the process raised awareness and, I believe, resulted in greater attention to tradecraft requirements at each step of the process, beginning with the drafting analyst(s).

These were positive developments but we did not want to rely solely on self-initiative and informal acquisition of tradecraft and evaluative skills. Skills can and should be taught. Awareness of IC demographics, especially the relative youth and limited experience of more than half the analytic workforce, underscored the need to put in place multifaceted training programs as quickly as possible. This was hardly a new idea. Most agencies had training programs for new analysts and some had training for midlevel and senior managers, but the amount and quality of instruction were highly uneven. Large agencies with many people generally had longer and more rigorous programs than did smaller agencies, but for too many across the community, training effectively consisted of being tossed into the deep end of the pool with little instruction, or medieval-like apprenticeships with more seasoned analysts. The latter were increasingly difficult to sustain because the number of wizened veterans was small and dropping rapidly. We had to develop a better system.

Training and Tradecraft

OVER THE PAST FEW DECADES there has been recurring debate over whether intelligence, specifically intelligence analysis, is or should be considered a discipline or profession.[1] I was and am basically agnostic with respect to how one characterizes jobs or individuals. In my judgment, there are both advantages and disadvantages to conceptualizing intelligence analysis as a distinct field or profession. Potential advantages include inculcation and reinforcement of a professional ethos that emphasizes objectivity, eschews pursuit of personal agendas, and accepts the responsibilities and limitations of working in the national security enterprise. Disadvantages include excessive and counterproductive isolation from non-IC experts working on similar topics and temptation to accord disproportionate weight to clandestinely acquired information.

My agnosticism about whether intelligence analysis should be considered a professional discipline predisposed me to give short shrift to arguments urging me to make "professionalization" part of the ODDNI/A transformation agenda. The issue arose as we began to think about what role we (the ODDNI/A) should play in the reform and expansion of IC training programs. Exactly what our role should be was left unresolved by the initial division of responsibilities among the four ODNI directorates. Responsibility for establishing a "National Intelligence University (NIU)" was assigned to the Deputy DNI for Management, but early in the process of standing up the ODNI, the four deputies met daily to, among other things, talk through the allocation of responsibilities and how best to fulfill them.[2] I think it fair to say that we generally treated this as an "important but not urgent" responsibility.

Questions about training became more urgent, at least for me, as we gained better understanding of IC demographics and the requisites of greater collaboration. The youth and inexperience of the analytic workforce made apparent that we had an immediate need to teach tradecraft skills and inculcate professional norms. The numbers involved, equal to more than half the total number of analysts, overwhelmed the capacity of existing agency training programs. The challenges of bringing newbies up to speed and inculcating IC-wide tradecraft requirements were compounded by the paucity of midlevel analysts and the fact that many senior analysts were in administrative positions and unable to mentor new arrivals. Demography made it impossible to rely on the guild-like mentoring and apprenticeship arrangements long followed in many agencies to supplement the substantive knowledge newcomers brought with them by providing instruction in Intelligence Community rules, norms, and procedures.

Establishing the National Intelligence University was not my responsibility, but the inadequacy of training programs for new analysts was a huge impediment to reaping benefits from reform. Moreover, we had already judged that we needed new forms of training to prepare analysts with limited experience who would rise to management positions more quickly than in the past and without hands-on experience and on-the-job training of the kind long used by many agencies. A third factor that converted the inadequacy of training from someone else's problem to my problem was the stand-up of analytic units in the FBI and the Department of Homeland Security (DHS). As entirely new units with responsibilities new to their parent organizations, the FBI's Intelligence Branch and DHS's Office of Intelligence and Analysis did not have senior or mid-career veterans capable of training newcomers. Given the high profile and obvious importance of combating the terrorist threat to the nation, we—specifically the ODDNI for Analysis—had no choice except to make training a priority. Others in the ODNI did not have the same sense of urgency.

Establishing the type of training we envisioned proved more difficult than anticipated. To me, the need for such a program was obvious, urgent, and an opportunity to score an early win for the presidentially mandated NIU. The Analysis Directorate needed the program, but we did not want to build or own it. Given all the other startup challenges we faced, I hoped and expected that we could describe our needs to colleagues in the Management Directorate and rely on them to build and run the course that quickly became known as

"Analysis 101." Indeed, I expected that they would jump at the opportunity. This expectation proved wrong, and members of my staff had grown increasingly impatient with their counterparts by the time Nancy Tucker joined us as the ADDNI/Analysis for Analytic Integrity and Standards.

Nancy was an "outsider" with no patience for what she regarded as unnecessary and counterproductive bureaucratic behavior. The first time that she came to me to complain that NIU staff seemed more concerned about bureaucratic process—how the new course would be organized, vetted with analytic components, codified in IC Directives, and so on—than in developing a workable pilot, I told her to help them understand how they could use this course to demonstrate to the Hill that the ODNI "got" the message on training and to IC components that it could do things for the Community more effectively and expeditiously than the structures it had replaced.

They didn't get it, and Nancy soon came back to me to argue that we must and could develop the course as an ODDNI/A project. Her argument included both a disparaging assessment of the ODDNI/Management staff responsible for NIU and a forceful rehearsal of things I had said about eschewing efforts to develop a perfect plan in favor of getting started and learning from our mistakes. She closed with, "You've developed new courses and know that the only way to get the bugs out is to teach the material and make changes in response to student complaints and performance. We know how to do this so let me do what needs to be done."[3] Though reluctant to add yet another task to my DDNI/A job jar and to alienate colleagues in other components of the ODNI, I told her to go ahead and that I would explain to Pat Kennedy why we could not wait for NIU to develop a course for us. Ever the pragmatist, Pat blessed our assumption of this responsibility.

We designed Analysis 101 with three objectives in mind. One was to provide training in proper analytic tradecraft. As once and future professors, Nancy and I believed strongly in the value of instruction and that it was better to teach people how to do things correctly than to rely on trial-and-error learning or mentoring by more senior analysts. Mentoring in the Intelligence Community was unsystematic and highly variable from one agency to another. Moreover, the existing demographic profile with many new analysts, few mid-career people, and a fast-dwindling number of baby boomer analysts made it impossible to inculcate critical skills and attitudes through on-the-job training.

A second objective was to use the initial training course to build a community of analysts through joint training at the beginning of their careers in the Intelligence Community. The idea here was not just to have all new analysts take the same course, it was to have them take the same course together with counterparts from all IC components. We envisioned this as a partial corrective to the bureaucratic pathologies of agencies that fostered organizational *esprit de corps* by disparaging other IC agencies and personnel.[4] Joint training was intended to help analysts across the Intelligence Community to understand that their counterparts elsewhere were just as smart, just as green, and just as committed as they were, and to reinforce this with direct knowledge that colleagues had received the same training in analytic tradecraft. We believed strongly that such knowledge of counterpart abilities would facilitate trust in their competence and the quality of work done in other agencies, and that this, in turn, would facilitate divisions of labor and more effective collaboration.[5]

Our third objective was to facilitate networking among analysts and agencies. The idea, which was borrowed from senior training programs in the US military services and the now-defunct national security Senior Seminar, was that getting to know people from other services or agencies provides an effective means to identify, contact, and collaborate with counterparts working on the same or similar issues. The underlying idea is that it is easier and more productive to seek assistance from unknown counterparts in another agency by contacting an Analysis 101 classmate in that agency than it would be to search organizational directories and approach someone without an endorsement from a friend in that agency. The goal was to shorten and make more efficient the development of multi-agency professional networks and analytic teams.

Members of my staff and I announced these objectives at every opportunity because we wanted analysts and managers to understand what we were trying to do. I did so on visits to agencies and ODNI-sponsored events, but my primary target audience was the Analysis and Production Board. As with many other elements of the transformation agenda, success required understanding, support, and ideas from senior analytic managers in all agencies. I tried to be as transparent as possible and to make what I did as DDNI/A help them and their agencies to perform their missions more efficiently and effectively than was possible in the past. The set of activities subsumed under the Analysis 101 rubric was a good illustration of what we were trying to do, and it won broad support from all but one agency. During my tenure, CIA never allowed more than token participation in Analysis 101. The agency argument was that its Kent School offered a more rigorous and more extensive training program for new analysts (which was true) and that the need to put their new analysts to work precluded them spending time in both the ODNI and the CIA training programs. Sadly, this "we can do it better by ourselves" attitude prevented CIA analysts from obtaining the community- and network-building benefits of joint training and made it more difficult for analysts in other agencies to connect with their CIA counterparts.

Training, building a community of analysts, and networking were the most important and most often articulated reasons for promoting Analysis 101, but they were not the only reasons. In addition to the substantive benefits we expected from the joint training, I saw an opportunity to score political or public relations points. Inculcating skills, improving the quality and utility of analytic products, and rebuilding morale and confidence in our work were all critically important, but they were also intangible and largely invisible to key constituencies. Analysis 101 was, in part, my answer to the question, "What have you done to improve analysis?" Granted that it was an input, not an outcome, but standing up the course and instituting joint training checked important boxes on the checklists of Congressional staff assigned to report on our progress. We could show them the syllabus and invite them to sit in on classes, so they could see for themselves that from the beginning we included analysts from across the Intelligence Community. The existence of Analysis 101 also provided a useful talking point with the President's Intelligence Advisory Board and journalists interested in how the ODNI was implementing the intelligence reform legislation.

I also saw the rapid stand-up of Analysis 101 as a way to address the skepticism of colleagues and former counterparts eager to discover whether the ODDNI/A would do anything for them or be just another layer of bureaucracy. Having spent much of my career in INR, I was acutely aware of how difficult it was for small agencies to find the time or the money for formal training programs. On-the-job-training was not the preferred way to teach analytic tradecraft and the unique requirements of intelligence analysis but there was no real alternative. I saw Analysis 101 as a way to provide something of value to all analytic components, especially the new and smaller ones, and judged that my colleagues and former counterparts would view the course as a sign that the ODDNI/A might be more useful to them than the Community Management Staff and other nominal "community" organizations had been. In other words, I saw it as a way to erode skepticism and score points with constituencies important to the success of what I had been asked to do. That judgment proved to be only partially correct.[6]

Although the logic of what we were trying to do was widely understood and largely welcomed by new analysts, senior managers in many agencies continued to push back against our efforts to forge a single corporate identity embraced by all IC analysts. There were rough analogs to resistance from each of the services to the goals and requirements of the 1986 Goldwater-Nichols Department of Defense Reorganization Act.[7] In both the IC and the DOD cases, individual components acknowledged the need for and generally wanted more effective integration, but they did not want to degrade—let alone surrender—their individual identities and capacity to perform core missions. It took a long time to substantially reduce service resistance to Goldwater-Nichols' mandated jointness, so it is unsurprising that resistance to deeper IC integration remained strong when my tenure ended.

Transforming the *PDB* into a Community Product

THE MANDATE TO TRANSFORM the *President's Daily Brief* from an exclusively CIA product into one that incorporated the views—including alternative views—of the Intelligence Community as a whole was clear but without formal authorization or instruction. The Intelligence Reform and Terrorism Prevention Act does not mention the PDB at all, and the sole reference in the WMD Commission recommendations accepted by the President says only that it "should be restructured."[1] Though not explicitly required or authorized, however, making the PDB a community product was widely judged to be appropriate, desirable, and necessary.[2] It was appropriate because the IRTPA had made the DNI "the principal adviser to the President . . . on intelligence matters related to the national security."[3] It was desirable because a principal rationale for intelligence reform was to enhance the quality of intelligence support by integrating the insights and expertise of all IC components.

The idea that it was necessary had at least two dimensions. One emphasized the severity of the terrorist threat to the nation and the need to integrate information and insights from foreign and domestic intelligence components. The other reflected a sense that CIA's privileged access to the President and senior White House advisers gave added weight to its analytical judgments even when analysts in other agencies with access to the same information had reached different conclusions. Some who held these views also thought that CIA had abused its privileged access via the PDB and should be punished for misleading the President and senior White House advisers about WMD in Iraq and/or skewing PDB analysis to satisfy the President or Vice President.[4]

The idea that the PDB should have more community input was gaining momentum even before passage of the IRTPA legislation in December 2004. Senior analytic managers had begun to talk informally about ways to broaden participation in the preparation of articles for the PDB, but without a mandate to make, or even to explore, structural and procedural changes required to achieve that objective, these discussions could not and did not make much progress. Participation in these discussions and brainstorming sessions proved valuable several months later when I was given the task of transforming the PDB because they gave me better understanding of the PDB process and specific impediments to expanding participation.

Making the PDB a community product was not discussed at all in my initial conversations with John Negroponte about what a yet-to-be-named deputy for analysis should do, or about what I should do after I had accepted the job. That it was not attests to the magnitude and complexity of the challenges confronting us, and the fact that neither he nor I had yet focused on whether the PDB would or should be in my portfolio of responsibilities. It was not until a week or so after I'd accepted the job (and while I was still at the State Department) that Negroponte told me he wanted me to take responsibility for the PDB. I had not thought much—or at all—about how supervising the PDB might fit with my other rapidly expanding responsibilities. Indicative of the incremental way in which we worked together, I responded with something like, "Are you sure? That is a big job and doing it will have to take precedence over other tasks in my portfolio." After a slight pause, John replied, "Yes, it is a big job and it has to be done right. But the most important part of the job is providing good analysis to the President, and analysis is what you are good at. You've got it. It is your responsibility. But I don't want you spending any [meaning much] time on it."

The nature of our relationship was such that I could have challenged the decision, but ego whispered in my ear that it would be cool to oversee the PDB so I simply responded, "OK." I was already beginning to think about how to manage this new task and how to interpret the assignment of responsibility and injunction not to spend much time doing it. Neither John nor I said anything further about it, but I was confident that it meant that I should select a good deputy and delegate day-to-day responsibility to him or her. As noted earlier in the section on building a team, the willingness of Steve Kaplan, a career CIA analyst, to become my deputy for the

PDB ensured that "new ownership" would not disrupt arrangements that had evolved during the four years that President Bush had shaped PDB priorities and practices.

Although there was much about the PDB as process and product that I did not understand when I assumed overall responsibility, I was acutely aware that what I wanted the PDB to be was far less important than what the President wanted it to be. After more than four years in office, he knew a great deal about the issues that warranted White House attention, had met and spoken with other world leaders (often numerous times), and had clear priorities for his second term. The knowledge of what he knew, what he cared about, what he wanted to know, and how he wanted to receive information and analytic judgments was crucial to the ability of the IC to provide useful intelligence support to the "first customer" and other senior officials. Kaplan had that knowledge and a passionate commitment to meeting the intelligence needs of the President.

Steve Kaplan's understanding of the process was critical to ensuring a smooth transition from DCI to DNI ownership of the PDB, but it was also critical to the success of efforts to make it a community endeavor. I was and am very grateful that his commitment to providing the best intelligence possible to the President and other senior officials was greater than his institutional loyalty to CIA, where he had spent his entire career. He was justifiably proud of the Agency, but meeting the intelligence needs of the national security enterprise, especially those at its head, was his highest priority. I would like to say that I recognized this immediately, but I didn't. I did not know Steve before I became DDNI for Analysis. Although I was very glad that he was willing to stay on and provide badly needed continuity, I had no basis for determining whether he would be fully supportive of the ODNI and its missions or eager for the new arrangements to fail so that things could revert to what they had been before passage of the reform legislation. It was no time at all, however, before I recognized that Steve was fully committed to the intelligence mission and the reform agenda.

Continuity and responsiveness to the President's requirements did not mean stasis. Transformation of the PDB into a community product was one of the indicators that oversight bodies, Hill staffers, and intelligence junkies would use to assess the efficacy of the ODNI. Recognizing this, I moved quickly to create the appearance and reality of ODNI leadership and multi-agency participation. I have placed appearance ahead of reality in the preceding sentence because demonstrating that things had changed in important ways was as or even more important, in the short term, than the substantive effects of changes that would not be felt for some time.

One step with both substantive and symbolic importance was to establish a multi-agency advisory body for the PDB. The core for such a body already existed in the form of the informal group that had convened a number of times prior to the stand-up of the ODNI. The group included senior managers from CIA, DIA, INR, NSA, and the National Geospatial-Intelligence Agency who had come together voluntarily to discuss ways to improve analysis and analyst collaboration across agency boundaries. Others were added to the group over time, but the initial participants represented all of the "all-source agencies" and most of the analysts with expertise on subjects likely to be worthy of coverage in the PDB. Most but not all. Given the importance of terrorism analysis and protection of the homeland, and in line with the IRTPA mandate to combine foreign and law enforcement information to produce "national" intelligence, I immediately added FBI and the National Counterterrorism Center to the advisory board. This group was a convenient and effective vehicle to convey information about PDB requirements and procedures that would help agencies other than CIA to understand how to plug into the process and what would be required of analysts from those agencies who wished to serve as authors, editors, or briefers.

Establishing the advisory board as a principal channel of communication between the PDB and analytic components addressed one dimension of the transformation to a community product but it was not sufficient. A key feature of the PDB process is the daily meeting at which those who have briefed PDB readers discuss observations and questions raised by "their" readers and convey requests for additional information or analysis. This feedback mechanism plays an important role in setting the agenda for future articles and products tailored to the specific concerns of individual readers. Heretofore, the results of these meetings were shared only with analysts in CIA. We had to develop mechanisms to share them across the IC without jeopardizing the trust and confidentiality that were critical to the process.

The default setting when such tensions arise between sharing to improve the product and restricting knowledge to protect confidentiality was to sacrifice quality for confidentiality. This challenge arose in many forms and arenas, but I faced it for the first time as DDNI/A in the PDB arena. If we were to make the PDB a community product, we had to devise a way to include representatives from other agencies in these post-morning-briefing meetings because without knowledge of what readers were working on, worried about, and trying to accomplish, writing for the PDB would be an exercise in throwing pieces over the transom in the hope that some might prove timely and relevant. We had to do better than that. The solution we developed was for each agency to name one to three analysts entrusted to participate in the meetings (usually via secure video) and to relay only the relevant portions of the discussion to analysts who could contribute on specific topics.

A third immediate challenge was to devise ways to share drafts and collaborate at a distance. Heretofore the PDB had been produced on a special system isolated from even the highest-security systems used to share intelligence across the IC. If we were to engage analysts outside CIA in the process, we had to have mechanisms that would allow them to do so without having to spend several hours at CIA headquarters. Otherwise they could not perform their "normal" writing, briefing, collaborating, and other duties in their home agencies for extended portions of the day. That would have made contributing to the PDB a zero-sum game in which managers were likely to give priority to supporting primary missions and customers. Even if managers encouraged them to support the PDB, many analysts would be likely to see the opportunity cost of doing so as too high.

The solution to this part of the problem was the obvious one, namely, to share drafts and draft-related communications via secure email. Doing so required resolution of long-standing issues impeding the electronic transmittal of sensitive information across agency boundaries. What I could do with respect to the PDB was shaped—and initially limited—by counterintelligence objections to connecting the highest-classification computer systems of IC agencies. I took the problem to the DNI's weekly senior staff meeting and argued that we had to find a way to solve it. Dale Meyerrose, the Associate Director of National Intelligence and Chief Information Officer, heard my argument, and DNI John Negroponte asked him what he could do to solve it. My problem had become Meyerrose's problem.

For almost a decade, IC CIOs had been arguing that it was technically possible to connect the highest-level security systems across the community and security specialists had argued that it would not be prudent to do so. Among the losers of this long-running battle were analysts who could not share intelligence reports, drafts, and other work products with counterparts in other agencies who held the same security clearances. Cleverly, Negroponte had appointed Meyerrose as both IC Chief Information Officer and Chief Computer Security Officer. I do not know whether Meyerrose was personally conflicted about whether to connect the systems, but he authorized doing so for the PDB.

This decision removed what was potentially the most serious impediment to making the PDB a community product and opened the door for much broader integration of the analytic community. If we were to deepen and broaden the scope of analytic collaboration, as I believed was critical, we had to be able to share products on the full range of issues being worked by the Intelligence Community. The need and potential for collaboration were far more extensive on issues that did not meet the PDB threshold of relevance to the President's agenda, responsibilities, and stated requirements. I immediately went back to Negroponte and Meyerrose to argue that if we could move PDB materials securely on the system, we could surely use the system for materials and subjects that were less sensitive. I did not have to argue very hard. Although it was not my initial intent, which was simply to reduce barriers to PDB collaboration, I was happy to use the status of the PDB to obtain decisions with much broader and more consequential impacts on IC analysis.

To demonstrate progress on the reform agenda, I could and did point to the PDB advisory board and steps taken to incorporate all analytic components into the preparation of analytic products for the President and other senior officials. But transformation was a long and slow process. Among the reasons that it was slow, I concluded at the time, was that analysts outside of CIA continued to accord highest priority to their primary customers and missions. For most, that was not the White House or cabinet-level officials outside the department in which they were embedded. This was not because they considered the President to be less important than their traditional customers. A more important reason was that many judged that CIA had the White House covered and, therefore, that the President would get what he needed without their contribution. If they too made the President the "first customer," top officials in their own agency would be less well served by the Intelligence Community. According to this logic, if they were "diverted" from their primary responsibilities, there was no one and no mechanism to provide intelligence support comparable to what they provided. This did not surprise me because such thinking had been part of the ethos of service and dedication to the Secretary of State and diplomacy more generally during my years in INR and was true in spades for military intelligence components. The lesson I drew from this was that more fully transforming the PDB into a community product required better integration of the IC analytic enterprise.

Over time, analysts from across the IC became PDB briefers and input from agencies other than CIA on certain topics (such as counterterrorism and military topics) became more common, but when I left the ODNI in December 2008, the vast majority of PDB articles were still drafted by CIA analysts. I found that neither surprising nor troubling. One reason was that a substantial part of CIA analytic effort was oriented toward production for the PDB. Only a small portion of analytic pieces made it into the PDB, but many were prepared in the hope that they might be. For CIA analysts, writing for the PDB was not a diversion from other responsibilities, as it was for counterparts elsewhere in the IC, it was their top priority. Moreover, production of the PDB remained at CIA headquarters and it was much easier for Agency analysts to respond to questions from editors, insert new information, or be available to help briefers to understand the background and context for their piece. As in many other matters, proximity mattered.

Before explaining why continued "CIA dominance" of the PDB did not trouble me, it will be useful to digress briefly to say a bit more about why we (the ODNI, with me in the lead) decided to leave the PDB at CIA headquarters. Moving it elsewhere would have underscored the transition to DNI "ownership" and responsibility, but making such a move for primarily symbolic reasons would have been both risky and foolish. For starters, the ODNI was a "homeless" organization for many months. We did not have a facility of our own, and staff were scattered across temporary spaces in multiple parts of the DC area. Even if we had had a home of our own, it would have been highly inefficient to duplicate capabilities available at CIA and structured to support the PDB process. These capabilities included a 24/7 operations center, a graphics shop, a motor pool, and communications equipment needed to support briefers when the President or other recipients traveled. Beyond inefficiency, it would have been foolish to risk disruption or additional problems of any kind in the delivery of intelligence to the most senior officials in the government merely to make a symbolic point. Moreover, the diversion of effort that would have been required to establish a new PDB location would have made it more difficult, if not impossible, to achieve other requisites of standing up a new organization.

Now, back to the primary narrative. The reason that I was not troubled by the continued high percentage of CIA pieces in the PDB was that the way they were produced was different in two important ways. One difference was procedural. In the past, soliciting comment from analysts outside of CIA was not required. One of the first procedural changes that I mandated after becoming DDNI/A was that all pieces for the PDB (and prepared by the NIC for White House meetings) must be circulated to knowledgeable analysts across the IC.[5]

Specifying that drafts were to be circulated to "knowledgeable" analysts was vague but deliberate. Concerns about protecting confidentiality and limiting counterintelligence vulnerabilities noted above caused me to eschew requiring that all drafts be sent for comment to "all" IC components when I knew from years of experience that relatively few agencies had real expertise on most subjects. It made no sense, at least not to me, to send a draft on North Korean military maneuvers, for example, to the intelligence units of DHS, Treasury, or the FBI. Instead of disseminating drafts in a "dear boxholder" fashion in the hope that the recipient agency would relay it to a true expert in the agency, I decided to utilize the less formal mechanism of reliance on drafters' knowledge of who their counterparts were in other agencies, and on the ability of PDB editors to go to appropriate National Intelligence Officers for guidance if they thought the list of recommended reviewers was inadequate. Willingness, and over time even eagerness to receive comments from counterparts was encouraged by my guidance that the purpose of this review was limited to identification of factual errors or failure to consider new or other relevant intelligence (in other words, to catch errors before misinforming the President), and to determine whether other analysts with access to the same information had reached different analytic judgments. My guidance instructed that analytic disagreement was not grounds to hold up a piece that was time-sensitive (although analysts could decide among themselves to delay publication in order to explore why they had reached different judgments), but that the existence of alternative judgments had to be acknowledged as soon as they were discovered. Phrasing the guidance in this way implicitly placed responsibility for weeding out frivolous or poorly supported objections on the PDB representatives from each agency. If they, usually in consultation with analytic managers in the dissenting agency, considered the alternative assessment to be well-founded, they authorized or instructed PDB editors to include a note indicating that analysts with access to the underlying intelligence did not agree on how to interpret it. I was confident that most would act responsibly, and that confidence proved justified.

A major source of dissatisfaction with the PDB process before Intel reform was that other agencies did not learn that the White House and other senior officials had been given an assessment with which they disagreed until it was too late to do much about it. I had learned early in my INR career that it is very difficult to "correct" a mistaken analytic judgment after a policymaker has internalized it and even more difficult after he or she has spoken about or acted on that erroneous judgment. The procedural change described above was designed to address that problem, and I believe that it did so quite effectively.

Another reason that I was not troubled by the prevalence of "CIA" articles was that an increasing percentage were prepared with input from analysts in other agencies. Obtaining multi-agency agreement on a piece was difficult because of the layers of review involved and understandable desire of managers in any given agency to make the piece as helpful as possible to their own primary customers. Analysts discovered this and decided it was not worth the hassle to add the logo of their own agency to a piece with which they agreed. They became "silent contributors" who enhanced the quality of the piece without seeking or receiving credit. I know this because the PDB is like professional baseball; it keeps stats on everything. This diligent tracking of information revealed a steady increase in the number of instances in which the background materials submitted with an article revealed that it had been reviewed and/or included input from named analysts in specified agencies. By the time I left the ODNI, more than 70 percent of published articles had this type of multi-agency origins.

A subset of such articles was suggested or even drafted by analysts outside CIA but submitted by a colleague in the Agency. When I learned of this practice, I decided to explore why it was happening by contacting analysts who had worked for me in INR. The answers from all were very similar. They thought they had identified something that the President should know but did not want to take the time or go through the hassle of working it through the process themselves so they sought out a colleague at CIA and worked together to produce the piece, which the CIA counterpart could work more easily after the draft was submitted to the PDB. I considered this a very sensible and desirable form of collaboration because it focused on accuracy and quality, not who or what agency received credit. This form of collaboration worked better for INR than for others, principally those supporting military missions, in which the number of items produced and published was more directly relevant to performance evaluations and promotion.

Management of the Analysis Mission

THE OVERARCHING MISSION of the intelligence establishment is to provide information and insight to policymakers, military commanders, and a wide variety of government officials with diverse operational responsibilities. Subcomponents of this mission include collection, analysis, covert action, and warning. All dimensions are important, but from my perspective, analysis and the roles and responsibilities of intelligence analysts are critical to the success of collectors, warning mechanisms, and covert activities. Not everyone shares this assessment, but whether they or I am most correct is less relevant here than the fact that my conception of how analysis fits into the broader intelligence enterprise is what shaped my priorities and approach to intelligence reform.[1]

Forced to think systematically about improving the quality, utility, and efficiency of the analytic enterprise, I immediately recalled an old Herblock cartoon depicting the Intelligence Community as a jury-rigged construction of disparate agencies. Each addition to the edifice was constructed differently than those erected previously, and there appeared to be no integrating logic or common purpose. The intelligence reform legislation was passed a decade after Herblock drew this cartoon, but commentary before and after passage of the 2004 intelligence reform legislation indicated that many expected the Director of National Intelligence to rationalize and restructure the intelligence edifice to eliminate duplication and enhance collaboration.

To the dismay of some, I quickly dismissed calls to consolidate functions and/or reduce the number of analytic components. One reason was that

Herbert Block, "What We Need Is an Architect." *Washington Post*, December 30, 1994. A 1994 Herblock Cartoon, © The Herb Block Foundation.

I (we) did not know enough about the missions, customers, and capabilities of individual components to realign responsibilities or propose changes to the IC organization chart. Mapping who did what was a prerequisite for informed consideration of structural changes (see the earlier chapter "Taking Stock"), but even before I knew how long that would take, I had decided to foreswear moving missions, responsibilities, and people. As noted earlier, one reason for doing so was to assuage concerns among the analytic workforce that we intended to make changes that would jeopardize support for key customers and missions, disrupt careers, and have an adverse effect on analysts' commutes to and from work. Since I could not prove or promise that proposed structural changes would bring rapid improvements in performance, I judged that failure to foreclose major reorganization would exacerbate morale problems and make it harder to secure analyst buy-in for the changes I did intend to make.

Another reason for dismissing calls for structural change was that my experience in INR and decades of interaction with counterparts in other agencies had convinced me that the risibly untidy IC organization chart was the result of considered efforts to ensure timely and tailored intelligence support to important national security missions. New components had been grafted on to the existing structure to meet specific intelligence requirements. To a degree seldom appreciated by outside commentators, different missions and customers require different types of intelligence support. The Secretary of Defense requires different types of information and insights than does the Attorney General, the Secretary of the Treasury, or an ambassador or trade negotiator. One-size intelligence fits nobody. The fact that sixteen different components had been established attested to both the perceived need to have them and the political clout of the Cabinet-level officials they supported. I judged that it would be imprudent to risk even temporary degradation of the intelligence support provided to powerful officials and critical national security missions, and that fighting battles I was unlikely to win would make it more difficult to implement reforms likely to have greater positive impact on performance.

Improving the performance of legacy foreign intelligence components by improving analytic tradecraft, information sharing, and collaboration among analysts was a daunting challenge, but it paled in comparison to two others created by the IRTPA legislation.[2] The former distinction between and separation of foreign intelligence and domestic law enforcement information was abolished by the 2004 legislation. In place of these two distinct realms separated by law, practice, and a metaphorical "wall," the IRTPA established the new category of "national intelligence."[3] Among other consequences for the ODDNI/A, this meant that we had to establish and integrate analytical components of the Federal Bureau of Investigation and the Department of Homeland Security. It also meant that we needed to change the way we thought about intelligence support and how we used information from new and very different sources.

My normal approach when tackling new and/or complex challenges is to disaggregate them. The obvious first task here was to help build new analytic capacity in FBI and DHS. Both agencies had already begun to recruit people, hire contractors, and define the scope and requirements of their analytic responsibilities. They welcomed help, but I recognized that there was a fine line between valued assistance and unwelcome meddling. Staying on the right side of that line posed a triple challenge. One challenge was to develop mechanisms to help FBI and DHS stand up new capabilities while building the ODDNI/A from scratch. Lacking institutions, on-the-shelf formulas, and even a rough draft strategy for integrating law enforcement and foreign intelligence analysis, we of necessity adopted an incremental approach in which we built our own capabilities, in part to address needs identified by the agencies we were attempting to help.

A second challenge was to learn what each of these agencies had already done to build new analytic capacity and why they had adopted the approaches they were using. I viewed this as a critical step for three reasons. One was to avoid unnecessary duplication of effort. I took it as a given that the managers leading the effort knew more about their missions, customers, and existing capabilities than we did, and that we did not need to start again from scratch. A second reason was my perceived "need for speed." I was constantly aware of the need to demonstrate results quickly in order to satisfy the demands of oversight bodies, intelligence professionals who questioned the utility of reform and the ODNI, and customers whose view of intelligence support had been tainted by post-Iraq-WMD criticism of IC analysis. The third reason was pragmatic; I judged that we could be more effective if we were perceived as providing value-added assistance than if we were perceived as arrogant interlopers.

When I began to assemble my senior staff, I judged that I needed a senior military officer to serve as explicator, communicator, and liaison to military intelligence units. As we began to understand the challenges of building capacity in and collaboration with the law enforcement community, it quickly became apparent that I needed similar understanding of and dedicated points of contact for FBI; DHS; and, eventually, state, local, and tribal police jurisdictions.

From the daily meetings of the ODNI deputies, I knew that other ODNI principals had reached a similar conclusion and were in the process of recruiting an experienced police officer to serve as liaison to the community of sworn officers. I saw this as an opportunity to utilize capacity developed elsewhere in the ODNI to achieve analysis community goals, but I also recognized that the ODDNI/A needed to have a designated point of contact for both the ODNI law enforcement liaison and for the analysis-related components of FBI and DHS.[4] Ron Rice willingly and ably added these responsibilities to his portfolio and became our (the ODDNI/A's) go-to person for interaction with the law enforcement community.[5]

The third challenge was to develop mechanisms and train analysts to integrate foreign intelligence and law enforcement information. From experience, I understood how important and how difficult it was to do so. A few days after 9/11, I was asked to oversee preparation of the official USG determination of responsibility for the attacks. Among other purposes, the report was to be used in diplomatic demarches explaining why the United States assigned responsibility as we did and why we would respond as was being planned.[6] This was the first time that law enforcement and foreign intelligence analysts sat together and presented all of the evidence they had that might be germane to the question of culpability. I, along with every other foreign intelligence analyst in the room, was amazed to learn what our law enforcement counterparts brought to the table. They reacted similarly to the materials we had assembled. That experience and the proven capacity to develop better understanding of complex events by integrating information from what had been two different worlds separated by a high wall made an indelible impression. Although I did not yet know how to ensure that materials from the two worlds could be shared and used effectively, I made doing so a "must do" task.

Two brief examples illustrate the advantages and difficulties of better integration of law enforcement and foreign intelligence. When I became Chair of the National Intelligence Council, one of the first estimates I was asked to review had been initiated before passage of the IRTPA but reworked in accordance with the new mandate for "national intelligence." I interpreted the meaning and purpose of the change as requiring a seamless transition from developments originating abroad (the subject of foreign intelligence collection and analysis) that come into the United States in the form of people, contraband, and so on (the subject of border controls) and endanger life and/or property inside the US (a law enforcement responsibility). When I received the draft of the estimate on the transport of illicit drugs into the United States, it contained a graphic with bold red arrows depicting the flow of drugs from various producer countries in South America through Mexico and Caribbean transit countries, and stopping at the Rio Grande.

Among other judgments, the text assessed that corrupt politicians and law enforcement officers facilitated the flow through Mexico and other transit countries. Thinking of the new mandate for national intelligence, I asked why the arrows stopped at our southern border, how drugs made it from the border to cities across the country, and whether transit inside the US was facilitated by corrupt police and politicians. The estimate had been prepared by experienced foreign intelligence analysts who had been taught that the Intelligence Community did not examine or make judgments about the United States and that they had therefore not attempted to trace the flow of drugs inside the country. We had to change analytic tradecraft to facilitate and encourage end-to-end analysis of transborder problems, of which international terrorism was the most obvious and most dangerous.

The second illustration is from a workshop that my analytic transformation team organized to explore ways in which law enforcement officers and foreign intelligence specialists could assist one another.[7] The desired forms of collaboration were unlikely to happen spontaneously. The workshop involved approximately thirty people, half from the federal government and half from state, local, and tribal police departments. Participants were "locked up" together for a month during which they were to deepen understanding of what each did and to discover how each could be more helpful to the other. Several participants commented to me that many of the specific requests for information and insight were obvious after they were articulated but simply had not occurred to the other community until they were. For example, a police officer observed that cops watch for anomalous ("just doesn't look right") behavior and that his city now had a large community of immigrants from Somalia. He assumed the foreign Intelligence Community knew more about Somalia and Somali customs than people in his department, and that it would be extremely helpful if people from the IC would tell his cops what behaviors were normal so they would be able spot anomalous or perhaps worrisome activity. The immediate response was, "We can do that." An obvious implication of this exchange was that we needed to develop mechanisms, including points of contact, through which police could pose questions and IC analysts could provide answers. This same example also illustrates how the integration of law enforcement and foreign intelligence transcends the traditional bounds of intelligence analysis and required intervention by other parts of the ODNI.[8]

Before turning to other dimensions of the analysis mission, I will interrupt the narrative to highlight a recurring dilemma that I faced and, I believe, must be confronted by any leader of a complex undertaking with multiple moving parts. In any complex undertaking, what can be achieved in specific subcomponents or issue arenas often depends on what can be—and is—achieved in other arenas. Improving analysis within IC law enforcement components and improving analysis across the Intelligence Community depended on and was constrained by progress in domains beyond the purview of the ODDNI/A.

At times, I felt hamstrung by the failure or slow pace of changes being implemented by colleagues in other ODNI directorates. I write this not to criticize them, but to emphasize that divisions of responsibility often lead to different prioritization of tasks affecting more than one organizational component. I have no doubt that my priorities and rates of progress also affected what they were able to do and how they attempted to do it. During my tenure in the ODNI, there was exceptionally good communication and collaboration among members of the leadership team, especially during the first two years. But our assigned and assumed responsibilities were prioritized primarily on the basis of what must be and could be achieved within a particular directorate. Often the pace at which the team could move forward was determined by the speed of the slowest horse.

One way around this dilemma is to reassign responsibilities or encroach on the turf of a colleague. The ODDNI/A's assumption of responsibility for Analysis 101 (discussed earlier) illustrates this type of solution. When those responsible for improving education across the Intelligence Community could not develop the analytic tradecraft course we needed as quickly as we wanted it, we developed it ourselves. Some viewed this as encroachment and empire building; we viewed it as a necessary expedient. Happily, members of the senior team generally were less worried about turf and had a shared commitment to rapid reform so this did not become a nagging or divisive issue. Lower-ranking staffs were less sanguine and sometimes less cooperative.

Integration of analysis across the law enforcement-foreign intelligence divide was heavily dependent on the pace and character of integration at the institutional level, and that proved to be one of the more difficult missions of the ODNI's first years. Although I might have been tempted to seek transfer of responsibility for higher-level institutional integration to my directorate, daily meetings at which the deputies shared information on what we were doing and what we wanted others to do so that we could achieve our objectives had convinced me that the opportunity cost of adding yet another task to my portfolio would exceed the benefits of doing so. Instead, I adjusted the goals and timelines of the analysis management agenda to fit the constraints resulting from the pace of progress in areas beyond my control.

One could easily imagine situations in which stress and rivalry among members of a leadership team become a significant constraint on progress or skewed action in particular directions, but that was seldom the case for our senior team. Professionalism and common purpose trumped individual ambition and, within days of our first meeting, mutual respect and genuine friendship became the hallmark of our interaction in and outside the work environment. I was lucky. Things could have been much worse.

Calls for better integration of analysis and collection are one of the hardy perennials of commentary on and criticism of the Intelligence Community. The basic premise, namely that analysts know best the kinds of information needed to answer analytic questions and address the needs of their policy customers, and that collectors should be guided by what analysts say they need is, of course, correct. But the premise is much easier to articulate than to implement.[9]

Although I certainly supported the idea that analysis should "drive" collection, I did not understand the logic of those who argued the necessity of structural integration, that is, placing leadership of the analysis and collection missions in a single ODNI directorate. Among other reasons, I did not regard this as a magic bullet fix to the problems of the Intelligence Community identified by SSCI, 9/11 Commission, and WMD Commission studies. I certainly did not see structural integration as the quickest or most effective way to improve the quality of intelligence analysis, restore policymaker confidence in our work, or address morale and retention problems in the analytic workforce. Indeed, quite the opposite. Decades of bureaucratic experience had persuaded me that attempting such integration would be difficult and time consuming, and would impede progress to address more immediate and consequential problems.

I never endeavored to find the sources of pressure for structural integration, but there was a palpable sense at the time that, for some, integration of analysis and collection had become a litmus test criterion for assessing the efficacy of the ODNI. Negroponte and Hayden seemed to share my judgment that placing analysis and collection in the same directorate would interfere with the achievement of higher-priority goals because they had already decided to establish separate directorates by the time I was asked to become deputy for analysis. I was somewhat surprised, therefore, when Mike McConnell revisited the issue when he succeeded Negroponte as DNI in 2007. He mulled the idea for a long time and repeatedly asked my collection counterpart Mary Margaret Graham and me to explain why we opposed combining our directorates before finally deciding to maintain the then-existing structure. My principal objections were two. The first was that managing the challenges in the collection directorate was so formidable a task that it would crowd out virtually all ability to manage the still important tasks of analytic transformation. The second was that naming a deputy director for a combined directorate with deputies for analysis and collection would be seen as adding an unnecessary level of bureaucracy when the ODNI was already being criticized for bureaucratic bloat and unnecessary layers while at the same time appearing to downgrade the importance of analysis (and collection) when we faced serious morale, retention, and reform fatigue problems. The original structure endured until DNI Jim Clapper combined them under a single deputy for intelligence integration in 2010. In doing so he encountered the problems Mary Margaret and I had anticipated and more.

Before describing the steps that my team took to enhance analytic guidance to collection and the reasons we took them, it will be useful to outline briefly some of the experiences, perceptions, and priorities that shaped my thinking. Probably the most important influence was conviction that the Intelligence Community had to make the transition from a model and procedures predicated on discovering secrets to a model focused on obtaining information that would help answer critical questions. It was always the case that analysts provided "wish lists" to collectors of the information they wanted to obtain, but the basic understanding in the community was that collectors would give priority to obtaining "secret" information on a relatively short list of high-priority topics. In the course of doing that, they often picked up other information that might or might not be passed on to analysts. Whether it was distributed depended in part on whether anyone had articulated a "requirement" for such information.

To increase the chances that they would obtain information that might be helpful to them, analysts put in requirements for more or less everything they could think of. The strategy made sense until collection became better, authoritarian regimes crumbled or relaxed in ways that made more information available, and the information technology revolution made available vastly larger amounts of information. We no longer had a situation in which analysts were starved for information, thankful for any intelligence they received, and devoted much of their analytic effort to understanding and explaining what had made its way to their in-boxes. By the turn of the century, we were awash in data and could not possibly make sense of what we had without relatively clear understanding of the developments we wanted to track, the questions we wanted to answer, and the puzzles we wanted to solve. This made it more important—imperative—for analysts to provide targeted and prioritized guidance to collectors. It also required making the process more agile and updating collection priorities more frequently than in the past.

Addressing the several dimensions of this challenge required a multifaceted approach. One dimension focused on (re)training analysts to key information requests to a limited set of analytic questions. Analysts who had joined the Intelligence Community during the Cold War and later entrants socialized into procedures developed before 2001 rarely provided targeted guidance to collectors. Those who worked on the Soviet Union and its allies were most interested in secret information that adversaries worked hard to protect. The subjects of greatest interest and concern to policymakers were well known and accorded high priority by both analysts and collectors. Collectors went after hard-to-obtain secrets with mixed success but often picked up additional information along the way. Analysts were grateful for any information that helped them to understand their "targets" and requested collection on more or less everything to ensure that the fruits of incidental collection were not left on the cutting-room floor. Analysts whose portfolios included lower-interest, low-priority places and puzzles were thankful for anything they could get. To maximize the chances of actually obtaining useful information, they too requested collection on "everything." Both those with hard-target accounts and those with low-priority subjects effectively left it to collectors to determine where to look for the information analysts wanted.

That strategy and the resultant procedures made sense in the last century, but they were rendered unnecessary and counterproductive by the demise of the Soviet Union, dramatic growth of the need for information on previously low-priority places and problems, and the explosion of publicly available information and restricted access data useful for understanding issues of interest to the United States.[10] Advances in collection and storage capabilities compounded greater availability of information. For many analysts, information drought became an information deluge. We were awash in data with limited ability to find needles in an ever-larger haystack. The only sensible way to manage the challenges of this new situation, I believed, was to narrow the scope of collection requests and to focus them more tightly on obtaining information that would provide the most insight.

Instead of effectively asking for "everything" and being grateful for "anything you can give me," analysts had to decide what information, if it could be obtained in a specified timeframe, would provide the most insight into the place, problem, or situation they and their customers most wanted to understand. Learning to do this required shedding old habits and acquiring new skills. Such skills could be taught and, I believed, we had to make teaching them a priority task of analytic transformation. I envisioned—and attempted—providing the requisite training through the promulgation of tradecraft standards and what came to be known as "Analysis 101" (see the chapter "Training and Tradecraft") and by using NIC products and procedures to demonstrate what was desired.

Learning to ask the "right" questions was only part of the challenge. If—or because—collection targets were to be more focused and, by definition, more urgent, analysts had to provide more precise guidance to collectors. Simply including the more focused topics on the wish list given to collectors was not enough. For this new system to work, analysts had to be able to tell collectors where to look. In other words, all analysts had to assume greater responsibility for providing targeting information based on their knowledge of the countries or issues in their portfolios. To illustrate and underscore the change in approach that was needed, I decreed that analysts would no longer be able to give collectors unconstrained wish lists like those children give to Santa Claus. Instead, they should think of their collection colleagues as genies able to accept only three wish requests at a time and demanding that the wish be accompanied by guidance on where to seek the desired information. A wish without a target would have to be replaced by one with information on where to start the search for relevant information.

To my surprise and delight, this demand for change met with essentially no pushback from IC analysts. They understood what we were trying to do, and, as we developed procedures to implement the new system, the guidance we provided to collectors became more focused, more helpful, and more productive.

Changing the way analysts thought about providing guidance to collectors was a necessary first step, but we also needed to change the procedures for submitting and prioritizing collection requests. The IRTPA assigned responsibility for collection requirements to the DNI, but (wisely) it did not specify how this authority was to be exercised. When the ODNI was created, there were two mechanisms for providing collection guidance. One was the National Intelligence Priorities Framework (NIPF), a formal matrix of intelligence topics that assigned priority scores for dozens of topics for every country and many transnational organizations. The NIPF was created a few years prior to the passage of the IRTPA to provide a structured and more transparent way to prioritize the hundreds of analyst requests generated by the "Dear Santa" wish list approach.

The second mechanism was informal to the point of being largely serendipitous. To improve the quality of analytic input to the collection process and the timeliness and utility of intelligence, analysts were encouraged to "get to know" their counterparts in the collection agencies and to provide direct input when they needed new or additional information. Though reasonable in theory, the result was a pronounced tendency for analysts in particular agencies to deal exclusively with collection counterparts in the same agency. We joked at the time that this resulted in prioritization by friendship and speed dial. There was abundant room for slippage in this system. Diligent collectors sometimes contacted their counterparts in other collection disciplines to alert them to the special request. This sometimes resulted in a six-year-olds-playing-soccer-like effort by multiple agencies to obtain what had been requested by a single analyst with minimal regard for the relative efficacy of different collection methods. If the first collector contacted did not bring counterparts into the loop but instead went after the requested information within his or her own system, the result might be failure to obtain the desired intelligence because the methods used were not the most appropriate for the subject. There had to be a better way than everyone running for the ball or collection based on personal ties.

Although the Assistant Director of Central Intelligence for Analysis and Production originally administered the NIPF and most of that portfolio of responsibilities (and staff) was reassigned to the ODDNI/A in 2005, prioritizing collection priorities was assigned to the DDNI/Collection. For reasons that I have forgotten, the placement issue was revisited in 2006 and responsibility for the NIPF was moved to my directorate. When that occurred, the matrix of topics and priorities had something in excess of fourteen hundred cells. Not all of the cells were filled, but most of them were. When I learned that I would henceforth have responsibility for the process, my first reaction was that I could not possibly keep a straight face while trying to explain or defend why the US Intelligence Community had more than fourteen hundred prioritized collection topics. Shortening the list, and establishing meaningful priorities, proved very difficult.

Though risible, the matrix did accurately reflect the scope and scale of policymaker concerns and issues of interest to IC analysts. When the Cold

War ended, demand for information and insights from the Intelligence Community expanded dramatically. Among other reasons was the breakdown of the stability that had resulted from the bipolar divide. Constraints on client states in each camp weakened, internal cleavages became more acute, instability spawned disruptive migration, and policymakers found that they could and must devote time and attention to issues such as infectious disease, water and energy availability, and dozens of other issues long seen through bipolar lenses. Analysts did make a good faith effort to rank order topics to guide collection, but as a practical matter, all topics with a priority classification lower than 2 (on a scale ranging from 1 through 5 with 1 being highest priority) were neglected by collectors. There simply was not enough capacity to collect on everything of interest.[11]

I confess that working this problem did not rise very high on my own list of priorities, but fortunately for the ODDNI/A and the Intelligence Community, John Keefe saw it as a worthy challenge for his extraordinary managerial skills. Heretofore analysts made decisions assigning priority to topics relevant to particular regional or functional portfolios. In theory, they were guided by explicit input from the policymakers they supported, but the exercise was generally regarded as too esoteric or unimportant to command much time and attention from customers. Instead, they instructed the analysts with whom they worked most closely to define and rank collection priorities on the basis of the analysts' understanding of what the customer needed to know and wanted to achieve. This gave at least the pretense of policymaker guidance, but it also reflected a fact of life with respect to the relationship between analysts and their customers.

Intelligence is a support function in the United States Government, and the most frequent (and in that sense most important) place in the system where policymaking and intelligence support converge is in the relationship between customers and analysts. Analysts are supposed to, and in my experience usually do, understand the wants, needs, and objectives of the officials they support. That being the case, the arrangement summarized above was not merely a contrivance to give the appearance of policy input; it was as close to the desired policy guidance to collection as one is likely to achieve.

NIPF priorities were established through a process that became more systematic and routine with each iteration. Policymakers (acting through the Joint Intelligence Community Council created by the IRTPA) reviewed, revised, and approved the entire matrix, but generally (and sensibly) focused on only a subset of top priorities. After senior policymakers approved the priority matrix, collectors undertook to implement it.[12]

The NIPF process worked reasonably well for providing overall guidance but was inadequate to meet the ever-changing array of what we referred to as "pop-up targets" for collection. To provide the timely and targeted support required—and demanded—by policymakers and military commanders, we judged that we needed a process or mechanism to tweak collection. John Keefe devised a very effective mechanism that enabled analysts to translate needs and requests from their customers into short-term collection requirements. The mechanism worked as follows. Every two weeks the National Intelligence Officers contacted senior analysts across the community to determine whether they saw a need for short-term collection on particular topics.[13] The analysts they contacted were supposed to check with their customers before making recommendations, and I believe that happened at least some of the time. NIOs were entrusted to assess, alter, and endorse (or not) suggestions from their contacts.

The NIO recommendations were submitted to John Keefe and his counterpart in the ODDNI/C, Sylvia Copeland, for a second round of evaluation and submission to the collectors. Rather than establish an entirely different mechanism, John and Sylvia piggybacked on the arrangements they cochaired to coordinate the assignment of topics and targets to collection agencies. The process they developed was efficient, nonbureaucratic, and respected by both analysts and collectors.

Transforming Analysis

EINSTEIN FAMOUSLY DEFINED INSANITY as doing the same thing over and over and expecting different outcomes. This observation doubtless contributed to my disinclination to adopt the recommendations of well-meaning people who argued for minimal and cosmetic changes to the way the Intelligence Community operated. I agreed with their argument that the IC as a whole and analysis in particular were not nearly as bad as critics contended, but I disagreed with those who argued that changes were more likely to be disruptive, dysfunctional, and deleterious to mission than they were to produce significantly better performance. The Intelligence Community, in my view, was the best in the world but not nearly as good as it could or should be. Continuing to do things in more or less the same way was unlikely to result in significantly better analysis or analytic support to the national security enterprise.

My bias for change was balanced, however, by my judgment that too much change or changes that were too disruptive (however defined) risked alienating the workforce and deterioration of support to critical missions and customers. Anticipating the question, "What missions and customers are critical," I will simply say, "All of them." The National Intelligence Priorities Framework prioritizes intelligence topics and is supposed to reflect Cabinet-level determinations of what subjects are most important to the nation, but analytic support is a retail activity, and the concerns of particular customers are critical to those customers and, derivatively, to the analysts that support a customer and mission. Collectors must and do prioritize, but analysts respond to the needs and priorities of their primary customers. This recognition, which was also a strong conviction, underscored my sympathy for those who argued the importance of not doing anything with the potential to degrade current support. Squaring the circle required small-step reforms to improve existing arrangements while pursuing parallel actions to achieve broader and deeper transformation.

Terminology matters. It matters because how one refers to a goal or other phenomenon shapes how users define the concept and how others perceive it. My task, narrowly defined, was to implement the analysis-related portions of the 2004 intelligence reform legislation and WMD Commission recommendations endorsed by President Bush. The bumper sticker formulation of this task was to reform and improve intelligence analysis. Neither term is self-explanatory, and the words implied different things and different courses of action to different people. For some, reform was a euphemism for simplification of the IC organization chart and reduction of the number of analytic products. Other ways of conceptualizing the task focused on information sharing; coordination and/or collaboration of effort; and greater transparency with regard to sources, assumptions, and analytic methodology. Those wishing to minimize structural and procedural departures from the existing system sought cosmetic change that preserved much of the status quo ante. Others seemed to argue for major changes that would demonstrate the authority and advantages of the newly created Office of the Director of National Intelligence regardless of how disruptive change would affect ongoing missions, workforce morale, or the quality of analytic products.

I was certainly aware of these and other competing conceptualizations of reform before I accepted John Negroponte's invitation to become Deputy DNI for Analysis, but I had to think about them in a more systematic way when I accepted responsibility for implementing mandated reforms. Reflections and conversations about *how* to achieve mandated goals quickly expanded to include consideration of purpose or *why* particular changes were desirable (some more desirable than others) and how they could contribute to improved performance by analysts, agencies, and the Intelligence Community as a whole. I had no interest in change for the sake of change or intended primarily to check a box on reform task lists. Quite the opposite; I was predisposed to make any and all changes that promised to improve the quality of analysis and analytic products and contributed to integration of the Intelligence Community, and to eschew "reforms" that were more cosmetic than constructive.

Thinking about what I needed to achieve in order to satisfy IRTPA and other formal requirements, and what I wanted to achieve from the once-in-two-generations opportunity to make intelligence analysis more useful to our customers overlapped with the recruitment of senior staff. "What do you want me to do?" conversations generated ideas that shaped the vision and goals of the ODDNI for Analysis. The more we talked, first in pairs and later as a group, the more we realized that we had both an opportunity and an obligation to transform the analytic enterprise into something very different from the arrangements that had evolved during and since the Cold War. From that point on, transforming analysis became the mantra and the overarching goal of the ODDNI/A.[1]

We now had a new overarching objective but only the dimmest conception of what it would entail and how to achieve it. In many respects, our problem was similar to that of developing a strategy and measures to improve IC analysis by improving the performance of all agencies and analysts. In both cases, we had a concise statement of what we wanted to achieve but lacked a strategy or roadmap to reach the desired destination. The two facets of "reform" were different, but had to be approached as an interconnected whole. For example, improving the performance of individual analysts required better training and enforcement of rigorous analytic tradecraft. This could be achieved through incremental improvements to existing procedures. Achieving other performance improvements, such as those resulting from greater collaboration among analysts in different agencies, required more fundamental and transformative changes such as the removal of impediments to sharing information across agency boundaries and interacting with experts outside the Intelligence Community. Recognition that we could not achieve our most ambitious "reform" goals without fundamental—transformational—changes to the way analysis is conducted in the Intelligence Community gave rise to our transformation agenda.

Reducing Barriers to Collaboration

Collaboration and information sharing were central to the reform "strategy" enshrined in the IRTPA legislation and WMD Commission recommendations. As important, they were essential components of my evolving vision of how analysts could and should support the national security enterprise. Declaring them to be essential and mandating improvement was easy; reducing impediments to and enhancing mechanisms for collaboration and information sharing were more difficult.

Reducing impediments to information sharing was a necessary but not sufficient condition for significantly enhanced collaboration. Early discussions with my new team made clear that we had to think about transformation as a multifaceted process that identified and alleviated existing barriers and established new rules, mechanisms, and procedures to facilitate collaboration across agency boundaries and with experts outside the Intelligence Community. We knew from experience what some of the key obstacles were but quickly decided that it would be useful to seek input from analysts across the community. We did so for three reasons: to ensure that we did not miss anything that might derail the effort, to demonstrate to the workforce that we were prepared to tackle problems that analysts considered to be the most important obstacles to doing their jobs as they believed they should be done, and to obtain buy-in for what we were trying to do. We wanted to make the point early on that our goal was to do things *for* IC analysts, not simply to do things *to* them.

Asking for input on problems and obstacles became a part of my parish call visits to individual agencies and a more systematic undertaking by members of my team. The results surprised me but were obvious to most of my deputies. Having spent most of my career in INR and long ago made the transition from working analyst to senior manager, I was unaware of the extent to which existing rules and procedures restricted the dissemination of intelligence reports to many other parts of the community. What others knew and our initial surveys confirmed was that many types of reporting that INR received as a matter of course were not widely disseminated to or in other agencies, and that the number one impediment to collaboration identified by experienced analysts was the application of originator-controlled (ORCON) restrictions on distribution.[2] I badly underestimated how hard it would be to solve this problem.

My first reaction to learning that analysts wanted us to tackle ORCON problems was to recall the words of the comic strip character Pogo, who summarized a situation by stating, "We have met the enemy and it is us." If IC rules had created the problem and the new post-IRTPA dispensation required much greater information sharing, it should be relatively easy to change the rules. Wrong. This proved to be one of the most vexing problems of my tenure.

Illustrative consequences of ORCON restrictions included prohibitions on sending particular intelligence reports to counterparts in other IC agencies working on the same place or problem, prohibitions on linking databases to facilitate identification of patterns and collaboration among analysts, and prohibitions on discussing the content of restricted reports with other USG officials holding the same clearances and knowledgeable about the subject matter of the report. These (and many other) counterproductive consequences were so obviously inconsistent with the goals of the intelligence reform legislation that I thought alleviating, if not completely removing, the restrictions within the IC was a no-brainer that could be accomplished quickly to give us an early and important "win" for the ODNI. I could not have been more wrong about how hard it would be.

Over time, I began to think about the need for and impediments to alleviating ORCON restrictions as a prime example of why "reform" of existing mechanisms and procedures would be inadequate to achieve our objectives, and why we had to think in terms of "transformation." We—certainly I—recognized that this was a more demanding aspiration than merely "fixing" problems with the extant system, but it was also more exciting because it required greater imagination and climbing higher bureaucratic mountains. We—the ODDNI/A leadership team—could get more excited about making big changes than merely tinkering to achieve minor improvements and create the illusion of greater change than was actually achieved. However, pursuing transformation entailed significant risks.

One risk was that we would alienate or disillusion the analytic workforce. As noted earlier in this book, we recognized that analysts were confused and uneasy about what "reform" would mean for them and their agencies and missions, and my initial parish calls were designed in part to assuage concerns and provide assurances that we did not envision major reorganization of the IC or major transfers of missions and personnel. Our task, as we recognized the need for transformation, was to reassure analysts that what we envisioned would make it easier for them to do their jobs without jeopardizing missions or careers. In other words, we had to persuade a skeptical workforce that our vision was both conservative (preserving what was important to them) and revolutionary (entailing big changes that would transform for the better the way they did their jobs). We understood that this would be a difficult argument to sell to the workforce but hoped that transparency and early gains would help to make the case.

In retrospect, we over-promised on ORCON reform. What we hoped would be an early win became a symbol of impotence and inability to deliver on what analysts considered a key commitment. I did not anticipate either the extent to which collectors would dig in their heels to preserve the ability to determine who did and did not see particular reports, or that my ODDNI senior counterparts would accord higher priority to achieving other objectives than to ORCON reform. I did not and do not fault their decisions to defer action on ORCON in order to achieve other goals, and I am sure that they wished that I had prioritized my own agenda somewhat differently in order to facilitate attainment of their objectives. There was nothing nefarious in the way this played out, and communication and cooperation among members of the senior team were such that we always understood what each directorate was trying to do and why each pursued the approach that it did. To a commendable degree, our activities were coordinated and mutually reinforcing, but synchronization was complicated by the perceived need to give first priority to issues and expectations in individual directorates. We all understood and respected the choices made by others, and I do not recall any instances in which the perceived need to pursue different priorities and timelines became a source of tension, although it easily could have. It is testimony to John Negroponte's skill in selecting deputies with both the expertise and the personalities to advance the overall reform agenda despite obstacles and opposition.

One area in which there was early and consequential collaboration across the ODNI centered on the integration of top-secret computer systems. Allowing the systems to be connected was a *sine qua non* requirement for collaboration among analysts. Doing so had been technically possible for a long time, but counterintelligence concerns had prevented approval of complete email connectivity until 2005 (achieving full connectivity took until 2007). IC CIO Dale Meyerrose's decision to certify all systems to the same classification level and to connect them made it technically possible to begin sharing documents and collaborating in cyberspace, but it did not ensure that all intelligence documents could be disseminated and shared over the now integrated system, or that all analysts with the same clearances could exchange information and collaborate virtually. Meeting those requisites for collaboration across agencies required additional measures to transform the Intelligence Community.

Intelligipedia

One of the first steps we took to facilitate collaboration at a distance was to adopt and invigorate the CIA's Intellipedia concept. The basic idea undergirding Intellipedia was to create a classified (at the secret level) version of Wikipedia. Initially it was to be little more than a repository of published IC assessments and unclassified information on topics of interest to the Intelligence Community. This conception of what it should be did not attract much interest from or use by analysts. It was essentially "just another tool" with more promise than utility. Mike Wertheimer and Andy Shepard saw an opportunity to transform

Intellipedia into an initial test bed for digital collaboration. The idea they brought to me had been suggested during our initial effort to determine what analysts wanted us to do to make their professional lives easier.

Since the initial version of Intellipedia was limited to documents classified at the secret or lower levels, we did not have to contend with still extant restrictions on sharing more highly classified information. The innovative use of the capability suggested by analysts was to post drafts, share ideas, and use blogging capabilities to develop collaborative understanding of specific issues without having to obtain higher-level review and approval to send them to analysts in other agencies. Intellipedia was not used initially to produce formal finished assessments, but it quickly became a repository of first-take analyses and works in progress that provided an unprecedented way for analysts to discover colleagues elsewhere in the community working on topics in their own portfolios.

Initial use of Intellipedia encouraged my analytic transformation team and confirmed judgments that they and I had made about the analytic workforce. A large majority of our analysts had joined the IC after 9/11, most of them were young, and virtually all were more tech savvy and comfortable operating in cyberspace than I was (and still am). To say that younger analysts took to this new opportunity for virtual collaboration like a duck to water trivializes what happened, but the fact of the matter is that it underscored how ready and how eager the majority of analysts were to use tools and collaborative mechanisms in their work lives that they had grown up with, used in college, and utilized regularly in their lives outside the workplace. I saw this as both an opportunity and a necessity to move quickly from the world of paper to the digital universe.

The nature of the opportunity requires little elaboration. Most of our workforce was tech savvy and accustomed to interaction and collaboration at a distance with people they had never met face to face. Collaboration in cyberspace was more unnatural for older analysts, especially if they did not have a prior personal connection. The lesson for me was that we could move to higher levels of virtual collaboration without a great deal of instruction and preparatory work, and that it was unnecessary to use the aptitude and acumen of more senior analysts as the pacing element for transition to new forms of collaboration.

The second lesson I drew from our initial experience with Intellipedia was that if we did not act quickly to replace existing ways of doing analysis and collaborating at a distance, we risked losing a significant portion of our young workforce. Initial comments about Intellipedia and our vision for the future of analysis indicated both high receptivity to what we hoped to achieve and considerable impatience to get there. In other words, I viewed the transformation agenda, which was still being fleshed out, as an integral part of our strategy to retain younger analysts who would soon—very soon—replace the tiny cohort of middle-aged analysts and larger but dwindling number of baby boomers.

An unanticipated (certainly by me) benefit of adopting Intellipedia and championing analyst-proposed ways to use it was that doing so made clear our willingness to welcome and work with ideas that did not originate with the ODDNI/A. In other words, it was an early demonstration that our goal was to improve performance and make it easier for analysts to do their jobs. This enhanced our credibility with our key constituency.

A-Space

One of the things that we learned from our early interactions with analysts across the community was that they had little appetite for new or more "tools." Indeed, "analytic tools" had become dirty words for a variety of reasons.[3] One was that all had over-promised and underperformed. Presented as "magic bullet" solutions to the explosive growth of information; new issues and customers; and escalating demands for greater precision, granularity, and timeliness, most tools were widely derided as more trouble than they were worth. Another tools-related problem was that they exacerbated differences and tensions between "have" and "have not" components of the Intelligence Community. Agencies with big budgets could afford—and bragged about—their new analytic tools. Poorer agencies went without and envied their better-funded colleagues even though many of those colleagues had nothing good to say about the tools.

As my senior team and I wrestled with the challenges of how to use digital connectivity to facilitate collaboration and information sharing, we recognized that our initial solution had to work well, do the things that analysts wanted it to do, and be immediately available to analysts across the community. The latter requirement was doubly important because it would provide concrete evidence that the IRTPA and the authorities granted to the DNI could better integrate the Intelligence Community than the structures they had replaced.

As with so many other challenges, designing, acquiring, and using an entirely new mechanism for meaningful virtual collaboration entailed multiple interconnected requirements. Moreover, we had to get this one right. The new system had to work well right out of the box. The way we developed what came to be known as A-Space was messier and more iterative than suggested by this summary account written to highlight my or our thought process rather than the sequence of developments. Mike Wertheimer, Andy Shepard, and their team did all of the heavy lifting. My role was to ensure that what they were doing fit into and contributed to the larger vision for analysis that we had developed jointly, to explain and endorse the project to the workforce, and to provide top cover within the ODNI and in our dealings with the Hill and the President's Intelligence Advisory Board.

The first requirement for the collaborative enterprise we envisioned was that it had to be able to access, move, and protect intelligence up to the Top Secret/Sensitive Compartmented Information level. Prior certification and connection of the high-level IT systems of all IC agencies was a necessary prerequisite, but it was essentially a dumb electronic pipe for moving data from one point to another. We wanted and needed far greater capability than the ability of an analyst in one agency to send information via an email attachment to specific counterparts elsewhere in the IC after determining that the intended recipient was authorized to receive it (a manifestation and consequence of the ORCON problem).

This is not the place to describe all of the considerations and requirements that shaped our request for proposals and the changes demanded during development, but I think it is worthwhile to summarize how I thought about the project and how I interacted with Wertheimer and his team. Although I do not recall ever prioritizing requirements in a formal way, the most important as far as I was concerned were that the new capability had to be easy to use, qualitatively better than anything currently available to IC analysts, and able to better integrate the analytic community. It had to—and did—do much more than this (for example, it could identify other raw and finished intelligence on the subject and other people who had worked on that topic), but my goal was to deploy a markedly better capability as quickly as possible, and to use A-Space to demonstrate improvement in the quality and utility of analytic products produced through informal collaboration across agency boundaries.[4] I also wanted to use it to demonstrate to skeptics inside and outside the Intelligence Community that the ODNI was serious about and capable of leading transformational change.

Like everything else that we undertook, the development of A-Space was an incremental process that built on prior achievements, lessons from both failures and successes, and the step-by-step approach of our "think big, start small, fail cheap, fix fast" mantra. For example, having discovered that solving the ORCON problem was going to take longer than we were willing to wait, we decided to settle for "half a loaf" partial solutions. In the case of A-Space, that meant winning approval for a "pilot" that would allow us to use A-Space to access documents in most agency databases regardless of ORCON restrictions, and to make them available to all IC analysts with the clearances necessary to access the system. This satisficing solution still precluded easy access to the expertise of other IC professionals and USG officials with the requisite clearances but lacking ORCON approval, but it removed an enormous hurdle to analytic collaboration.

We also used the "pilot" or test bed argument to overcome counterintelligence objections to making "all" intelligence available to all analysts.[5] This was not a gimmick that ignored legitimate counterintelligence concerns; it really was an opportunity to test the efficacy of the tracking and anomaly detection software (adapted from what is used in the financial industry). It was not easy, but we secured approval for a pilot that would include a small percentage of people holding special access clearances. Analysts represent such a small percentage of all IC professionals (let alone the much larger number of defense contractors and other non-USG personnel with such clearances) that we could easily include 100 percent of IC analysts in the A-Space pilot.

Prior creation of the Analytic Resources Catalog (ARC) provided the basis for determining who would be given access to A-Space. Anyone who was in the ARC was considered an analyst (recall earlier discussion of the debate over who was entitled to be considered an analyst and the inclusive way in which we resolved that debate). But we added another requirement, namely holding a current Top Secret/Sensitive Compartmented Information clearance.[6] Consistent with our goal of making A-Space easy to use, we automated the process, making it very easy and fast for analysts to gain access. The mechanics of how we did this are less important than the fact that they complied with my requirements for ease of use (in this case access) and accessibility by all analysts.

Existing arrangements (after all high-level IC systems were connected) made it possible to collaborate with persons known to be working on specific topics; we wanted to be able to tap the expertise of people who were not known personally by the analyst seeking assistance. A-Space made that possible by suggesting the names of others who had used a report or worked on similar topics. It also made it possible to issue general inquiries of the "Does anyone know anything about . . . ?" variety. Early examples of productive responses to such queries included the explanation of an Urdu phrase provided by a native speaker and deconstruction of the photo of a new weapon by an analyst who stated, "I do not know anything about that country or advanced weapons, but I know a lot about photography and that has been photoshopped. Here is how it was produced." There were many more that said, in essence, "I do not know you and did not even know that your unit worked on these issues but we are studying the same thing and I think we can work together."

My insistence that our new system work the first-time analysts used it and that it do what analysts wanted it to was taken to heart by Mike Wertheimer and his team. The starting point was to assemble a group of analysts to discuss what they wanted and what they liked and disliked about available tools. Developers were brought into the process and told to build capacity based on what analysts said they wanted. We also insisted that the system use as much off-the-shelf commercial software as possible.[7] This was in marked contrast to the prevailing procedure in which developers built in as many bells and whistles as they could imagine and told analyst they would find them helpful. That had contributed mightily to "tool fatigue" and hostility to having to learn yet another new system. The first prototype delivered by our contractors was subjected to rigorous testing by slightly more than one hundred early adapter analysts. The bottom line was that they didn't hate it, but they also didn't want it. The testing group provided more than 125 specific complaints and suggestions, which our developers took to heart. They "borrowed" a subset of our analysts to work directly with them to build a second prototype. The second one was subjected to more rigorous testing by analysts who evaluated its utility to help them to address the problems they were working on. The second version still had bugs, but they were fixed to the satisfaction of our early adapters. Only at that point did Mike propose that we open A-Space to all analysts.

By the time we were ready to open A-Space to participation by all analysts, my team and I had been previewing our vision of what we hoped it would do and providing updates on progress for several months. I recognized that there was an element of risk in talking about A-Space before it was ready, especially if it performed much worse than we anticipated, but I wanted to build a sense of expectation and excitement and give analysts, Hill staffers, and other skeptical observers of the ODNI experiment better understanding of what we were trying to accomplish and what transformation could mean for them.

Despite the protracted buildup of expectations, and confidence that we had a system that would work well from day one and quickly win over skeptical analysts wary about yet another "magic bullet" tool, we decided to eschew automatic or mandatory enrollment in favor of voluntary and gradual expansion of participation. The reasons for doing so were partly psychological (I judged that we would engender less reluctance and resistance if we made participation voluntary rather than mandatory), and partly prudential (if there were serious problems, I wanted to be able to find and fix them before their existence soured too many analysts).

Based on adoption rates for new platforms on the Internet, we anticipated a slow start (consisting mainly of early adopters) and gradual growth. To the surprise of everyone, there was a stampede to sign on. Hundreds had signed on within a few days, and the number swelled to thousands within a few weeks. The principal incentive to do so was word of mouth; those who tried it first told colleagues about the experience and urged them to take advantage of the services and capabilities it offered. We had a winner, both with the analytic community and with those monitoring ODNI and ODDNI/A progress.[8]

Library of National Intelligence

A perennial divide in the Intelligence Community was that between those (mostly analysts) who wanted greater transparency into and access to "all" available information, and those (mostly counterintelligence specialists and some collectors) who considered it imperative to obscure sourcing information and limit access to those with a "need to know." The ORCON fight was one manifestation of this enduring division and dilemma, but it was not the only one. Although I certainly recognize the importance of protecting sources and methods and the desirability of limiting how much adversaries know about US concerns and capabilities, my own experience, the letter and intent of the intelligence reform legislation, and the logic and requisites of analytic integration put me squarely on the side of greater transparency and accessibility.

As has been noted several times already, Intelligence Community managers had begun to draw and apply lessons from the way intelligence was handled before 9/11 and from the flawed estimate on Iraq's WMD capabilities. One such lesson was that analysts, or more specifically some analysts, needed to know more about the "raw" intelligence provided by collectors than had previously been allowed. DCI George Tenet took a small but important step to address this need when he mandated, shortly after the flaws of the Iraq WMD estimate became apparent, that the NIOs and a few other senior analysts must be given more information about the intelligence reports undergirding the analytic judgments in NIC products. I welcomed this step but considered it inadequate. Building on this small step to provide much more information to "all" analysts became both part of my vision for a community of analysts and a specific goal of analytic transformation.

By the time I had been given the opportunity to shape and implement intelligence reforms intended to improve the quality of analytic support to USG missions and officials, I had already added three access-to-information goals to my imaginary "things that I would do if I were king of intelligence" list. One was to bridge the divide between analysts and collectors so that we could all operate as members of the same team and take full advantage of the expertise and insights each possessed.[9] In the name of protecting sources and methods, and reflecting practices antedating creation of the modern US Intelligence Community in 1947 that relegated analysis to a lower status than espionage, collectors (and rules governing distribution) determined which analysts needed a given piece of intelligence and what the analysts needed to know about how it was obtained. In essence, standard operating procedures required analysts to accept collector judgments about the accuracy and reliability of specific developments and observations contained in intelligence reports, and collectors often took umbrage and were relatively unresponsive when analysts asked for more information or challenged anything in a report. This effectively precluded dialog between professionals on each side of the divide who had subject matter knowledge and a shared responsibility to provide the best possible intelligence support to the national security establishment. I believed strongly that each side could help the other far more than was occurring, and that efforts to deny information to adversaries were having a perverse and negative impact on the ability of USG decision makers to understand developments, protect our nation, and advance US interests.[10]

A second goal was to reduce—ideally remove—the pernicious effects of "if you knew what I know" arguments to justify analytic judgments challenged by analysts in other agencies or another part of the same agency. This also was a multifaceted problem. ORCON (and other) distribution restrictions often prevented analysts in some IC components from having ready access to reports available to their counterparts in other components even though all had the same clearances. Another manifestation resulted from understandable and justifiable decisions to restrict certain reports to far smaller numbers of people. Among other perverse and deleterious consequences of this practice was that some highly restricted reports were shown to senior decision makers in a given agency but not to the analysts who supported them. Other consequences were exacerbation of institutional rivalries that impeded collaboration and unwarranted impressions that the analyses of particular agencies must be superior to those of others because they had access to additional, more restricted information. I regarded all of these as pathologies that had to be addressed if we were to restore confidence and morale, improve analytic support, and integrate the analytic community.

The third problem I wanted to address was the difficulty of knowing whether one was working with all of the information on a given topic that was available in the Intelligence Community, and the related problem of knowing whether distinct reports had come from one or multiple sources. For an analyst trying to understand developments and to determine the accuracy and validity of available information, it is useful, even essential, to know whether one is working with corroborating information from multiple sources, multiple reports from the same source, or different versions of the same report classified at different levels because of additional or omitted detail. I viewed this as both a substantive and a processing problem.

Collector judgments about the access and past reliability of a given source did not automatically ensure the accuracy or interpretation of specific reported developments. Moreover, my own experience had taught me that analysts are more comfortable with information that can be corroborated than with information from a single source, and that they want to know whether multiple reports on a topic disseminated over time are from one or multiple sources. The process dimension of the problem was that individual analysts had to spend sometimes large amounts of time assembling reporting on a given development when better (and simpler) metadata and appropriate software could allow computers to assemble all relevant data (both raw reporting and finished analysis) so that analysts could devote more time to assessing what it means.

Writing this reminds me of another example of change that I thought would be of obvious value and easy to implement that proved to be unachievable during my tenure. That seemingly simple reform was to standardize the format of HUMINT, SIGINT, Imagery, and other types of raw intelligence reports. For whatever reasons, basic identifying information (for example, date of information, subject, location of what was being reported) was located in different places on different types of reporting. I saw standardizing the format as an easy way to demonstrate that the ODNI could do things to integrate the community and to simplify the training and tasks of analysts and proposed making the change at one of our first ODNI staff meetings. Everyone agreed that the change would be desirable, but it never happened. This may be a trivial example, but it illustrates the fact that others had different priorities and that I was not prepared to challenge their judgments about what they needed to do within their own areas of responsibility. The ODNI senior team thought corporately, but we each had to make judgments about priorities and sequencing within our individual purviews and all had sufficient respect for one another (and had more than enough other tasks) that we were reluctant to intrude too far onto one another's turf or to appear to know better than they how to achieve collective objectives. This was in the "nice to do," and I believed "easy to do" category, but it was not of high importance to any of us.

Desire to address the problems summarized above predisposed me to support Mike Wertheimer's proposal to create a fully searchable and discoverable Library of National Intelligence (LNI) that would contain all raw and finished reports disseminated in digital form by the US Intelligence Community. For some agencies, digital reporting began in the early 1980s; other agencies (notably in the law enforcement world) still maintained most information in nondigitized case files. Though favorably disposed, my limited understanding of information technologies caused me to ask in all seriousness, "How many servers will that take?" I was surprised and pleased when Wertheimer responded that search engines and software would be able to find and integrate reports without moving them.

Mike and his team had already done a great deal of work on this project before they brought it to me. What they had done demonstrated exactly the kind of initiative and focus on transformational changes that I considered essential. They understood what "I" wanted because we had developed a shared vision to which everyone contributed and each member of the senior team had wide latitude to explore ways to achieve that vision. Far from being troubled because they had acted without asking or telling me, I was thrilled that they had done so. I saw my role in this undertaking as cheerleader and facilitator-in-chief. As with Analysis 101, the ARC, and A-Space, I saw my role as ensuring that the LNI was consistent with and contributed to the overall vision, explaining what we were doing and generating enthusiasm within the analytic community and oversight bodies, and ensuring that my colleagues on the ODNI senior team understood what we were trying to do and how it might impact their own responsibilities and plans.

I could contribute little, very little, on the technical side, but I was able to play a larger role in other arenas. As in so many other of the decision arenas discussed in this book, ideas and methods emerged through cumulative discussions among members of the senior team, with counterparts elsewhere in the ODNI, and consultations with managers and working analysts across the Intelligence Community. I no longer remember—if I could ever distinguish—which of the ideas summarized here originated with me and which I appropriated from others or emerged organically, but this is a book about what I was thinking so I will focus on how I viewed the issues involved.

Probably based on earlier decisions about how to organize and pay for training and evaluation programs, Mike's original proposal to create the Library of National Intelligence specified that the ODDNI/A would cover all costs to convert the products of component agencies to formats that could be utilized by the LNI. Advances in information technology made this task much easier than it would have been even a few years earlier. If we succeeded, which we did, it would constitute a giant step toward IC integration, comprehensive information sharing within the Intelligence Community, and better IC analysis.

The decision—and ability—to pay for the conversions made the process a free good that agencies were generally happy to accept. Experience had shown that even the larger, better-funded agencies would be reluctant to commit resources to activities that benefitted other agencies more than themselves, and that smaller agencies would never have the money to fund this. Using ODNI funds to build the LNI enabled us to do something important that we could not otherwise achieve but, as important, it provided a concrete example proving that the ODNI was more than just another layer of bureaucracy. We were demonstrably doing things that had not been possible under the old structure and authorities, and we were doing things that advanced the explicit goals of intelligence reform.[11]

One of the goals and reasons for creating the LNI was to make all intelligence discoverable. This did not mean making all reports available to all analysts, but it did mean that all analysts could discover the existence of reporting on the topic of their research. If a report had been disseminated at a classification level and compartment they could access, the LNI would provide the information needed to find it. If distribution were more restricted, they would discover that information existed that they had not seen, but it also provided a way to seek permission to see it on a "need to know" basis. Procedures were developed to seek limited access or information on who within the analyst's chain of command had access to the reporting. The context for seeking access was the shift from traditional "need to know" to "responsibility to provide" guidance issued by then DNI Mike McConnell.[12]

SHARP and RASER

Intellipedia, A-Space, and the Library of National Intelligence were "big" innovations, but the transformation agenda also included smaller steps intended to capitalize on lessons learned in parts of the Intelligence Community. One such step was to build on NSA experience running summer workshops that focused attention and effort on specific, hard to solve problems. The basic idea was to bring together a relatively small number of specialists from inside and outside the Intelligence Community who would work together for several weeks with the twin goals of trying to solve specific problems and developing collaborative relationships that would persist after the workshop. My analytic transformation team proposed, and I readily supported, convening similar workshops under the auspices of the ODDNI/A.

Dubbed the Summer Hard Problems Program, or SHARP, the month-long workshops brought together people with overlapping interests and a range of experiences who would not normally have occasion to work on problems of common interest. We recognized from the beginning that we would have to learn as we went along, and successive workshops became both more focused and more productive. Some of the topics we explored were patterns of transition from individual unhappiness to organized dissent to mobilization for terrorist activities; ways in which extremists do or might use the Internet to move money, coordinate activities, and recruit followers; how to reduce vulnerability to terrorist attack on the food supply; how to better integrate the capabilities of foreign intelligence, border security, and law enforcement to provide end-to-end coverage of potential threats; and determination of culpability for nuclear terrorism.

The sessions generated more insights than answers, but in some cases provided the starting point for novel approaches and techniques with applicability beyond the initial topic. Perhaps the most important product was recognition that there was much to learn from one another and much to gain from collaboration across the "inside the IC-outside the IC" divide, and much that intelligence analysts could learn from unclassified sources and colleagues without security clearances. An ancillary benefit was that several of the non-USG participants continued to work on "our" problems after the workshop ended because they recognized their importance and had become hooked on trying to find solutions.[13]

The Rapid Analytic Support and Expeditionary Response (RASER) project was a very different adaptation based on IC experience and intended to address future requirements. One inspiration for this program was the proven utility of small multi-agency analytic teams deployed to support military and diplomatic missions.[14] The basic idea was a simple one, namely, that a small group of experienced analysts deployed close to the mission being supported could determine among themselves how best to reach back to home agencies to obtain collection or analysis to address urgent requirements. Their knowledge of home agencies and ability to exploit personal and bureaucratic relationships could dramatically shorten response times and provide more focused answers to high-priority questions. A second inspiration was the escalating demand for deployment to Iraq and Afghanistan of nonmilitary intelligence professionals able to provide timely and targeted support to military operations, counterterrorism, and nation-building efforts.

The RASER pilot was designed to train cohorts of young analysts who could deploy immediately to stand up multi-agency support teams and/or serve as key members of agency-based task forces. Their joint training was designed to enable them to operate without becoming a burden to the units and missions to which they were assigned, work collaboratively with other members of their team to achieve synergy and efficiency, and utilize their reach-back and networking capabilities to provide optimal intelligence support to missions in the field. The program was also designed to move young analysts up the learning curve faster than could be achieved through traditional on-the-job training and occasional assignments to another component of the IC. Goals of the program included accelerated training, building long-term capacity to catalyze and organize cross-agency collaboration, and preparing teams for immediate deployment domestically or abroad.[15]

Analytic Outreach

Having spent the first ten years of my professional career teaching at Stanford and nineteen years in INR, I was amazed to discover the degree of disinterest if not antipathy toward interaction with outside experts in most other components of the Intelligence Community. In academe, referencing the work of other scholars and, as possible, consulting with them on subjects of common interest is both a natural and required part of the scholarly enterprise. People being people and competition for recognition naturally cause some to hold back ideas intended to feature prominently in a forthcoming book or article, but this still leaves broad scope for mutually beneficial exchanges, and most experts are eager to talk about their work and to offer comments on that of others. In INR, maintaining contact with experts inside and outside government known to be knowledgeable about subjects of common interest was normal and expected.

Subjects worthy of examination by the Intelligence Community are inherently complex and consequential, and both customers and analysts know they almost never have as much information as they would like to have in order to draw conclusions helpful to customers. I believed strongly that tapping the information and insights of many experts is likely to lead to greater understanding and better support to national security customers than reliance on a small number of IC analysts, many of whom have limited expertise and experience and rely primarily on classified information. I saw expanding contacts with experts outside the Intelligence Community as a cheap, easy, and quick way to improve the quality of IC analysis. I am still convinced that I was right in terms of the potential benefits but was very wrong in my judgment about how easy it would be to change this dimension of IC culture.

In the Intelligence Community, the term "analytic outreach" was generally understood to refer to interaction with scholars, think tank experts, journalists, and others working outside the US Government. I thought about it in broader terms that encompassed collaboration of IC analysts across agency boundaries and interaction with non-IC USG officials. The ARC, A-Space, NIC, and PDB procedures, and efforts to change ORCON restrictions, had multiple objectives, but all were parts of my "master plan" to enable IC analysts to collaborate with one another. Making it easier for analysts to tap the expertise of USG officials who were not part of the Intelligence Community was another part of this scheme to improve analysis.[16] Allowing, encouraging, and facilitating interaction with outside expertise was the final building block in this "grand scheme."

One of the first steps that I took to enhance outreach was to hire Ken Roberts, the recently retired former director of INR's outreach program, to prepare an inventory of existing contacts and contract mechanisms across the Intelligence Community. This effort was in many ways analogous to the mapping exercises described earlier to identify analytic expertise and the character of work performed in each IC component. The results filled a three-inch-thick binder. His findings confirmed that we had a lot to work with. A logical next step was to ascertain whether individuals or entities that had regular contacts with analysts in one IC agency would be willing to make themselves available to analysts in all agencies, and to build a database (similar to the ARC) with the names, expertise, and contact information of all who were willing to be included. That would be a useful but insufficient condition for expanding outreach.

A second prerequisite was to change agency rules and cultures with the objective of developing a single permissive and supportive set of rules governing such contacts. That proved far more difficult than I had anticipated. One impediment was the insistence by a portion of one agency that it alone was authorized to contact and report conversations with non-USG experts. I considered this claim to be ridiculous and was confident that we could end the self-proclaimed monopoly, but it took time and effort to do so.

The reason the agency took that position was not simply a matter of defending its turf. The more substantive—if to me unconvincing—rationale was that only a subset of specially trained professionals could be trusted to discuss matters of interest to the Intelligence Community with people who did not have clearances. The implicit—and sometimes explicitly stated—concern was that ordinary analysts would unwittingly (or carelessly) reveal classified information as well as the fact that the USG was interested in a particular topic. I knew from my experience supervising INR analysts for almost twenty years that they were fully capable of distinguishing between information about sources and methods obtainable only through classified means and generic information, questions, and insights about the matters in their portfolios. It is entirely possible to discuss the trajectory and drivers of developments in a particular country or transnational arena without talking about how one knows about a development or why the analyst wants to understand it. Moreover, we did not have to rely on chance and good intentions; interacting with outside experts is a teachable skill that could and would be added to the tradecraft toolbox of all IC analysts.

In addition to the kinds of structural and procedural obstacles summarized above, there were also cultural impediments that could not be ignored if we were to fulfill our responsibility to protect sensitive information and raise the comfort level of analysts instructed to confer with outside experts. Training them to use instead of eschew such contacts would have to be part of any solution, but there were other elements as well. One was the result of channeling "all" information to analysts on highly classified computer networks. Some did not have separate access to the Internet, and even though there was no direct link between the Internet and IC classified systems, much of the information on the classified systems was, in fact, unclassified and labeled as such. However, it was natural, and probably inevitable, for analysts to think and act as if "everything" that they knew about a subject was based on classified intelligence.

Another dimension of the problem resulted from the way analysts in many agencies were expected to write and brief. Overstating only slightly, there was a bias in most agencies to write and disseminate products at high levels of classification. There were probably many reasons for this, but I suspected that two of them were at least a subliminal belief that products would be considered to be better informed and/or more accurate if classified at a high rather than a low level. Every beginning analyst and new customer is instructed that classification reveals nothing about accuracy or reliability; it is supposed to apply only to source sensitivity and possible damage to US national security if revealed without proper authorization. But human nature often acts as if higher classification signals greater reliability, and at least some analysts and some agencies seek to exploit that tendency.

My perspective on this dimension of the problem was also shaped by my experience in INR. The Bureau received and used the full spectrum of intelligence, from unclassified media through HUMINT, SIGINT, Imagery, and other classified collection mechanisms, but it always sought to write at the lowest possible level of classification in order to make its products and briefings as useful as possible to its primary customers, most of whom were not cleared to the highest levels. There was an implicit compact between INR and its customers that assured the people it supported that INR analytic judgments had been informed by all available intelligence even if they did not refer to Top Secret or compartmented sources. If customers with the requisite clearances wanted to see such information, it would, of course be shown to them, but the shared goal was to produce analyses that could be stored in customer spaces or IT systems and used by and with officials who did not have high-level access. This compact procedure forced INR analysts to be more attentive to unclassified sources of information on subjects also covered in classified intelligence.[17]

Despite the to me obvious advantages of facilitating and expanding interchange with outside experts, some agencies (one in particular) fought doing so with all the means at their disposal. After literally years of effort, we finally secured approval for *Intelligence Community Directive 205: Analytic Outreach* on July 16, 2008. The directive was symbolically important but something of a Pyrrhic victory because it gave agencies broad discretion in implementation.[18]

Roads Not Taken

PREVIOUS CHAPTERS have attempted to describe the way I defined, prioritized, and pursued a number of mandated and self-initiated components of intelligence reform. Since the book was conceived as a case study, not a history, it has focused more on why I made the decisions that I did than on the content and consequences of those decisions. The examples are illustrative, not exhaustive; we attempted—and achieved—more than has been described. I hope, however, that the examples given are sufficient to illustrate and clarify the general guidance summarized in Part II. But the case study is still incomplete because it has not yet examined the important subject of roads not taken or, more accurately, decisions to walk away from fights on issues that others thought more important than I did.

One of the most important challenges facing any leader or new appointee is to find the right balance between undertaking all tasks critical to success in high-priority areas and undertakings that are nice but not necessary and are likely to entail more costs than benefits. There is a limit to what any leader or team can do in the amount of time available and, as a rule of thumb, the more tasks pursued simultaneously, the more difficult it is to achieve success in any. But if achieving high-priority goals requires prior success in other areas, the prerequisite tasks must be undertaken early in the process. Those that are not essential should, generally speaking, be deferred or avoided. Every attempt to restore or reform bureaucratic institutions or procedures encounters resistance and demands attention. Some fights are best avoided.

Earlier chapters explained my thinking when I decided to foreswear attempts to make structural changes involving the transfer of responsibilities and people from one analytic component to another, forego potentially disruptive changes to the *President's Daily Brief*, and ignore calls to punish those "responsible" for the flawed estimate on Iraq's WMD. Here I will focus on decisions that were not discussed previously.

Responsibility for Terrorism Analysis

Terrorism, more specifically the "failure" of the IC to predict and prevent the attacks of 9/11 and determination to prevent a recurrence, was a prime mover and major shaper of the reforms I was tasked to implement. It was also an omnipresent part of the context within which we had to operate. An implicit, if not explicit question about every action we proposed was, "How will this contribute to the war on terror?" As a result, it was advantageous and to a considerable degree necessary to frame proposed changes in terms of how they would affect the Intelligence Community's ability to discover and disrupt terrorist plots. Moreover, nearly half of all IC analysts had joined the Intelligence Community after 9/11, many of them with the stated intent to combat the terrorist threat to our country and our people. Given the importance of the counterterrorism mission, the psychological and political imperatives to protect our country, and the express desire of agencies and analysts to contribute, it is necessary to explain why I did not endeavor to make the ODDNI/A more central to the war on terror.

Nothing underscored the centrality of terrorism in the mandate to reform intelligence more forcefully than the language in the Intelligence Reform and Terrorism Prevention Act of 2004 that established the National Counterterrorism Center (NCTC) and specified that it was "[t]o serve as the primary organization in the United States Government for analyzing and integrating all intelligence possessed or acquired by the United States Government pertaining to terrorism and counterterrorism excepting intelligence pertaining exclusively to domestic terrorists and domestic counterterrorism."[1]

The IRTPA language did not make NCTC the exclusive agency responsible for analysis of terrorist-related information and developments, but its intended primacy was unambiguous, a point that its first director, Vice Admiral (retired) Scott Redd, made repeatedly and forcefully. The reform legislation did not terminate counterterrorism analysis in other components of the Intelligence Community. The nearly simultaneous stand-up of NCTC and the ODNI, and the strong opinions of many in the analytic community, posed several issues that I had to consider and, ultimately, to address. I chose to sidestep most of them.

One of the first issues that arose was triggered by the need to staff the newly created NCTC. The IRTPA legislation had transferred some functions and personnel from CIA to NCTC (specifically those previously housed in the CIA's Terrorism Threat Identification Center), but the legislation did not mandate or provide a framework for staffing other planning and analytic functions. The importance of counterterrorism as a national security priority and the primacy assigned to NCTC made it imperative to fill its hundreds of positions as quickly as possible. But the fact that all agencies retained residual responsibility for terrorism-related analysis of developments germane to the primary missions they supported made them reluctant to transfer any analysts—let alone their best ones—to NCTC.

The DNI had authority to transfer analysts across agency boundaries, but John Negroponte never suggested to me that he had considered using that authority to staff NCTC, and he never asked me to consider involuntary transfers for that purpose. I would have been very reluctant to do so for three reasons. One was my general concern to avoid actions that might degrade current capability to support critical missions in hope of reaping greater benefit in the future. A second reason was that I considered terrorism-related concerns to be too important to put all analytic capacity in a single (and unproven) agency. I believed fervently in the value of multiple and independent evaluations of information and analysis of its meaning and implications, and understood the logic of redundancy in coverage of important issues and the need for tailored support (including on terrorism) to the diverse missions and customers of the national security enterprise. The third reason was less important but still significant, at least to me. As noted much earlier in this book, during my initial parish calls to analytic components I had sought to reassure analysts worried about how intelligence reform would affect them that I did not plan to make major structural changes or to transfer analysts from one agency or mission to another. I considered it important to honor this commitment for reasons of morale and DDNI/A credibility.

Although almost every analytic component did work on terrorism and had issues with NCTC, CIA and the FBI were most unhappy and most significantly affected by the stand-up and declared missions of the National Counterterrorism Center. The issues involved pride, personnel, and mission, but for understandable reasons, arguments were framed primarily in terms of potential negative impact on each agency's ability to perform critical missions in the war on terror. In some respects, this was a classic case of reluctance to jeopardize current performance by making changes that might (or might not) lead to better performance in the future. Given the salience of the terrorist threat and praiseworthy determination not to let anything like the events of 9/11 happen again, CIA and FBI concerns about mission were understandable and justified, not merely self-serving. So were arguments on the other side contending that what we had done before was obviously inadequate and could not be trusted to prevent another devastating attack.

As a deputy director of national intelligence, I shared responsibility for implementing IRTPA reforms and preventing another terrorist attack. This meant that I was drawn into virtually every senior-level ODNI discussion of these issues and expected to take positions that, inevitably, would favor one side or the other. On this issue, my experience and instincts predisposed me to favor protection of current capabilities rather than pursuit of potentially better arrangements with the risk of temporarily degrading our ability to detect and disrupt terrorist plots. But implementation of mandated reforms was an explicit part of my job description, and the lessons I was learning in my first weeks on the job were deepening my commitment to transformational change. I confess to being pulled in two directions on these issues.

My thinking was also colored by negative perceptions of all three contenders. For reasons alluded to above and developed more fully below, I was displeased by the way NCTC leaders were describing and pursuing their mandate with respect to analysis. Suffice it to say that it galled members of my staff who worked on issues germane to terrorism and struck me as unnecessarily if not wrongheadedly arrogant and counterproductive. In other words, the attitude and actions of NCTC seniors disinclined me to support their arguments. That inclination was—or might have been—reinforced by what I knew about CIA's steps to enhance its own stature and capabilities and the FBI's struggles to build analytic capacity. However, positive incentives to support CIA and FBI were offset by negative sentiments fueled by the almost daily litany of complaints about CIA and FBI obstructionism shared in meetings of the ODNI senior staff. In the case of CIA, obstructionism and refusal to cooperate were experienced repeatedly by my own staff and often involved initiatives that I had launched or endorsed. The perhaps perverse result was that I was disinclined—and did not—weigh in strongly in support of any contending party.

My calculus and responsibilities with respect to terrorism and counterterrorism were further complicated by my concurrent position as Chair of the National Intelligence Council. The NIC and its National Intelligence Officer for Transnational Threats had both legacy and new responsibilities to serve as the convener and coordinator of analytic work performed in all IC components.[2] As DDNI/A, I had an obligation to be objective about the roles and capabilities of constituent agencies, but as Chair of NIC, I had specific obligations to that organization and its people. NCTC essentially wanted to assume all terrorism-related tasks and responsibilities previously exercised on behalf of the analytic community by the NIO for Transnational Threats. The NIO and his colleagues on the NIC did not want that to happen. This was more than a matter of pride and turf. Terrorism, like all transnational concerns, is inextricably entwined with regional, national, ethnic, religious, economic, and other attributes of the international system. Terrorists do not exist is a separate universe; they can only be fully understood in the cultural, social, economic, and political settings in which their views were formed and they choose to operate. Divesting responsibility and capability for terrorism would degrade the capacity of the NIC to address the myriad issues remaining in its portfolio. Moreover, since meaningful understanding of terrorists and terrorism requires understanding of context, the "only" way for NCTC to master its narrow responsibilities was to duplicate capabilities already extant in NIC.

The summary above simplifies the issues but I believe is sufficient to illustrate the crosscutting and contradictory pressures and considerations shaping my decisions on whether, how, and with what objectives I would join the fray centered on the stand-up of NCTC. But the list is incomplete because it omits overarching considerations of context and opportunity cost. Context is both an objective and a subjective factor; conditions are what they are, but objective reality is always viewed through subjective lenses that shape how that reality is perceived. It was a fact that NCTC had been established by the intelligence reform legislation as a quasi-silver-bullet fix to correct identified and imagined deficiencies responsible for the failure of the USG to detect and prevent the events of 9/11. It was also a fact that the legislation made the NCTC director a Senate-confirmed appointee who reported directly to the President on counterterrorism operations and to the DNI on budget, intelligence, and other matters.[3] In addition, it was a fact that I perceived terrorism to be *a* if not *the* most important concern of the administration in which I served and the oversight committees to which I was accountable.

Taken together, these aspects of the political context made it imprudent to appear to oppose or act counter to the intent of Congress and the President on matters related to the role of NCTC in keeping our country safe from terrorist attack. Rightly or wrongly, I did not judge that siding with CIA, FBI, my NIC colleagues, or other analytic components would jeopardize my own position. In other words, I was not worried about losing my job because of how I handled NCTC-related issues. But I did judge that appearing to be on the "wrong" side on these issues could and probably would produce significant risks to the position of DDNI/A and my ability to obtain and maintain high-level support for our transformation agenda. Despite the urging of respected colleagues who saw these as litmus test issues and wanted me to take a strong stand in defense of the status quo, I judged that doing so was a fight I was almost certain to lose and that waging it would jeopardize other undertakings that were more important to me and, I believed, to the success of what we were trying to accomplish.

Opportunity cost was a second consideration. My job jar was already overflowing, and I did not see how I could hope to have a meaningful impact on the structure, staffing, and performance of NCTC analytic capabilities without devoting a great deal of time, attention, and political capital to the effort. I could not simply walk away from the fight, but I could—and did—limit my participation to pro forma and defensive moves. The most important considerations in my calculus were perceived importance of the issues (I judged that, in the end, none of the possible outcomes would have a decisively positive or negative impact on analytic performance or IC work to combat terrorism), amount of time and effort required to make a difference (and the opportunity cost of devoting that effort to this issue), and likelihood of success (in other words, that I could achieve the goals that others wanted me to champion).

Consciously or unconsciously, I applied essentially the same framework to calculate the costs, risks, and potential benefits of different courses of action with respect to many other issues. In each case, I tried to calculate the actual and relative importance of the issues involved, the amount of effort likely required to make a difference and the opportunity cost of devoting limited resources to those issues, and the likelihood of achieving the outcome for which I was to fight. Sometimes, as was the case with the fight over NCTC, I decided that it was best to avoid the fray or adopt a low profile.

Open Source Intelligence

Not all issues are contentious. The one I will discuss here centers on where to locate responsibility for open source intelligence within the nascent ODNI structure. Unlike many activities that could easily be assigned to the directorates for analysis, collection, management, or the catchall of community support, open source intelligence did not have a natural home. Open source intelligence—what people outside the Intelligence Community correctly refer to as information or unclassified information—constitutes the largest category of information collected by the United States Government. There is absolutely nothing clandestine or nefarious about this collection activity; it is simply—but importantly—the collection and compilation of information from media accessible to all with the ability to pay for or receive it. The US Government has enormous capacity to collect unclassified information, and, for historical reasons and convenience, much of that capacity resides in the Intelligence Community. Think of a giant vacuum cleaner on steroids that almost indiscriminately sucks in TV and radio broadcasts; newspapers and magazines; and online versions of academic papers, professional journals, and vast amounts of other material disseminated electronically or in print.

Unclassified information is as important for IC analysts as it is for academic researchers, think tank scholars, corporate strategists, and myriad other types of analysts. At a minimum, it provides baseline information and context necessary to understand classified intelligence and real-world developments. On many topics, especially those with low collection priority, it constitutes the largest—if not the only—source of information. Obtaining it is relatively easy; translating, organizing, storing, and integrating this information is more difficult. These tasks, as well as ascertaining the accuracy and implications of what is reported, are the responsibility of analysts. Very little information of any kind is self-evident. Determining whether it is accurate, what it means, and whether it is important is what analysts do.

Very early in the life of the ODNI, Negroponte, Hayden, the four deputies, and a handful of others took up the question of where to locate responsibility for open source activities. The initial conversation went something like, "Who wants it? Give it to collection because that is where it was placed under the existing structure. Maybe it should be moved to analysis because analysts use it and have best understanding of what is needed." No deputy felt strongly that these activities belonged in his or her directorate, and none raised strong objections to having it. The question floated for a few days without resolution, not because of contention but because it was less urgent than many other problems in our individual and collective in-boxes.

The pace at which we were making decisions, hiring staff and assigning responsibilities, and executing our new responsibilities was such that non-urgent matters, like where to place open source activities, were effectively deferred until we had to decide them. By the time we reached that point, the real options had narrowed to analysis and collection, and the magnitude of what we had taken on was becoming clearer to all of us. On the margins of a meeting about something else, Mary Margaret Graham, my counterpart for collection, suggested that I take responsibility for open source activities and that we claim doing so as a concrete step to have "analysis drive collection," which had become something of a totem in the drive for intelligence reform. I recognized the symbolic utility of what Mary Margaret had proposed and was confident that my team could develop ways to prioritize and manage this information, but I did not jump at the chance to add yet another responsibility to my portfolio.

By the time we had this conversation, each of us had developed better understanding of the magnitude and complexity of our portfolios and the inherent challenges of our mission to reform and/or transform the Intelligence Community. Neither of us thought of open source as a snake pit or undesirable set of tasks; both of us wanted to ensure that it was well managed and received the priority attention it needed. But by this time, both of us recognized that our portfolios were beginning to overflow and worried that the addition of open source could be a proverbial straw on the camel's back. We discussed this without rancor and with a good deal of humor, and in the end decided to leave it where it was under the old regime, that is, in collection. We also agreed to revisit the decision at some point in the future and to work together as necessary.

At the time, we had not yet discovered or developed the formal mechanism of coordination epitomized by the collaborative way in which John Keefe from analysis and Sylvia Copeland from collection handled prioritization and deconfliction of collection requests from analysts. If we had, I'm sure we would have acted to put something like that in place right away, but discovery and proving the utility of this mechanism was still in the future. I was tempted to take responsibility for open source because I'd learned that open source collection utilized the same topic prioritization as did those responsible for clandestine collection. That, as far as most analysts were concerned, was the reverse of what it should be. The logic of analysts was that open source collection was even more important when a topic had low priority because the reality was that low priority effectively equaled no priority and topics with low priority obtained no intelligence. More—and more easily accessible—open source information would, I believed contribute to the improvement of analytic products, make them easier to share with policy customers, and facilitate interchange with experts outside the Intelligence Community. In other words, there was a temptation and a case for making open source activities a more integral component of my transformation agenda. I resisted this temptation and the importuning of others who, months after the initial decision to leave it in collection, wanted to move open source activities to the ODDNI/A because I was convinced that taking on this responsibility would dilute my ability to lead and manage other parts of our already extensive agenda. The perceived opportunity cost was too high.[4]

There is more to the story. Although I declined to take responsibility for open source activities, including preparation of analyses based entirely on open source information and what became the Open Source Center repository of information available to researchers inside and outside the USG, I did help launch one new open source activity.[5] The genesis of what was dubbed Open Source Works was a conversation with friend and CIA Director of Intelligence (Analysis) John Kringen. I have forgotten the trigger for this conversation, which occurred when I needed a break from my computer screen and wandered down the hall from my NIC office to see if John was in, but we somehow turned to the problem of clearing people with critical language skills and substantive expertise needed to understand high-priority hard-target countries like Iran and North Korea. One of us opined that we needed a way to hire and utilize people whose clearances were sure to take a long time and might never be granted because they had relatives vulnerable to pressure from unsavory regimes or other problematic conditions. We both knew of people who needed a paycheck and took jobs because they could not afford to wait for the length of time required to obtain a clearance. We needed a way to hire them at once in a provisional capacity that would allow them to work with completely unclassified materials.

Kicking ideas back and forth convinced us that we needed and could establish a halfway house arrangement under which people we wanted to hire could use their special skills to analyze and write on important national security topics using only unclassified materials (mostly in their original languages). We decided to rent commercial space and establish a pilot program. Knowing that it would not get the attention it needed if I added this to my portfolio, I made CIA the executive agent and effectively delegated responsibility to John. Standing up the operation was more difficult and frustrating than we had anticipated (the downside of making CIA the executive agent), but we eventually did get it up and running and hired people with badly needed skills who might never have gotten a clearance but quickly demonstrated how much they could contribute using only their expertise and unclassified materials.

Mission Managers

The National Counterterrorism Center was not the only magic bullet solution enshrined in the intelligence reform legislation and associated documents. Another manifestation was the establishment of "mission managers" who would preside over all dimensions of a problem to ensure end-to-end coordination of collection, analysis, and operational programs. In addition to NCTC, the first wave of reform established the National Counterproliferation Center (NCPC) and freestanding mission managers for Iran and North Korea. Some of the challenges associated with the stand-up and mission of NCTC were described earlier. In contrast, the establishment of NCPC did not pose significant problems or issues for the NIC or the analytic community more broadly because it did not attempt to replace or duplicate analytic work done elsewhere in the community. It became a useful and effective partner rather than a rival.

Freestanding mission managers (that is, those without a "Center") were more problematic. Established at least in part for symbolic reasons, namely, to demonstrate administration concern about support for terrorism and the nuclear weapons programs of Iran and the Democratic People's Republic of Korea, these mission managers were also assigned responsibilities traditionally (and effectively) performed by National Intelligence Officers. Administratively, they reported directly to the DNI because their functions transcended the directorates for analysis and collection. Perhaps I should have paid more attention to them than I did, but almost before I knew it, both had acquired staffs far larger than those of the NIOs responsible for these countries. In the case of the mission manager for Iran, the staff eventually grew to almost the size of the NIC.

Early informal conversations among ODNI senior staff determined that we could and should treat the initial mission managers as a pilot that would help us determine whether more should be created or if they should be structured differently. This appeared to be a bounded and manageable problem. The first indication that it might not be arose approximately a year later. John Negroponte called me in to discuss a number of matters and, after we had done so, he asked what I thought about establishing a mission manager for Cuba and Venezuela. I responded immediately that we did not need one. He then asked if I thought it would be helpful to have a mission manager to guide collection and coordinate analysis on these countries. Again, I responded immediately that this task was being handled well by the NIO for Latin America and that we did not need to invite more criticism for bureaucratic bloat by creating an unnecessary staff. He returned to the subject a third time, stating that he thought we needed to have a mission manager for these countries. I replied, "Fine, we can double-hat the NIO for Latin America. He is a respected and highly capable officer and I'm sure he can do this."

I was clearly slower to realize why he was asking these questions than I should have been because his next sentence was, "What if I tell you that the President has directed me to establish a mission manager for Cuba and Venezuela and given me the name of the person he wants me to appoint." I replied that I still thought it was a bad idea and unnecessary complication but accepted that we would have a mission manager for Cuba and Venezuela.[6] The results were even worse than I had anticipated.

During my tenure, problems between the NIC and the ODDNI/A, on the one hand, and mission managers on the other remained more theoretical than real, but frictions increased over time. These resulted in part because of competition for the best experts on Iran and North Korea. IC component agencies needed their best people to support their missions and customers, and the NIC needed them to support the NSC and produce coordinated analytic products. The mission manager for Iran wanted a role in the preparation of a high-profile estimate on Iran's nuclear intentions and capabilities, but deflecting her request proved relatively easy.[7] Pressure on DNI Mike McConnell to create more mission managers was clearly increasing during the final months of my tenure, however. We had a number of brief conversations about the subject, in all of which I pushed back saying that the NIOs were fully capable of performing this role and could be double-hatted, as the NIO for Latin America was after the first mission manager for Venezuela and Cuba departed, and that as necessary I would add a deputy to each of the NIO offices with explicit responsibilities to liaise with and provide guidance to collectors in addition to that already being provided through the Analytic Mission Management mechanism (see the chapter "Management of the Analysis Mission").

My thinking with regard to mission managers was shaped primarily by three loosely interconnected but largely discreet considerations. One was the (mostly) inaccurate but ritualistically repeated criticism that the ODNI was a bloated and unnecessary layer of bureaucracy reflecting the empire-building proclivities of its senior staff. The size of the Iran mission management office validated this criticism even though it was an anomaly within the ODNI structure. I had spent enough time in organizations to be convinced that declaring a topic or function so important that it required a dedicated office headed by a capable individual virtually ensured that the office would grow as more people were deemed necessary to perform the high-profile mission for which it had been established. My rough mental calculation was that adding eight more mission managers (in addition to those embedded in NCTC and NCPC plus those for Iran and North Korea) would add a minimum of eighty people to ODNI rolls. I thought doing so would subject us to increased criticism that would divert high-level staff time and attention from pursuit of our substantive agenda.

The second and more important reason for opposing creation of additional mission managers with stand-alone staffs was that I regarded them as duplicative and unnecessary. This view was doubtless influenced by my perspective and responsibilities as Chair of NIC—I genuinely believed that the tasks for which some thought we needed more mission managers were and could be performed by NIOs with administrative support from other parts of the NIC. Duplication per se is not bad, as I noted much earlier in this book when describing why I decided not to seek consolidation of analytic portfolios existing in multiple IC components. At a minimum, useful duplication provides independent "second opinion" checks that reduce the dangers of single-point failure and groupthink errors. As important, it facilitates the provision of timely, tailored, and targeted IC analytic support to the diverse missions and customers of the national security establishment. Adding new units that duplicated functions that were, could, or should be performed in existing units in the NIC and elsewhere in the IC would be both unnecessary and incompatible with my vision and expectation that greater transparency into the analytic missions and capabilities of individual agencies and greater ability to collaborate across agency boundaries would eventually result in fewer, better concentrations of expertise. A third element informing this consideration was the knowledge (from the ARC, our mapping of agency foci, and our evaluations of analytic products) that the community was actually pretty thin in a number of important areas. Creating new units and new staffs would further dilute the available supply of regional and functional expertise.

The third consideration proved to be a miscalculation. I underestimated the strength of sentiment for creation of mission managers and the determination of advocates to make that happen. I had incorrectly calculated that if we demonstrated improved performance without creating more centers and mission managers, the demand to do so would diminish. In retrospect, I had clearly underestimated the degree to which at least some influential players had made mission managers a touchstone issue for the ODNI.

The bottom line of these considerations was that I considered creation of more mission managers to be unnecessary and detrimental to what we (the ODDNI/A and the ODNI more broadly) were trying to do, and judged that I could prevent that from happening without making it a high-profile issue. Instead of making the points summarized above in my interactions with staff and Members of our oversight committees, the President's Intelligence Advisory Board, and associational groups such as the Intelligence and National Security Alliance and the Association of Former Intelligence Officers, I chose to rely primarily on my own reputation and relationship with DNI Mike McConnell. I overestimated my own influence and/or underestimated the strength of pressure on him (and his successors) from those determined to establish mission managers. The result was that I managed to block this development during my remaining time in the ODNI but failed to build arguments and alliances that might have continued the fight after my departure.

The examples summarized herein are illustrative of the case-specific character of instances in which I had to decide whether (and if so, how) to join the fight or take on additional responsibilities. If there is a universal rule of thumb for determining when it is necessary to engage or prudent to walk away, I have not found it. Each situation must be evaluated individually. Leadership and management, like life, are incremental processes that must adapt to changing circumstances, feedback, and continuous learning. Individuals develop their own frameworks for evaluating issues, obstacles, and opportunities, and both frameworks and assessments often change over time. Learning is (or should be) continuous, and I now have benefit of hindsight that no one has at the time they make decisions. Unfortunately, we seldom have opportunities for a "do over" informed by experience and hindsight.

Others might—and probably would—have made different decisions than I did. We now know the results of some of those decisions and can assess their efficacy and, with lower confidence, the accuracy of my perceptions and calculations at the time. But we cannot know the results of roads not taken and the alternative but hypothetical decisions of those who would have followed a different course. Speculating about what might have been can be instructive, but I think there is more to learn from attempts to explain perceptions, priorities, and calculations with regard to specific decisions. No one will face the same context, constraints, and challenges that I did, but every decision maker must consider the relative importance (objectively and to relevant players) of the issues in play, the stakes involved, implications for other goals and undertakings, the resources required to influence outcomes, and the opportunity costs of engagement in particular ways. A decision to do nothing can be a consequential decision. Sometimes, however, that is the right decision.

Reflections and Lessons

WRITING THIS ACCOUNT of what I was thinking and how my approach to analytic reform and transformation evolved inevitably triggers a question that I have been asked many times in the years since I left the ODNI at the end of 2008. That question is, "Having gone through the experience and knowing what you do now, would you have done anything differently?" The short answer is, "Probably not." The reason for answering in this way is not, I hope, simply a reflection of personal arrogance and belief that I did everything right. Some of the changes made during my tenure have endured; others (for example, SHARP and RASER) were terminated shortly after my departure. I believe, and many concurred at the time, that we achieved our most important goals. Those goals included rebuilding confidence in the quality of analytic support to national security customers and missions, deepening integration of IC analytic components, restoring morale in the IC analytic community, increasing collaboration among analysts, improving the quality and utility of IC analytic products, and implementing reforms mandated by the 2004 intelligence reform legislation and presidentially endorsed recommendations from the WMD Commission. While doing so, we transformed the *President's Daily Brief* from a solely CIA to a genuinely IC product, maintained—and I would say improved—analytic support to warfighters and diplomats in Iraq and Afghanistan, and expanded the role of the National Intelligence Council to include support to the National Security Council and associated high-level meetings.

We accomplished a great deal and suffered no setbacks even remotely approaching the perceived failures of 9/11 and the Iraq WMD estimate. Could we have done things better? The answer is certainly yes, but would or should we have adopted a different vision for analysis; attempted major structural change and personnel transfers within the analytic community; or acquiesced to demands at the time to expand the number and role of mission managers, combine leadership of collection and analytic functions in a single directorate and individual, or "punish" analysts responsible for analytic errors? My answer is "No." We made errors along the way, but I still think that we got most of the big things right.

My retrospective assessment will and should be less important than the judgment of colleagues and customers at the time and the more objective observers who will give our activities in 2005–2008 the attention I think they deserve. The goal of such studies should not be simply to critique, but to evaluate whether the choices we made at the time were appropriate under the circumstances, accomplished or at least advanced the objectives they were intended to achieve, and contributed to later successes and failures. That analysis must be undertaken by someone other than me. What I can do, or more accurately, what I have attempted to do in this book, is to contribute to future assessments by specifying as accurately as I can recall the way I perceived the tasks I had accepted, the political atmosphere and conditions surrounding and shaping what I could and must do, and what I thought I was doing at the time.

Others may decide that I had a warped or imperfect understanding of the situation, prioritized tasks inappropriately, or should have pursued a different vision. Alternatively, future scholars might conclude that, under the circumstances, what we did was reasonable and reasonably effective. My goal in writing this book is not to push future scholars toward any particular assessment of our (including my) performance. Rather, it is to provide explicit answers to questions about perception, calculation, priorities, and rationale that normally must be inferred or deduced from actions and the impressions of others. I have attempted to explain the decisions I made, not to justify them, but to help anyone interested in intelligence reform or facing the challenges of a new appointment to understand how one senior individual thought about what to do and how to do it at a particular time in American political history and stage in the evolution of the US Intelligence Community.

When I accepted John Negroponte's invitation to serve as his deputy director for analysis, a number of friends reacted with mystification. Why, they asked, would I leave a terrific job at the State Department for the parlous and uncharted waters of intelligence reform? They predicted that my new job would be characterized by constant frustration and limited ability to achieve meaningful change. They were largely right with respect to frustration (especially with continuous resistance from some agencies) but underestimated the potential for change. Since these were friends, many hastened to add that their pessimistic prediction of what could be achieved was based on their assessments of the political mood in Washington and knowledge of bureaucratic behavior and the Intelligence Community and did not reflect low regard for my abilities. The more generous among them said something like, "This is almost certainly an impossible mission and feckless undertaking, but if anyone can make it work, that person is you. Good luck."

I interpreted their limited vote of confidence as more an expression of friendship than reflection of hardheaded analysis, but the words reminded me of a brief but impactful conversation with Mark Lowenthal more than a decade earlier. Mark, who had served in INR, including a stint as Deputy Assistant Secretary (DAS) for Functional Analysis, visited the Bureau's front office shortly after the Clinton administration's "right sizing" of government after the Cold War had resulted in the elimination of one of INR's DAS positions. He had learned (in his new position on the staff of the House Permanent Select Committee on Intelligence) that the Bureau intended to respond by creating a single DAS for Analysis who would assume responsibilities previously assigned to separate DASes for Functional and Regional Analysis. Mark argued that this was a bad idea because the resultant span of control and span of information requirements were too wide for one person to manage. He made a compelling argument, but closed by saying "You can do the new job because you are you, but it is a bad idea to restructure the Bureau around the abilities of a single individual. What happens after you leave?"[1]

The well-meaning cautionary notes about likely frustrations, span of responsibility challenges, and the difference between individual and institutionalized capability stuck with me and shaped my thinking about the position, responsibilities, and future of the Deputy Director of National Intelligence for Analysis (DDNI/A). Although I had held many leadership positions before taking on DDNI/A responsibilities, I am first and foremost an analyst. Leadership and management can be rewarding, but I love the challenges of analysis in general and intelligence analysis in particular. That is the reason I jumped at the opportunity to serve concurrently as Chair of the National Intelligence Council. I knew that the rewards of substantive intellectual engagement on complex and consequential analytic issues would be a counterbalance to the frustrations of the DDNI/A portfolio. That expectation proved accurate and personally important, but it also proved critical to the way I thought about and pursued the challenges of reform.

The fact that my multiple and disparate responsibilities as DDNI/A limited the amount of time I was able to devote to the NIC was good for me but may have been detrimental to the NIC. Being double-hatted gave the DDNI/A direct access to the most senior analysts in the community, both at the NIC and, through the NIOs, across the IC. It also gave the DDNI/A position a stature that it would not have had otherwise because far more people inside and outside the Intelligence Community knew of and respected the position of NIC Chair than knew about me. However, my divided loyalties and responsibilities probably prevented me from taking a more activist position in defense of NIC interests with respect to mission managers and NCTC.[2]

It would be an exaggeration to claim that I would have been tempted to quit as DDNI/A were it not for the psychic rewards of leading the NIC, but it is certainly true that in my final months at the ODNI, I gave much thought to whether my successor in the DDNI/A position should also be double-hatted. As noted earlier in this book, I could and did leverage my NIC position to achieve DDNI/A objectives. Whether my successor would need the same leverage was uncertain. On balance, I thought it better for the NIC, the IC, and the USG to end the double-hatted arrangement. Despite the very real benefits to me and my efforts to define and empower the DDNI/A, I always worried that effectively making the NIC Chair a part-time position had diminished its stature.[3] Separation of the two positions I held would clearly be beneficial for the NIC; I was less confident that it would be good for the DDNI for Analysis.

Lowenthal's cautionary words about excessive reliance on an individual rather than institutionalized arrangements had influenced my decisions from the beginning of my time as DDNI/A, and they resounded as I thought about whether to recommend splitting my portfolio. The position of DDNI for Analysis was brand new and completely undefined when I accepted it. It had no history, ambiguous authority, and no organizational structure or staff with shared experience in executing the missions within its purview. In a very real sense we—I—had to invent these things in the course of implementing mandated reforms and executing continuing analytic missions. I initially tried to bolster the status of the DDNI for Analysis by issuing statements in the name of the position and instructing my deputies to think about institutionalizing the position and eschewing use of my name as a basis for seeking cooperation or compliance. As noted earlier, that proved a bridge too far and, at John Keefe's suggestion, we shifted to greater reliance on my reputation and concurrent status as Chair of NIC.[4] I thought about but never resolved how to use personal reputation and stature derived from a different position to embody the Deputy Director of National Intelligence for Analysis with institutionalized stature and authority.

In the event, my musings about whether my portfolio should be retained or subdivided proved to be largely irrelevant. My departure roughly coincided with the inauguration of the Obama administration and appointment of a new Director of National Intelligence with both ideas and mandates different from those of Negroponte and McConnell. The new DNI, Dennis Blair, quickly separated the positions of DDNI/A and NIC Chair, and his successor, Jim Clapper, soon replaced the deputies for Analysis and Collection with a single deputy for Intelligence Integration. When Mike McConnell had proposed the latter change, I argued forcefully that transformation of analysis was incomplete and too fragile to be subsumed in a structure that would almost certainly favor collection. That assessment appears to have been substantially correct. I will not second-guess the decisions of Blair and Clapper, both of whom are good friends. Whether either one would have made different decisions if I had stayed on is irrelevant because I had made clear that I would step down at the end of 2008. But their choices, like mine, were shaped by the interests and attributes of the people who were available and the way they defined and prioritized their most important tasks.

When I accepted the DDNI/A position, I did not give a great deal of thought to the question of how long I wanted to serve. Every position I had held since 1988 had an indefinite tenure—I served at the pleasure of an Assistant Secretary or higher-ranking official—and I assumed that the DDNI/A position would be the same. I also had relatively definite plans to retire from the USG when I reached my sixty-third birthday in January 2009 so that I could resume the academic career I left in 1986. These became relevant considerations when prospective members of the team I was building asked me how long I planned to stay in the job.

The reason for this question and my answer were important because I was asking good people to leave what they were doing in order to join an unstructured and untested organization. As it became clear that some were willing to accept the risks of doing so because of the role I would play and would accept only if assured that I did not plan to bail out at the first opportunity, I realized that I had to make decisions about how long I intended to serve. I thought it imprudent to telegraph plans to retire in 2009 because that would make me a lame duck from day one, but I also felt it important to state that I did not intend to stay indefinitely.

I had served in the INR front office for eleven years. Some thought that was a good thing because it contributed to stability and predictability. Others saw it as clogging the system in ways that limited promotion opportunities and stifled innovation. These and other considerations persuaded me to set a notional four-year endpoint. That happened to coincide with my tentative retirement plans, but it also reflected my judgment that it would take about four years to accomplish what I hoped to achieve as DDNI for Analysis. If I could not do so in that amount of time, I should step aside and let someone else take over. Conversely, if I succeeded in achieving most of my transformational objectives, they would not be institutionalized if they appeared to be dependent on my tenure. In other words, to succeed, the changes we made had to survive transition to a different leader and leadership team. That became both my goal and my promise: four years unless fired before then.

My calculation of how long it would take to achieve the vision we were developing was completely hypothetical. I had never before attempted to build a new organization and reform multiple bureaucracies of the US Government and did not know of anyone who had attempted what we were about to undertake. But I was certain that the road ahead would have many obstacles and pitfalls, that everything would take longer than anticipated or hoped, and that we would have to backtrack and restart as we learned from experience. Although based on seat-of-the-pants judgments, the four-year timeline became an increasingly significant factor in my calculations of what to attempt and what to avoid. It also became a promise that I felt obligated to honor. For example, when Secretary Rice asked me to return to the State Department to serve as Director of Policy Planning, I was momentarily tempted to accept because the invitation came at a time of greater than usual frustration with the challenges of reform and I knew that I would have enjoyed the chance to again work with my former Stanford colleague. But, as I told her, I felt duty bound to honor my commitment to remain in the ODNI through 2008. I do not regret that decision.

Teamwork

Revisiting challenges and decisions now more than a decade in the past reinforced my gratitude for the contributions and collegiality of my counterparts in the ODNI and, especially, the members of my senior team. This is a book about the way I perceived matters, prioritized tasks, and decided what to undertake and how to do so. Electing to structure the book in this way necessarily exaggerates my own role and diminishes the contributions of others. Had I chosen to write a history of the ODDNI/A's formative years, I would have said far more about the contributions of specific individuals and the ways their ideas and efforts shaped the vision and actions pursued in my name. Everything we achieved was the result of collective thought, collaborative decisions, and coordinated action. Earlier sections of the book have described how I assembled my senior team; here I will focus on how I attempted to transform talented individuals into effective team players and, more important, how to mold all of us into an effective team.

The people I selected for my senior team (deputies, chief of staff, and staff assistants) were experienced and talented individuals, but few of us had worked together previously. My selections were based on individual capabilities, not judgments about compatibility. David Gordon (Vice Chair of NIC) and Steve Kaplan (Deputy for the PDB) were recruited with specific responsibilities in mind, but I wanted and needed them to play major roles in the broader undertakings of the ODDNI/A. The prospective roles and responsibilities of Nancy Tucker (analytic integrity), Mike Wertheimer (analytic transformation), John Keefe (analytic mission management), and Ron Rice (liaison) were much vaguer. So too were the prospective roles of Jan Karcz (Chief of Staff) and Sherry Hong (staff assistant). Defining portfolios and developing specific and prioritized tasks were urgent tasks if we were to build confidence, momentum, and support for what we wanted to achieve.[5]

The obvious first requirement for developing strategies and building support was to develop a shared and reasonably clear vision of what we wanted to accomplish. Early expectations—or perhaps hopes—that I had been given or developed a reasonably well-articulated strategy were quickly dashed. At best I had a partial vision in which we would rebuild confidence and improve analytic support to the national security establishment by improving collaboration, the work of each agency, and the capabilities of every analyst. An equally vague goal was to build a community of analysts eager and able to collaborate across agency boundaries. Step one was to flesh out this vision. Step two was to determine what was necessary to achieve that shared vision. Step three was to implement mandated and desirable reforms in ways that would help us to realize our vision. I developed this sequence mentally, but even before I shared it with my nascent team, I realized that it was missing step zero. Step zero was to create conditions conducive to taking all subsequent steps.

Some people like to convene or attend meetings. I am not one of them. To me, meetings are a necessary evil, but when thinking about how to create conditions for collaborative action, I immediately recognized that sitting down together was probably the best way to get everyone on the same page, develop programs, work out divisions of labor, and capture feedback.[6] Almost from day one, members of my senior team met at 8:00 a.m. to bring one another up to date and up to speed. If deputies could not attend, they sent one of their deputies. The meetings had three purposes: they provided a chance for me to share information on ODNI matters and my thinking about timely issues in the IC and in my activities with respect to the transformation agenda; they were the vehicle through which everyone else shared information on what they were doing, what problems and opportunities they had discovered, and what they needed from others on the team or elsewhere in the ODNI; and they were the primary vehicle for development of a shared vision and concrete measures. Anyone could offer ideas on any topic. When necessary or appropriate, I made decisions and issued guidance.[7]

I tried to be as explicit as possible when thinking out loud about points raised in these meetings because I wanted others to understand how and why I viewed matters as I did. My goals for doing so were to minimize the potential for misunderstanding, to make it easier for teammates to identify possible flaws in my logic or downsides to tentative proposals, and to make it possible for everyone to act on the basis of understanding rather than instruction. There was an element of a "What would Fingar do?" rationale for this approach, but a more important purpose was to enable every member of the team to act on my behalf if I was not available.

The latter point was important because of the scope of what we were doing, the number of times that I would have to divert from my scheduled activities to substitute for the DNI or attend an unexpected meeting or event, and the near-constant need at the top of the national security enterprise for instant decisions and immediate action. One of the few "rules" that I articulated early on was that anyone needing an immediate response from the DDNI/A would get it. If I was unavailable, the call or task would be redirected to one of the deputies who would provide an authoritative ODDNI/A response. For this to work, I assured my deputies that I would stand behind any decision they made when acting in my stead. Their decision became my decision. I pledged not to countermand or second-guess what they had done. It also required that they understand the big picture considerations and thought processes discussed in the morning staff meetings. We kept things moving, and I never regretted empowering my deputies to act.

Concluding Observations

The concatenation of circumstances, challenges, personalities, skill sets, and interactions described in this book was unique to a particular time and place. Another person in my position with a different—or even the identical—team of colleagues might, and probably would, have perceived the situation and acted differently than I did in 2005–2008. The way in which this hypothetical counterpart framed issues and the choices he or she made would almost certainly be different; whether they would have yielded better or worse outcomes is impossible to say. My experiences in the USG taught me that there are multiple good and bad ways to do things, and that it is often difficult to know whether a particular strategy or approach is producing desired or counterproductive results until sometimes difficult to reverse or revise steps have been taken. Searching for perfect solutions is certain to be a feckless exercise, and attempting to retrace the steps or even to apply the template used by someone else is unlikely to yield the same results. There are simply too many variables and too many possibilities to have confidence in a cookbook formula for success.

The disutility of "do it this way" recipes does not mean, however, that one cannot learn from the experience of others. Most of the time, explication of key players' perceptions, priorities, and thought processes must be inferred from actions, documents, and/or the recollections of people with partial and indirect knowledge. That characteristic, in my experience, makes it difficult to draw lessons from what others have done because it simplifies or obscures key elements of the principal actor's thought process. This book is my attempt to fill that gap in the belief that enhanced understanding of what I was thinking might provide more useful lessons than a detailed narration of what we did to transform analysis in the US Intelligence Community.

Hindsight knowledge of what happened after I left the ODNI at the end of 2008 facilitates evaluation of the efficacy and durability of the changes we introduced and/or implemented. I have not attempted to do that here because I cannot be completely objective and because I lack detailed knowledge about what has continued, what has changed, and how national security customers have evaluated subsequent performance. Though unwilling to do a retrospective evaluation of our performance, I want to close this section of the book with a short description of how I thought about the efficacy and durability of what we were doing at key junctures of my tenure.

Three times during the period described here I wrestled with the question of "What happens if I leave now?" The first time was when I was invited to head the Office of Policy Planning at the State Department. I have already provided a partial summary of my thinking, specifically my belief that I must honor the commitment that I had made to the senior colleagues who had agreed to join the ODNI experiment at least in part because of their confidence in me. But that was only one part of my calculation. Another, and equally important factor was my judgment at the time that the ODDNI/A and analytic transformation were not yet ready to stand on their own. Many of the steps we had initiated were still in an early stage and their viability and utility were not yet proven. Rightly or wrongly, I judged that the organization we were building and the vision we were trying to implement still needed the training wheels or props of my reputation and the leverage that accrued to the DDNI/A from my being double-hatted as Chair of the NIC.

The sentence above sounds more egotistical than I want it to be, but the story would be misleadingly incomplete if I did not acknowledge the impact on my thinking of comments by my staff, IC colleagues, and key members of Congress and the 9/11 and WMD Commissions asserting that they supported what we were doing because they trusted me. I judged at this point in 2007 that we had not yet converted trust in me into trust in the institutions and activities we were building.

The second time that I gave more thought to what would happen to the ODDNI/A and our transformation agenda if I left was later in 2007 when DNI Mike McConnell several times suggested merger of the directorates for analysis and collection. I concluded from the conversations that he thought I might head the combined directorate. The position was never offered to me but I made as clear as I could that I would not take it if it were offered. The reasons I took such a strong position were that I did not want to lead or be responsible for the difficult challenges in the collection basket, and that I feared de facto subordination of analysis to the much larger collection arena would hurt analyst morale and derail our agenda.

There was also a personal reason for wanting nothing to do with the prospective joint directorate. I am an analyst with no experience or expertise on collection issues. As far as I was concerned, this should have disqualified me as a candidate to head a merged directorate. Could I have learned what I needed to know and obtained help from a more qualified deputy? I'd like to think that the answer is yes, but I had no desire to end my government career trying to climb a steep learning curve involving skills and activities that did not interest me. In addition, I knew from daily interaction with Mary Margaret Graham (and later Glenn Gaffney) that obtaining buy-in and cooperation from the law enforcement and collection components of the IC was proving far more difficult than was integration of the analytic components. This looked like a challenge I did not want or need.

I also knew from daily interactions in the ODNI that collection received far more scrutiny and second-guessing from oversight bodies (SSCI, HPSCI, and the President's Intelligence Advisory Board) than did analysis. The reasons, I believe, are that collection (and covert action, which was in the same directorate) involves vastly more money, greater risks, and much sexier toys. I simply did not see how analysis could be other than a neglected stepchild if incorporated into a joint directorate. For reasons of professional pride, concern about analyst morale and retention, and continued conviction that analysis still needed top cover and support, I concluded that I must stay longer.

When I briefly thought that I might lose the argument to maintain separate directorates, I did give fleeting thought to development of a "Plan B." That plan was never fleshed out, in part because I considered it a poor alternative, but it would have left me as Chair of NIC and transferred some level of responsibility for analytic transformation to that position. The more I thought about it, the more I was convinced that it would be bad for the NIC and even more frustrating for me than the existing double-hatted arrangement.

The final time I thought about the future of IC analysis and the ODDNI/A without me was in the months immediately prior to my retirement. I had already made a commitment to return to Stanford, which I left in 1986 intending to spend only two years in Washington, but was (perhaps arrogantly) confident that I could remain in a senior ODNI position after the change of administration. I again recalled my thinking and statements about leaving after four years in order to institutionalize the organization and program I'd been tapped to build in order to avoid over-personalizing the endeavor and to clear the way for others to advance their careers. Unlike my assessments twelve to eighteen months earlier, I now judged that we had built something that could endure without reliance on the ad hominem support that I had provided. That judgment might have been self-serving because I was not willing to extend my time in Washington, but I chose to believe at the time that it was also an accurate assessment. We had built something of which I could be—and am—proud.

Lessons for New Appointees

THE CONTEXT AND CONSIDERATIONS described in Part I were unusual if not unique, but developments in the years since have made my once-unusual experience more relevant to the challenges facing most new appointees to United States Government positions. Fifteen years ago, inside-the-Beltway attention was focused on fixing real and perceived problems in the Intelligence Community, and the challenges I faced could be treated as something of a special case. Activities in other parts of the federal government, including the installation of new appointees and routine bureaucratic operations, took place below the radar of media and the public and beyond the realm of partisan politics. The Intelligence Community was declared to be broken and in need of reform, but most of the government was expected and assumed to function with an acceptable level of competence and efficiency. That is no longer the case.

What was once unusual will—must—become the new normal. The federal government is widely perceived to be—and is—broken and badly discredited. Jokes about dumb bureaucrats and dysfunctional bureaucracies have been a staple of American humor since the earliest days of the republic. They used to be funnier than they are today because confidence that the institutions of government work reasonably well most of time and can perform adequately if not superbly in times of crisis has been badly eroded. New appointees to positions across the federal government will face challenges more akin to those I faced than to those of their predecessors. The generalized "lessons" summarized in the following pages are intended to provide tips that I wish I had had when I accepted the Deputy Director of National Intelligence for Analysis position.

Climbing Out of a Deep Hole

Many institutions of government were in need of renewal before the election of President Trump, but the assertions, antics, and actions of his administration exacerbated the situation by inflicting unprecedented damage to government capabilities and public confidence in federal officials and institutions. The founding fathers constructed a system of checks and balances to limit the scope of federal authority and the power of would-be autocrats, but Trump's disdain for the Constitution, disinterest in governance, and disregard for the views of anyone who did not pander to his narcissism badly undermined the foundations of government and the capacity to recover. The caliber and personal agendas of many appointees to senior positions and deliberate efforts to weaken the capacity of federal agencies by leaving key positions vacant made already existing problems worse. Diatribes against the "deep state" and attacks on agencies and career professionals that caused many experienced public servants to leave government have left a path of destruction that will take years of sustained effort to repair.

The election of a new president will not automatically repair the damage. New presidents (it will take more than one to restore confidence and capacity) must set the tone and champion restoration and reform, but the hard work of rebuilding institutions, restoring competence and morale, and implementing reforms needed to address new challenges will be the responsibility of lower-level officials. The federal government is a huge and diverse enterprise with responsibilities ranging from public health to the safety of food, pharmaceuticals, and drinking water; from national security to management of natural resources and national parks; and from collection of taxes and distribution of social security payments to administering the census and monitoring outbreaks of disease. Each of the government's hundreds—thousands—of responsibilities is entrusted to specific components of one or more departments or agencies. Every one of these components has been impacted by delay of necessary reform, partisan paralysis, and Hurricane Trump. Primary responsibility for assessing the damage, setting priorities, and developing and implementing plans for recovery and reform rests with the newly appointed heads of departments, agencies, and other major components of the federal bureaucracy. This chapter was written to help bridge the gap between "I'm thrilled to accept this position" and "This is what we need to do."

Understanding the Challenge

In normal times, transitions from one administration and team of appointees to another is facilitated by the existence of reasonably well-functioning organizations and a large contingent of experienced public servants who understand their institutional and individual responsibilities. Career public servants have ideas about what could be done to improve performance, and most are eager to help new appointees to achieve administration objectives. Under the best of circumstances, which admittedly seldom exist, the agency or component is functioning with a reasonably high level of efficiency and effectiveness and new appointees need do little more than slide into the seat vacated by a predecessor. Even in less than ideal normal times, it requires only a short time to become familiar with key missions, staff, and standard operating procedures. But these are not normal times.

Every administration has priorities and blind spots, and no administration has appointed uniformly good people to all components of the federal government. But Trump was in a league of his own as an omnidirectional disrupter. Some may consider that a good and necessary focus of his administration, but after four years, it can be said with little danger of contradiction that there is no component of government that does not function less well and have fewer well-qualified people than it did when he was inaugurated. His administration was a hurricane wrecking damage everywhere in its path. The answer to the question, "Which parts of the federal government are most in need of massive rebuilding?" is "All of them."

The instruments of governance are in shambles. Trump diminished the pool of experienced and committed public servants, disrupted and degraded procedures developed over many years to enhance the efficacy of government actions, dismantled bureaucratic structures and with them interpersonal ties and networks of people and agencies that provide agility and insurance against counterproductive decisions. One need look no further than the tragic incompetence of Trump's response to the Covid-19 pandemic for examples proving this point. Missions have been abandoned, downgraded, or ignored. Many parts of the federal government limp along with dedicated professionals operating below the radar when they can, working without or around routinized procedures and high-level guidance. That the system still works as well as it does—which is sometimes not well at all—is a tribute to the strength and value of bureaucratic inertia and the commitment of the public servants who chose to remain on the job despite the chaos all around them. Virtually no new appointee will inherit a well-functioning organization.

Trump's inexcusable disparagement of hard-working public servants, many of whom eschewed more lucrative opportunities in the private sector because they believe public service to be a noble calling, has deterred able and ambitious young professionals from joining the federal bureaucracy and depleted the cadre of midlevel officials. The depletion of midlevel officials, who are the civilian equivalent of noncommissioned officers in the military, reduces the availability of experienced veterans who understand the mission and the reason for existing and abandoned procedures. The resultant deficit of experience makes it more difficult for new appointees to master their portfolios and limits the capacity to train and supervise the new employees who must be recruited to fill existing gaps.

Some may criticize this characterization of Trump's impact on the federal government as overstated and unproven. The former criticism might be accurate; the latter is certainly the case. But this is not a book about the Trump administration and its impact on the capacity and image of the federal government. Journalists have begun to chronicle the hurricane's impact on specific agencies and policy arenas, and scholars will soon add detailed and heavily footnoted studies of Trump's impact on our system of government, the Republican Party, professionals in public service, and the policymaking process. Even if subsequent studies discover positive consequences of Trump's disruptive behavior (which is likely) and conclude that the characterization above is exaggerated, that will not change the fact that one and perhaps more incoming classes of newly appointed senior officials will assume office at a time when

- Even before Trump upended the game board, many attributes and priorities of federal agencies had become outmoded, inefficient, or in other ways in need of replacement or reform.
- Large majorities of Americans distrust the federal government.
- Specific components and the government as a whole are perceived as broken and badly in need of transformative change.
- Many long-established procedures have been ignored or allowed to atrophy, and many of the people who understood the reasons for those procedures and how to make them work effectively have left government service.
- The federal workforce believes that it is understaffed, overworked, and underappreciated. Morale is low but aspirations for rapid positive change are high. If what they would regard as meaningful and

constructive "fixes" are not made quickly, many more experienced professionals will be tempted to join the flight to the private sector.

Taken together, these perceptions and realities of the situation new appointees will inherit mean that they cannot simply pick up where their predecessors left off, reinstate people and procedures discarded by the previous administration, or take months to develop strategies for restoration and reform. The precise circumstances of every appointment will differ because the disparate components of the federal government are broken in different ways and for different reasons. But the general characteristics of the political context within which they take office will—or certainly should—compel them to undertake a thorough but rapid assessment of their own particular situations and to move out smartly to remedy the most egregious or consequential problems.

Components of a "Checklist" for New Appointees

One of the attributes and advantages of checklists for specific tasks is that they subdivide complex undertakings into a prioritized sequence of steps. If step B must be completed before step C can be initiated, then step B must precede step C, and so on. The sequence is determined by efficacy and necessity. Many complex tasks can be subdivided and sequenced, but some entail interconnected subtasks that must be tackled simultaneously. Rebuilding and reforming bureaucratic institutions belong to the second category. That is the reason I have put "checklist" in quotation marks. What follows is a list of challenges that must be considered at more or less the same time, not a recommended sequence in which to tackle them.

Every new appointee, or at least every one that I have encountered, enters office with one overriding question: "Where do I begin?" My answer for those assuming positions in the federal government is that it is useful if not imperative to think first about the totality of the task one is about to undertake. Everyone enters office with goals they wish to achieve, general awareness of the political environment, some knowledge of the bureaucratic component they are to lead, and partial understanding of what is "broken" or no longer adequate to satisfy new requirements. That first-order level of understanding is insufficient; acting without greater appreciation of the many factors that will shape what you can and must do will make ultimate success more difficult to achieve. If there were an actual checklist, the first injunction would be, "Make a list of the factors and tasks that will enable or impede achievement of what you want to do." What follows should help a new appointee to get started.

The Importance of Context

Washington is not a neutral environment within which one can dispassion-
ately assess the situation; gather, assess, and integrate suggestions; or assume
support for contemplated or implemented actions. The context within which
new appointees must operate is always political and sometimes intensely partisan. The preceding paragraphs were written not only to present my personal
assessment of the Trump administration's impact on the federal government
but, more important, to illustrate one dimension of the political environment.
Some in the Congress, the career bureaucracy, the media, and other constituencies will share many of the views summarized above. Others will hold
diametrically opposite positions on the Trump legacy and what should and
should not be done to restore capacity and rebuild confidence in the federal
government. Still others will have hobbyhorse issues or special interests they
wish to pursue by influencing decisions in the purview of particular agencies
and appointees. You should expect that everything you say and do will be
immediately scrutinized, criticized, and subjected to pressures for changes in
line with the critic's own perceptions and priorities.

The nature of the scrutiny you receive; the intensity of resistance or support within your organization; and the methods used to encourage, frustrate,
or reshape your efforts will depend on where you work and what you are trying to accomplish, but they will never be entirely absent. Awareness of their
existence and understanding of their origins and objectives is not just useful,
it is essential for the achievement of your goals. No one can succeed without
allies or anticipation of and preparation for objections and opposition. As
you begin your new assignment, and more or less continuously throughout
your tenure, you should take stock of the environment within which you
must operate and recalibrate your strategy to incorporate useful feedback and
bolster external support.

I know of no available checklist of what to look for in the environment.
What follows is illustrative, not definitive or prescriptive. In preparing it,
I assume that every reader appointed to a specific position will have better
understanding of the political, oversight, bureaucratic, and platform promises dimensions of that particular environment than can be captured in any
generalized list of things to consider. You would not have been selected for
the position if you did not have—and were not thought to have—significant
experience and exposure in the most relevant parts of intersecting environments germane to the appointment. But experience and basic awareness of

the environment is not a substitute for up-to-date and targeted analysis of key actors, interests, and expectations. As in many other components of preparation for your new position, complacency is not your friend. What you "knew" the last time you served in government or when you wrote academic papers or lobbyist briefs on topics in your new portfolio may no longer be valid or as important as you thought previously. Things change. New people enter the fray and others move on to something else. Priorities change and, at the start of a new administration, especially one involving the shift from one party to the other, "everything" will be in flux. The better you understand the context within which you must operate, the better you will be able to use environmental elements to your advantage and, as important, to anticipate, avoid, or ameliorate hostile or unhelpful elements.

As politics in the United States has become increasingly partisan there has been a secular drift toward demonization or dismissal of everything undertaken by the other party or the previous administration. When George W. Bush succeeded Bill Clinton, people inside and outside the administration used the shorthand "ABC" (Anything but Clinton) to describe how the new president's team would approach recurring and carryover issues. Obama's efforts to close the prison at Guantanamo and end the detentions without trial of post-9/11 detainees have been characterized as "Anything but Bush." Trump went further in an effort to reverse or erase Obama's legacy.

Disparaging and attempting to reverse or in other ways change the policies of predecessors has a long history in the United States, but new appointees should avoid the twin traps of assuming that every change made by the Trump administration is bad and that every previously extant organizational, procedural, or policy arrangement should be restored. Having a mandate to "fix" problems should be more than a license to restore the status quo ante. Although it is certainly appropriate, even imperative to examine both recent and earlier decisions in order to understand why they were made, what they were designed to achieve, and how effective they were, automatic reversals and restoration would squander the opportunity to apply useful lessons and implement necessary reform.

Stereotypes about the propensity of bureaucrats to oppose change and accord high value to existing or preexisting arrangements have a basis in reality, but no one knows more about the missions, capabilities, strengths, and weaknesses of a government bureaucracy than the experienced people who work there. Most take pride in their organization, are committed to its missions, and have ideas about ways to improve performance. It would be a grave mistake not to solicit and listen to their arguments for continuity and proposals for change. After the disruption caused by Hurricane Trump, it would be surprising if many did not advocate at least partial rollback of recent changes and restoration of previous arrangements.

Bureaucracies and bureaucratic procedures exist to ensure reliable execution of recurring tasks. The nature of the tasks, and the recruitment and training of people to perform them, are keyed to the goals and requirements of specific organizational missions (such as to analyze signals intelligence, assess the risks and benefits of technology exports, or conduct the national census). Most structures and procedures have evolved over time to incorporate lessons learned, new technologies, and the different priorities of successive administrations. Ineffective and inefficient arrangements are eliminated or modified through a combination of natural selection and innovation. Some endure longer than they should because of inertia and lack of imagination; others persist because opportunities for change are constrained by circumstances, priorities, and the proclivities of key administrators. The point may be obvious, but it is seldom desirable or possible to attempt "big bang" comprehensive change or to assume that extant arrangements cannot be improved. The challenge is to determine what to retain, what to change, what to do differently, and when and how to initiate desired modifications.

There are both political and practical reasons for making changes in the first months of a new administration or appointment. Some of the political pressure for early change derives from the logic and rhetoric of electoral campaigns. When one party has displaced the other, hyperbolic criticism of the predecessor administration and pledges to "fix" everything that is broken raise expectations and the perceived urgency of rapid action. Such pressures are less intense but still present when an incumbent is reelected or succeeded by someone from the same party because elections are widely seen as a renewing process that reinvigorates our democracy and the federal government. Practical reasons for prompt action include the small and rapidly closing window of opportunity to investigate and act before being overwhelmed by day-to-day requirements (the so-called "tyranny of the in-box"). Receptivity to reform proposals will decrease as veteran employees and newly appointed subordinates settle into and become captured by existing routines.

Pressures to act quickly obviously conflict with the prudence of deferring action until one has a good understanding of the inherited situation. Acting without investigation and careful consideration of alternatives is seldom desirable, but delaying until one thoroughly understands the situation (and has a team in place and a reasonably coherent plan of action) risks missing the window of opportunity for major change. Tensions between imperatives to act quickly and desire to act wisely can be compounded by other considerations such as workforce appetite and tolerance for change. It makes a difference whether the people directly involved are eager for change (and whether they want to go back to the past or move on to a different future) or suffering from "reform fatigue" that makes them reluctant to adopt yet another set of new rules and procedures.

Gauging the attitude and appetite for change of specific components of the workforce is also useful for determining when to attempt and how to present proposed reforms. This should also be part of the calculus regarding priorities—what can or must be done right away and what can or should be deferred until later. Some changes will be easier than others to launch and, if initiated successfully, can build momentum and willingness to undertake additional reforms. Changes recommended by career bureaucrats, if consistent with where you think you want to go, can similarly be introduced early to build confidence in you and momentum for subsequent measures.

Suggestions and demands from the workforce are not the only alternatives you will have to consider. Others can include specific commitments made during the campaign; Congressionally mandated requirements; the hobbyhorse preferences of powerful Members of Congress; and the recommendations of special commissions, study groups, and think tanks. Some proponents of specific recommendations can be ignored more easily than others, but many of the ideas will have sufficient merit to be taken seriously. Unfortunately, no effort will have been made by anyone else to examine and integrate the sometimes-incompatible proposals of different groups. That task will have to be undertaken by you or people you designate, but for others to do the legwork, they must know at least generally where you want to go. This, of course, is another chicken-and-egg problem because you may not know what you want to do until you have collected and considered information about what is necessary and possible.

In addition to written reports and admonitions that can be studied by others or perused in your very limited leisure time, you should anticipate offers to "help" from Congressional members and staff, former officials, other notables it would be imprudent to ignore, and vendors eager to provide "exactly" the advice and services you need. All will be well-intentioned, many will have a personal agenda, and none will know the precise set of considerations that will shape what you can and must do to rebuild or transform your piece of the federal bureaucracy. Washington, especially the legislative branch, relies heavily on studies and recommendations from lobbyists and other special interest and/or for-profit organizations, and a wide array of "Beltway Bandits" are available to provide services that cannot be easily performed inside the government or for which you did not even know you had a need. Depending on your organization and your mission, decisions about whether to retain or end inherited relationships or to utilize contract support to launch new initiatives might be a part of your plans for the agency. You may well want outside help to do things other than what the waves of eager would-be providers will bring to your attention even before you move behind your new desk.

Scoping the Problem[1]

Desire and a mandate to "fix" structural, staffing, and procedural problems are necessary but insufficient guides to action. Few new appointees enter office with clear understanding of what individual components do, why and how they do it, where the strengths and weakness are, and precisely what is broken and what should or must be maintained. No one wants their initial moves to be perceived as making things worse. Indeed, it is often desirable to score early wins by addressing "easy" and widely acknowledged problems. But to do that requires understanding how problematic units, procedures, and people fit into the larger organizational matrix. For example, it is useful to know whether problems in a particular part of the organization are the result of "upstream" problems that might not be obvious and how changes in a "problem" component will affect the performance of "downstream" units and activities. It is also essential to assess the extent to which the problem is the result of defective procedures or inadequately trained people.

Understanding what individual components (and people) do and how the components fit together to perform required functions and achieve mission objectives is a prerequisite for identifying and prioritizing problems and opportunities and developing a strategy to fix defects, enhance efficacy, and restructure to pursue different objectives and incorporate new technologies. Whether one's starting point is a mandate to repair damage, restore capabilities, or rebuild for the future (or some combination of all three), early investigation is necessary to determine what works reasonably well and what is most in need of immediate attention, how disruption of current arrangements in a target or problem component will affect performance elsewhere in the organization, and what cannot be fixed without prior or concurrent changes in other components. The goal of such a scoping inventory and mapping operation is to inform judgments about what can or must be fixed or changed and to determine how difficult or time-consuming possible fixes would be.

Other scoping challenges and requirements include determination of how many organizational units and people are involved, whether and how their responsibilities and activities intersect, and what participants, customers, and others think are the reasons for the problems requiring attention. Scoping the workforce also requires information about the experience and capabilities of individuals and groups and other demographic information (for example, relative numbers of experienced veterans, midlevel people, and new additions to the unit). A separate information-gathering task is to inventory what components and individuals do. Without such information, it is impossible to assess whether redundancies exist and whether it is prudent or unnecessary to maintain such duplication of effort, whether specific tasks are no longer required or need more resources, and for what customers and what reason the tasks are performed.[2]

Somewhere in the process—not necessarily in phase one but certainly before significant changes are launched or decisions to retain or restore specific units, positions, and tasks are made—one should assess the quality of work done by each unit or individual. Among other reasons for doing so is to determine whether specific tasks are critical to your organizational mission or could be dropped or done as well or better elsewhere in the organization or in a separate but affiliated component of government. Stated another way, it is useful to determine what is currently being done, why and how well it is being done, and whether it is something that must be preserved, fixed, or reformed or can be discontinued or transferred elsewhere.

This scoping and mapping exercise can be undertaken in conjunction with efforts to collect information and ideas from the workforce, and to assess the utility of proposals and proffers from outsiders eager to "help" you. Like all other tasks on this notional checklist, the quest for thoroughness and perfection must be constrained by the need to do other things at the same time and the imperative to demonstrate action and accomplishment quickly.

Building a Team[3]

Probably the most important of the concurrent tasks you must undertake is to build a team of people able and eager to help you develop and implement plans, policies, and procedures. Given the initial premise that the organization you will lead requires some degree of rebuilding and reform, you do not have the option of simply sliding into the chair of your predecessor and overseeing business as usual. Disruption, uneven performance, the loss of personnel and experience, and the other maladies that make it imperative to do more than simply take over from the previous shift make this a job that requires an effective team. No one is smart enough, knowledgeable enough, or has enough time to do everything without help.

Building an effective team is the most important thing you will do; determining who should be on that team will be among the most difficult and consequential decisions that you make. There is no simple formula for selection of those with whom you will work and to whom you must delegate substantial responsibility and authority. The process is filled with chicken-and-egg challenges. For example, do you pick people because of past friendship and collaboration; specific expertise and experience; or proven ability to build, staff, and lead new organizations or tasks? What mix of insiders and outsiders do you need, and to what positions should they be assigned? Do you pick people to fill positions on an existing organization chart or do you select them for still ill-defined duties in a nascent and still-under-construction blueprint for the future?

If you think you know exactly what needs to be done you can subdivide responsibilities and pick people deemed able to perform assigned duties. But if you do not know exactly what needs to be done, you need people who can help diagnose problems, determine priorities, and develop solutions. These are different skills and do not always cohabit in the same individual. To an extent, the people you select will shape what you can do and how you can or must do it.

A team is more than a collection of individuals selected for their expertise, diversity (however defined), and previous relationship with you or someone else important to the success of your undertakings. Collegiality is important; how important is a function of how much diversity and dissent you are willing to tolerate, and how confident you are that decisions (yours and made collectively) will be implemented effectively even by those who may have preferred alternative approaches. Teamwork is essential, but it does not just happen and it is imprudent to merely hope for the best or be overly confident of your own leadership skills and managerial abilities. Teams are made, not born.

Getting Everyone on the Same Page[4]

Inertia and bureaucratic resistance are inevitable. Bureaucracies and bureaucratic procedures exist, in part, to ensure efficient performance of routine tasks and rapid response to crisis events. Most procedures and structures have evolved over time. Some are the result of "fixes" or "reforms" introduced by previous appointees but many derive from experience and bottom-up adjustments to enhance performance. Innovations that enhanced performance were retained, those perceived to have reduced efficacy were modified or dropped. The result of this evolutionary process is a set of arrangements that often works reasonably well. It also results in strong conviction on the part of those who utilize those arrangements that they are better than most alternatives. Attempts to change time-tested and familiar procedures tend to be viewed with skepticism and as endangering the effective performance of "mission."

In the post-hurricane environment that will follow the Trump administration, normal bureaucratic or organizational inertia and reluctance to change will be diminished because his chaotic administration disrupted normal procedures. Your problem will be less one of resistance to change than determination to restore what has been dismantled or disrupted. Simply restoring old institutions and procedures would be "easy" because much of the workforce would know what to do and support restoration of arrangements judged to have been more efficient and effective and/or more appropriate to the mission of the agency. But across-the-board restoration might not be the best course of action.

Bureaucratic evolution, like history, is a continuing process. Specific innovations introduced during the era of Trump might have antagonized the workforce or made things worse, but at least some of them were attempts to address real problems. No organization is perfect or capable of meeting changing requirements without periodic adjustments. Sometimes the situation calls for deeper and more extensive reform; knowing when such reforms are needed and determining when and how to make them is one of your responsibilities. Generally speaking, the best time to introduce change is early in your tenure. But that is the time when you will know least about your new organization and be most dependent on insights and information from the workforce you have inherited. Career professionals will want to change some things but be very reluctant to change others. You need their input and their cooperation.

Career public servants generally are strongly committed to the mission of their organization and predisposed to support and assist new supervisors. They want you to succeed because if you fail, their organization fails and they will have failed to perform the mission to which they have dedicated this phase of their careers. Gaining their acquiescence—if not their support—for the steps you decide to take is essential to your success. One way to begin to do so is by eschewing blanket criticism of existing arrangements and recent performance while announcing general goals that all can support. Such goals might include fixing problems that they identify, improving individual and organizational performance, restoring confidence in the organization and its people, and making it easier for people to do their jobs. The trickier and more important task will be to build support for making things better rather than simply returning to the status quo ante.

Doing this involves multiple subtasks. One is to seek input before demanding compliance. Even though career public servants are committed to helping every new administration and appointee to achieve both the enduring missions of the agency and specific objectives outlined in campaign platforms and the personal agendas of new appointees, veterans naturally assume that they understand the capabilities and responsibilities of the organization better than the newbie who has just arrived on the scene. You need them and you can profit from their experience and insights. Members of the permanent bureaucracy understand the organizational mission, and they have views on what works well and what doesn't and on the reasons for good and poor performance. It would be foolish to squander the chance to profit from their experience and desire for organizational success. Actively seek their input and listen to what they have to say.

The flip side of genuine solicitation of input is to delay articulation of specific changes and avoid triggering organizational antibodies by appearing to dictate substantive changes without prior consultation or explanation of how proposed changes are expected to enhance performance and address real concerns of the workforce. This involves striking a balance between appearing to dictate without proper investigation and consultation, and appearing to be completely adrift with no idea of what can, should, and must be done.

Selection of members of your senior team should be done with an eye to obtaining the benefit of people with diverse experience and perspectives willing to contribute ideas, critique ideas proposed by others, and embrace and implement decisions about how to move forward. Like the horses in a team, all must pull in the same direction while being attentive to the pace and problems of harness mates. This does not happen automatically.

Pulling in the same direction and ensuring that tasks and activities in the portfolio of one team member do not get too badly out of sync with those of others requires both deep understanding of and commitment to the program you want to implement. Understanding and commitment—as well as the quality and viability of plans for restoration and reform—are facilitated by collaborative decision making. People are generally more willing and better able to execute plans they have helped to formulate and in which they have a personal stake.

Division of labor and responsibility is essential because the tasks are too numerous and complex for anyone to do all that is necessary for success. Ensuring that everyone is on the same page requires awareness of what everyone else on the team is trying to accomplish, the progress and problems encountered in the course of implementation, and how what others are doing affects the ability of teammates to execute their plans. This requires clarity and buy-in throughout the decision-making process and effective mechanisms to acquire and act on feedback.

Getting everyone on the same page is not simply a matter for the leadership team; midlevel managers and the workforce as a whole must understand—and to a considerable extent support—what you are trying to do. This requires frequent and genuine two-way communication. Such communication requires clear explanation of objectives, and solicitation of ideas on the objectives themselves and how best to achieve them. It also requires that you solicit and be receptive to feedback identifying obstacles and indicating how well or badly new arrangements achieve their declared objectives. Securing buy-in is a continuous process requiring both quasi-formal mechanisms and constant attention by you and other members of the senior team.

Start Fast[5]

Notwithstanding the importance of building a leadership team, scoping the magnitude and specific dimensions of your rebuilding assignment, and the need to obtain insights and buy-in from key constituencies, delay in getting started can imperil success more than can beginning with imperfect and incomplete plans. The window of opportunity during which key constituencies inside and outside your organization will anticipate and be willing to contribute to the restoration and reform effort is short. You and everyone else will soon become captive to the in-box, and the workforce will drift toward utilization of familiar procedures as they focus more on mission than on restoration or reform.

Though theoretically desirable, you cannot defer explaining and executing elements of a "still under construction" strategy until you have consulted broadly, built your team, and devised the perfect plan. The workforce, counterparts across the USG, oversight committees, and, if warranted by your position and responsibilities, the media want to know, at least in broad terms, where you want to go and how you intend to get there. The need for remedial action is widely recognized, and you can expect strong support if you demonstrate that you "get it" and are prepared to act. Conversely, if you appear hesitant and unsure about what needs attention, confidence and patience will evaporate quickly and you will have to contend with more "helpful" advice and demands for action in areas that might not be high on your tentative "to do" list.

Many will demand, or at least ask for, detailed plans and timelines so they will know what you intend to do. How much you are prepared to tell them will depend in part on how quickly you are able to perform other tasks outlined in this checklist, but it should also depend on how much you want to expose preliminary ideas and tentative approaches to scrutiny and criticism from audiences that have neither the responsibility for implementation nor, in most cases, effective means to help you. Providing general statements of objectives and approach will serve until you have more specific plans and accomplishments to report, but it is better to report partial progress (and impediments) on a recurring basis to sustain interest and support for what you are doing than to wait until you have completed a detailed plan and/or implemented most major steps. Audiences that hear nothing about what you are doing will assume that you are doing nothing.

Prioritizing Tasks

Achieving meaningful and effective change is inherently a multifaceted process with many interconnected parts, but it is not possible to do everything at once. In order to make the overall task manageable and to increase the likelihood of success, it is imperative to prioritize the steps involved.

Prioritization has many dimensions. One involves deciding which tasks you will undertake personally and which you will delegate to other members of your team. For delegation to work, subordinates must understand and support what you (collectively) are trying to accomplish, but it must also allow broad scope for deputies to determine how to achieve shared goals, and to make modifications based on experience and interaction with other members of the team.

Sometimes—often—it is better to delegate particularly important tasks to other team members because your broader portfolio of responsibilities makes it difficult to ensure that you can give the priority task the attention it requires. Delegation also involves decisions about where to assign responsibility. This is in part a decision about which deputy is best able to achieve a particular goal, but it is also and inevitably a decision about organization charts and which subunit will have responsibility for execution of specific activities. Sometimes assignment of responsibility can be based on existing organization charts and selection of the "right" person to head a particular component, but many tasks could be assigned to two or more people and places.

It is usually better to locate tasks in the organizational subunits responsible for similar activities than to assign them to individuals elsewhere in the organization because doing so makes it easier to capture synergies and to explain what you are doing. This appeals to people who assign high value to having clear, logical, and nonduplicative organization charts. But having tidy organization charts should not automatically trump other considerations. For example, overloading the portfolio of whoever is responsible for a given subunit for the sake of organizational tidiness endangers the ability of that individual—and thus the subunit—to perform effectively. In addition to "load balancing" considerations, it sometimes makes sense to assign particular tasks to a less obviously logical subunit because the leader or other key person in that subunit has special expertise germane to those tasks. Overall efficacy and efficiency are the goals, not pretty organization charts.

Prioritization also involves decisions about sequencing. Some tasks must be substantially completed before conditions exist to execute other dimensions of an overall plan. Getting the sequence right can be critical. For example, before restructuring the organization to redistribute responsibilities or add or delete subunits, it is prudent to understand what each component does and how well or badly it is staffed to perform those functions. Similarly, if new procedures or methodologies are to be introduced, one should first ensure that mechanisms exist to provide instruction and evaluate performance.

Prioritization and sequencing will also be shaped by the character of the tasks involved. Some may be required by legislation or executive order; others may have had salience during the political campaign or be particularly important to the President or a cabinet secretary. Still others will demand early attention because the component or mission involved is seen by oversight bodies to be particularly important and/or badly broken. Generally speaking, if key players such as members of your Congressional oversight committee believe that you were appointed and confirmed to "fix" particular problems, attending to those problems should probably be a top priority. Doing so will likely garner approval and support for subsequent actions. Failing to do so will have the opposite effect.

Yet another consideration when prioritizing activities is the importance of securing and maintaining support for what you are trying to do, delivering concrete accomplishments, and building momentum. Considerations affecting how to do this include judgments about which tasks can be accomplished quickly and easily, and which require prior accomplishments or appear difficult and time-consuming to achieve. It is, of course, necessary to devote whatever time, attention, and political capital are needed to succeed at key tasks, but it is usually a mistake to pay the opportunity costs of devoting too much attention to difficult tasks that, if achieved, will have only limited positive impact on organizational performance. "Necessary to do" must trump "nice to do." Doing "easy" things first is often a good strategy to build support and momentum. But this cannot be at the expense of neglecting foundational steps required for sustained progress and ultimate success in rebuilding and reforming your institution.

Regardless of how you prioritize your tasks, it is important to telegraph and maintain transparency about where you are heading, what you hope ultimately to achieve, and how intermediate and instrumental steps pave the way for achievement of higher-order objectives. Simply doing things, however necessary or valuable they might be, is insufficient to build momentum and confidence. At every step of the process, it is advantageous to tell members of your leadership team, the workforce, counterparts elsewhere in your parent organization and other USG agencies, oversight bodies, and (sometimes) the media what you are doing, why you are doing it, and what it and other actions have achieved. This might sound like encouragement for self-promotion. It is. But it is far better to tell key constituencies what you are doing and to alert them to potential problems than to limit communication with them until you are ready to unveil a major success or insoluble problem. Again, if you tell them nothing, they will assume that you are doing nothing.

Utilizing Strengths and Eschewing Unnecessary Fights

Having been named to a position of responsibility bestows significant legitimacy and authority to reorganize, rebuild, and reform the structures and procedures in your portfolio. But success requires more than giving instructions and assuming that they will be executed exactly as you intended. Change is inherently disruptive, even when the changes involve rolling back ill-considered, disruptive, counterproductive, and widely criticized measures. Unless your mandate is a narrow one requiring only the restoration of what was dismantled or disrupted by the previous administration, you should anticipate uncertainty, reluctance, and resistance.

To secure buy-in and initial implementation, it is useful—necessary—to persuade people that you know what you are doing and that you have the ability and authority to do it. Nobody wants to engage in feckless activity that detracts from performance of mission and/or appears to have adverse consequences for organizational viability and individual careers. One of the most important assets available to most appointees is their reputation. If it were not at least reasonably good, you probably would not have been appointed.

Reputation matters. Everyone has a reputation, whether that reputation is an asset that you can use to build trust and confidence or a liability that makes people reluctant to incur short-term pain to achieve longer-term gain will affect your ability to lead. No one can change the reputation acquired in previous assignments, but what one does with that reputation is a different matter. Obviously, someone appointed to a position in an organization where he or she served previously or involving responsibilities similar to those exercised elsewhere in the USG or in the private sector enters the job with credentials that burnish the aura of "I know what I'm doing and have a track record to prove it."

Using your reputational assets, and those of your leadership team, can be extremely useful for reducing skepticism and obtaining provisional buy-in. The obvious caveat to this generalization is that utilization of one's reputation is not the same as egotistical bragging about past achievements. Your reputation is what it is; you cannot refashion it after the fact. As important, it may be the only thing that your new workforce and outside observers know about you, so it will be the starting point of early judgments about you and what you declare to be your objectives. People will respond to your observations and objectives based on what they think they know about you. If you have a positive reputation, you do not need to refer to it. If people know nothing about you, which is the functional equivalent of having a negative reputation, it is generally not a good idea to underscore or inflate past achievements. It would be better to look for early successes and use them to build momentum and a more positive image.

A stellar reputation can be an asset but should not be squandered on fights or tasks that will require more time, effort, and political (reputational) capital than they are worth. The flip side of seeking to build confidence and momentum through early (but meaningful) successes is avoiding early losses that deplete capital and impede achievement of more important goals. It is not always possible to know in advance which undertakings will prove to be "too hard" or not worth the cost, but one should always be alert to signs (and advice) that particular challenges should be deferred or abandoned. The words of the Kenny Roger ballad "The Gambler," admonishing a younger card player just how important it is to know when to fold 'em and when to walk away, are instructive.

No Magic Formula

If you were hoping for a roadmap to success or an ordered list of instructions telling you what to do and how to do it, this is the point at which you will be disappointed. Every situation and the assets of every appointee are different and there is no matrix arraying combinations of situational conditions along one axis and individual attributes on the other. Each person must figure this out individually. That does not mean, however, that I think the effort to provide general guidance is a waste of time. To the contrary, I wish that I had been alerted to the range and type of considerations that shaped and constrained my own efforts to meet the challenges of the positions I accepted in 2005. Having spent half my career as a teacher, I believe that the most important result of instruction is not mastery of facts but greater awareness of alternative ways to think about specific problems and puzzles.

My goal in writing this part of the book was to identify considerations that will affect the ability of new appointees to achieve their objectives. It does not specify what one should do, but I hope it does alert those about to assume new responsibilities to challenges and factors that must be considered when setting priorities, formulating plans, and implementing steps to restore or enhance capability and confidence in the federal government. My hope is that others can learn from my experience and make fewer mistakes than I did.

Notes

Prologue: Purpose and Perspective

1. On the evolution of intelligence analysis see, for example, Rebecca Fisher, Rob Johnston, and Peter Clement, "Is Intelligence Analysis a Discipline?" in *Analyzing Intelligence: National Security Practitioners' Perspectives,* 2nd ed., ed. Roger Z. George and James B. Bruce (Washington, DC: Georgetown University Press, 2014), chapter 4.

2. Examples include Roger Z. George, *Intelligence in the National Security Enterprise: An Introduction* (Washington, DC: Georgetown University Press, 2020); and Mark M. Lowenthal, *Intelligence: From Secrets to Policy*, 8th ed. (Thousand Oaks, CA: CQ Press, 2020).

3. On the utility of checklists, see, for example, Atul Gawande, "The Checklist," *The New Yorker*, December 10, 2007, https://www.newyorker.com/magazine/2007/12/10/the-checklist.

4. I taught and directed projects at Stanford from 1975 through 1985. When I left to head the China Division in the State Department's Bureau of Intelligence and Research in 1986, I expected to return after two years in Washington. Two years stretched into twenty-three, and I did not return to Stanford until 2009.

5. The other books were *Reducing Uncertainty: Intelligence Analysis and National Security* (Stanford, CA: Stanford University Press, 2011); *The New Great Game: China and South and Central Asia in the Era of Reform* (Stanford CA: Stanford University Press, 2016), editor; *Uneasy Partnerships: China,*

Japan, the Koreas, and Russia in the Era of Reform, (Stanford, CA: Stanford University Press, 2017), editor; and *Fateful Decisions: Choices That Will Shape China's Future* (Stanford, CA: Stanford University Press, 2020), coedited with Jean C. Oi.

6. There is one partial but notable exception to the general disregard for preparation of a historical record. Approximately one year into the process, after some of the heretofore scattered components and staff of the Office of the Director of National Intelligence (ODNI) relocated to temporary offices at Bolling Air Force Base, I invited ODNI historian Mike Warner to sit in on my daily staff meeting and any other meetings that he wanted to attend. He did so as his schedule permitted, but I have not consulted the notes he prepared at the time. To my knowledge, they have not been analyzed or declassified.

7. For example, IRTPA provisions requiring assessment of how well analytic products conformed to specified tradecraft standards required visibility into the work of every agency and created the capacity to identify and capitalize on strengths and to address weaknesses. In order to use this as a diagnostic tool, however, I judged that I had to meet the mandated requirement for an annual report to the Congress in a way that did not entail or invite invidious comparisons and unhelpful criticism of particular agencies. Provisions requiring assessment of analytic performance are at section 1019 of the *Intelligence Reform and Terrorism Prevention Act of 2004* (Public Law 108–458), December 17, 2004, https://www.nctc.gov/docs/pl108_458.pdf.

Intelligence Reform

1. The most detailed book-length study is Michael Allen, *Blinking Red: Crisis and Compromise in American Intelligence After 9/11* (Washington, DC: Potomac Books, 2013). See also Paul R. Pillar, *Intelligence and US Foreign Policy: Iraq, 9/11, and Misguided Reform* (New York: Columbia University Press, 2011).

2. An earlier version of my take on the 2004 reform legislation can be found in Thomas Fingar, "Office of the Director of National Intelligence: From Pariah and Piñata to Managing Partner," in *The National Security Enterprise: Navigating the Labyrinth*, 2nd ed., ed. Roger Z. George and Harvey Rishikof (Washington, DC: Georgetown University Press, 2017), 185–202.

3. Summaries of previous studies recommending IC reform can be found in Richard H. Immerman, "The Politics of Intelligence Reform," in *The Politics of Major Policy Reforms in Postwar America*, ed. Jeffery A. Jenkins and Sidney M. Milkis (New York: Cambridge University Press, 2014), chapter 10; and Michael Warner and J. Kenneth McDonald, *US Intelligence Community Reform*

Studies Since 1947 (Washington, DC: Center for the Study of Intelligence, 2005), https://www.cia.gov/library/center-for-the-study-of-intelligence/csi -publications/books-and-monographs/US%20Intelligence%20Community %20Reform%20Studies%20Since%201947.pdf.

4. See *The 9/11 Commission Report: Final Report of the National Commission on Terrorist Attacks Upon the United States* (hereafter *9/11 Commission Report*), July 22, 2004, http://govinfo.library.unt.edu/911/report/911Report.pdf; and Charles Perrow, "A Symposium on *The 9/11 Commission Report*," *Contemporary Sociology* 34, no. 2 (March 2005): 99–107.

5. See also Richard K. Betts, *Enemies of Intelligence: Knowledge and Power in American National Security* (New York: Columbia University Press, 2007), chapter 5.

6. See Robert Draper, *To Start a War: How the Bush Administration Took America into Iraq* (New York: Penguin, 2020).

7. For analysis of why calls for reform of the Intelligence Community in 2004 did not suffer the ignominious fate of so many previous studies, see Allen, *Blinking Red*, chapter 2; and Thomas Fingar, "Office of the Director of National Intelligence: Promising Start Despite Ambiguity, Ambivalence, and Animosity," in *The National Security Enterprise: Navigating the Labyrinth*, ed. Roger Z. George and Harvey Rishikof (Washington, DC: Georgetown university Press, 2011), 140–141.

8. See, for example, Eric Lichtblau, "US Warns of High Risk of Qaeda Attack," *New York Times*, August 2, 2004, http://www.nytimes.com/2004/08/02/ politics/us-warns-of-high-risk-of-qaeda-attack.html; the data cited in John Mueller, "The Iraq Syndrome," *Foreign Affairs* 84, no. 6 (Nov.-Dec. 2005): 44–54; and the sources cited in Richard K. Betts, "Two Faces of Intelligence Failure: September 11 and Iraq's Missing WMD," *Political Science Quarterly* 122, no. 4 (Winter 2007/2008): 585–606.

9. The reports of these review panels can be found at US Senate, *Report of the Select Committee on Intelligence on the US Intelligence Community's Prewar Intelligence Assessments on Iraq Together with Additional Views*, 108th Congress, 2d Session, S. Report 108–301, July 9, 2004 (hereafter SSCI 2004), www.intelligence.senate.gov/108301pdf; *9/11 Commission Report*; and *The Report of the Commission on Intelligence Capabilities of the United States Regarding Weapons of Mass Destruction*, March 31, 2005 (hereafter WMD Commission Report), https://www.gpo.gov/fdsys/search/pagedetails. action?granuleId=&packageId=GPO-WMD. The WMD Commission report was not due or issued for several more months, but I was sufficiently well

informed about its tentative conclusions to know that it too would contain a number of specific recommendations.

10. The fact that Fran Townsend chaired the meeting signaled to me that any reforms would focus more on combating terrorism than on the analytical problems of the Iraq WMD estimate.

11. For a more detailed exposition of my views on the Iraq WMD estimate, see Thomas Fingar, *Reducing Uncertainty: Intelligence Analysis and National Security* (Stanford, CA: Stanford University Press, 2011), chapter 6.

12. This generalization applies to both the Intelligence Community "drafting" sessions in the morning and the policy discussions held in the afternoon. In the first afternoon session, I backstopped Deputy Secretary of State Rich Armitage; after that, I substituted for him. When I pointed out that for me to represent him as State's policy official in the meeting to comment on the draft to which I had contributed in the morning would be a bit strange, he replied, in his inimical fashion, "You wanted to be a big shot, you can go to these lousy meetings. Just tell me what happened."

13. The particular lessons to which I refer were those in E. E. Schattschnei-der, *The Semisovereign People: A Realist View of Democracy in America* (Boston: Wadsworth, 1960, 1975).

14. Because this is a book about what I was thinking, not a history of debate within the administration over intelligence reform issues, I will not attempt to capture or characterize the positions of specific players. Personalities and memory of past fights played a role, but my judgment at the time and today is that most fights over intelligence reform were defensive struggles to protect valued prerogatives rather than power grabs by particular agencies or individuals. Those interested in these matters should consult Allen, *Blinking Red*, chapter 8 and the sources cited therein.

15. See Mark Leibovich, *This Town* (New York: Penguin, 2013).

16. SSCI 2004; and *9/11 Commission Report*. Examples of press commentary and speculation include David Ignatius, "Spy World Success Story," *Washington Post*, May 2, 2004, http://www.washingtonpost.com/wp-dyn/articles/A59794–2004May1.html; and Douglas Jehl, "The Reach of War: Intelligence; Bush Considers Replacing CIA Chief More Quickly," *New York Ttimes*, June 22, 2004, http://www.nytimes.com/2004/06/22/world/the-reach-of-war-intelligence-bush-considers-replacing-cia-chief-more-quickly.html.

17. On the early history of today's Intelligence Community, see C. Thomas Thorne Jr., and David S. Patterson, eds., *Foreign Relations of the United States, 1945–1950, Emergence of the Intelligence Establishment* (Washington, DC: US

Government Printing Office, 1996), https://history.state.gov/historicaldocuments/frus1945–50Intel. For a history of intelligence reform proposals, see Warner and McDonald, *US Intelligence Community Reform Studies Since 1947*; and Richard A. Best Jr., *Proposals for Intelligence Reorganization, 1949–2004* (Washington, DC: Congressional Research Service, September 24, 2004), http://fas.org/irp/crs/RL32500.pdf.

18. See Amy B. Zegart, *Flawed by Design: The Evolution of the CIA, JCS, and NSC* (Stanford, CA: Stanford University Press, 1999).

19. Commission on the Intelligence Capabilities, *Report to the President of the United States*, 6 (emphasis in original).

20. National Intelligence Estimate, *Iraq's Continuing Programs for Weapons of Mass Destruction*, October 2002, redacted version at http://nsarchive.gwu.edu/NSAEBB/NSAEBB129/nie.pdf. For examples of commentary on INR's relatively better performance, see Ignatius, "Spy World Success Story"; and Douglas Jehl, "The Reach of War: Intelligence; Tiny Agency's Iraq Analysis Is Better Than Big Rivals'," *New York Times*, July 19, 2004, http://www.nytimes.com/2004/07/19/world/reach-war-intelligence-tiny-agency-s-iraq-analysis-better-than-big-rivals.html.

21. As Principal Deputy Assistant Secretary, I became Acting Assistant Secretary when Carl Ford decided to retire. I was serving in that capacity when Secretary Powell proposed my nomination to the confirmed position and President Bush accepted that recommendation. That is the reason I was able to serve as Assistant Secretary before being confirmed.

22. Creating such a position had been proposed many times previously and rumors swirling at the time speculated about who might champion it in 2004. I knew at the time that members of the 9/11 Commission were likely to recommend such a position but learned only later that champions in the Congress included influential Senators Diane Feinstein and Olympia Snowe. See, for example, Eric Schmitt and Richard W. Stevenson, "Judging Intelligence: The Reaction; Admitting Intelligence Flaws, Bush Stands by Need for War," *New York Times*, July 10, 2004, http://www.nytimes.com/2004/07/10/world/judging-intelligence-reaction-admitting-intelligence-flaws-bush-stands-need-for.html.

23. I was asked additional questions a few weeks later when I had a second "confirmation hearing" in a closed session with members of the SSCI. For reasons having nothing to do with me, I was caught in a jurisdictional fight between the Senate Foreign Relations Committee (SFRC), which has oversight of the State Department, and the SSCI, which for the first time decided

to assert jurisdiction for appointments to head the Bureau of Intelligence and Research. When the hearing began, Senator Roberts thanked me for appearing at this confirmation hearing and Senator Rockefeller thanked me for coming even though I had already had my confirmation hearing before the SFRC. Despite its somewhat muddied origins and the fact that I had appeared before the committee many times before, the two hours I spent with members and staff as the only witness in a closed hearing was invaluable to me and, I believe, contributed to the generally excellent working relationship that I had with the committee after I became Deputy Director of National Intelligence for Analysis.

24. On the DCI's dual role and limited authority to manage other agency intelligence components, see Douglas F. Garthoff, *Directors of Central Intelligence as Leaders of the US Intelligence Community, 1946–2005* (Washington, DC: Center for the Study of Intelligence, 2005).

25. This was not a new position. Secretary of State George Marshall had taken the same position in 1947 during the debate that created the modern national security enterprise. He insisted that State must have its own intelligence unit reporting to the Secretary. As a result, what is now the Bureau of Intelligence and Research (then known as the Office of Intelligence Research) was established at the same time as CIA and the Office of the Secretary of Defense. For this reason, Marshall opposed establishing CIA, as did Forrestal at Defense. This opposition contributed to the construction of the IC as a confederation rather than as a community.

26. Secretary Colin L. Powell, "Opening Remarks Before the Senate Governmental Affairs Committee," September 13, 2004, https://2001–2009.state.gov/secretary/former/powell/remarks/36123.htm.

27. Ibid. I had a role in preparing Powell's testimony on intelligence requirements and, in that respect, his written submission previewed criteria that I would employ when setting priorities and designing implementation strategies as DDNI/A. It was useful, however, to justify what I wanted to do by being able to cite on-the-record views of the highly respected former Secretary, National Security Advisor, and Chairman of the Joint Chiefs of Staff.

28. The WMD Commission report was not issued until after the President had signed the Intelligence Reform Act, but most of its recommendations were fed into the process in draft form in order to influence—or at least appear to have influenced—the legislation that was approved before the commission had completed its work.

Sliding Toward an Offer I Couldn't Refuse

1. See Intelligence Reform and Terrorism Prevention Act of 2004 (Public Law 108-458), December 17, 2004 (hereafter IRTPA), https://www.nctc.gov/docs/pl108_458.pdf; and President Bush Administration Actions to Implement WMD Commission Recommendations, June 29, 2005, http://fas.org/irp/news/2005/06/who62905-wmd.pdf. The accepted recommendations were not codified in an executive order, but they were accepted and treated by the ODNI as binding requirements for intelligence reform.

2. SSCI 2004; WMD Commission Report.

3. For a more detailed exposition of my views on the Iraq WMD estimate, see Fingar, *Reducing Uncertainty*, chapter 6.

4. Key members of this informal group included John Kringen (CIA), Paula Causey (INR), Earle Sheck (DIA), Dave Shore (NSA), and Kate Hall (NGA). The unusual degree of camaraderie and shared commitment to do what we could to fix problems we had lived with for a long time without fully realizing how damaging they were until the Iraq WMD estimate and its aftermath galvanized us to take action and influenced my subsequent efforts to lead analytic transformation. They also made it easier than it might have been to overcome structural and cultural impediments to success.

5. Condi Rice and I have been friends since she came to Stanford as a postdoctoral student in 1980. In the early 1980s, we were both assistant directors of programs in what is now the Freeman Spogli Institute for International Studies. This was before first I, then she, and then the third member of our assistant director troika, Coit (Chip) Blacker (who served as National Security Council senior director for Russia and Eurasia in the Clinton administration), left Stanford to serve in Washington.

6. See, for example, Douglas Jehl, "Report Says Key Assertions Leading to War Were Wrong," *New York Times*, July 9, 2004, http://www.nytimes.com/2004/07/09/national/report-says-key-assertions-leading-to-war-were-wrong.html.

7. Names of outside experts that came readily to mind included Dick Betts and Bob Jervis at Columbia, Joe Nye at Harvard, and John Steinbruner at the University of Maryland.

8. The distinction I make between management and leadership is captured by the aphorism, "A good manager does things right, a leader does the right thing."

9. Thinking about this requirement reminded me of a comment made by one of my classmates in the Senior Seminar in 1992–1993. This program, which existed for more than forty years, was designed to forge ties among senior officials from across the national security enterprise who were expected to be elevated to assistant secretary, ambassadorial, or comparable positions. His comment was that we were almost assured of promotion because otherwise those who selected us for the program would have to admit that they made a mistake. The serious point here is that expectations of success often contribute to success.

10. For an example of the quotation, see *9/11 Commission*, chapter 8.

11. Writing about this exchange recalled another illustration of the way things often work in government and, I suspect, other large organizations. I encountered Kennedy in the State Department cafeteria one morning during the period when the US Information Agency (USIA) was being incorporated into the State Department. Pat, who was in charge of that project, took the occasion to tell me that he planned to assign the polling and media analysis portions of USIA to INR "because they are analysts." I thanked him for the heads up and asked him to hold off until I determined if this would be a good fit. When I did, I learned that then-current plans would have separated the analysts from their dedicated computer support personnel in order to tidy up organization charts. Ann Pincus, the head of the USIA unit, convinced me that the technical support needed to be embedded in the unit. I called Pat, explained this, and told him to give me everyone or no one in that unit. His immediate answer was, "You've got them all." That was clearly the right decision, and INR has benefited from the addition of the people and functions of the polling and media unit.

Blank White Board and Ticking Clock

1. When writing these sentences, I was reminded of a quip by Negroponte during one of our early staff meetings in which he noted that the number of agencies and other components subsumed under the ODNI was smaller than the number he had overseen in several of his ambassadorial postings.

2. See, for example, Michael Hill and Peter Hupe, *Implementing Public Policy: An Introduction to the Study of Operational Governance*, 3rd ed. (London: Sage, 2014); and Jeffrey L. Pressman and Aaron Wildavsky, *Implementation: How Great Expectations in Washington Are Dashed in Oakland*, 3rd ed. (Berkeley, CA: University of California Press, 1984).

3. For more on delegated authorities, see Intelligence Community Policy Memorandum 2005-200-1, November 9, 2005, https://fas.org/irp/dni/icpm/2005-200-1.pdf. This ICPM was later replaced by a new delegation reflecting subsequent changes to the ODNI structure.

4. Another reason for accepting the chairmanship of the NIC was that it is one of the best analytical jobs in the world. Where else can one work on the most difficult and consequential national security issues with the support of the best analysts in the Intelligence Community and the resources of the USG, and direct access to senior policymakers? For a student of international and comparative politics, it is the dream job. See Robert Hutchings and Gregory F. Treverton, eds., *Truth to Power: A History of the National Intelligence Council* (Oxford, UK: Oxford University Press, 2019).

5. If I had not fully appreciated the need for speed before, I certainly did after a one-on-one meeting with House Permanent Select Committee on Intelligence Chairman Peter Hoekstra in late May or very early June. I had asked to see him shortly after I was confirmed as INR Assistant Secretary, but the meeting had been postponed several times. I had accepted the DDNI/A position between the time of the last postponement and the scheduled date for this meeting, so I decided to keep the appointment even though my position had changed. In the meeting, I summarized my still very rough plans and priorities for analysis. Hoekstra commented that my ideas sounded good and asked what he could do for me. I asked for time to work out the details and to ensure that we did not screw things up when trying to make them better. He replied, not at all facetiously, that he could not do that, adding that it had already taken too long to get to this point. It was my third or fourth day on the job.

6. I was able to do this only because Director of Intelligence John Kringen and PDB Director Steve Kaplan did everything possible to ensure that the PDB process continued to work smoothly during (and after) the transition.

7. IRTPA); and President Bush Administration Actions to Implement WMD Commission Recommendations, June 29, 2005, http://fas.org/irp/news/2005/06/who62905-wmd.pdf.

8. I began my intelligence career in 1970 as a German linguist and analyst in the Office of the Deputy Chief of Staff for Intelligence at the headquarters of USAREUR and Seventh Army in Heidelberg, Germany.

9. Although I had been trained as a military policeman before being reassigned to USAREUR headquarters, I certainly did not think this gave me the

level of knowledge the ODDNI/A needed to achieve mandated and desirable integration with law enforcement.

10. More accurately, I thought that I had moved administratively when I submitted my letter of resignation to Secretary Rice and, I thought, to the appropriate part of the State Department personnel system. It was not until months later that I discovered that my resignation letter had been misplaced. Since I was paid the same amount and my government salary was regularly deposited in my bank account, I had not noticed the error. My "official" move to the ODNI did not occur until months later.

Building a Team and Building Support

1. Potential members of the ODDNI/A leadership team were not the only ones with questions about the planned organization and the specific responsibilities of individual team members and subdivisions. As will be discussed further on, I almost immediately began to receive similar questions from members of oversight committees on the Hill, the President's Intelligence Advisory Board, journalists who follow the Intelligence Community, and former members and staff of the 9/11 and WMD Commissions. The questioners were understandably curious and I'm sure eager to be helpful, but I quickly realized that the more detail I provided about my plans and strategy, the more time I would have to spend defending still-evolving ideas and deflecting "suggestions" to do things differently.

2. There were also other constraints and imperatives, including the mandate to make the PDB a "community product." The most important of these considerations will be discussed further on.

3. See Fingar, *Reducing Uncertainty*, chapters 5–6.

4. The two most detailed critiques of the NIE and its tradecraft are US Senate, *Report of the Select Committee on Intelligence on Postwar Findings About Iraq's WMD Programs and Links to Terrorism and How They Compare with Prewar Assessments Together with Additional and Minority Views*, 109th Congress, 2d Session, S. Report 109-331, September 8, 2006, http://intelligence.senate.gov/phaseiiaccuracy.pdf (hereafter SSCI Report); and the WMD Commission Report.

5. Despite spending eleven years in the INR front office, I had never seen a PDB. The best I was able to work out was to receive a sanitized table of contents each day so that I—and thus INR—would know what topics had been briefed to senior officials.

6. Despite the calls of some to "move" the entire PDB operation to the ODNI, it took me less than a pico-second to decide that that would be a

very bad idea. For starters, we did not even have a permanent home, let alone a twenty-four-hour watch, graphics shop, motor pool, or other elements essential to sustaining the PDB operation. As will be discussed further on, we made the PDB a community product by using other, more substantive means than physical relocation.

7. That was certainly the case with respect to the recommendations of the WMD Commission.

8. For more on this point, see Fingar, *Reducing Uncertainty*, chapter 5.

9. The exception is my decision to split the unit responsible for the Near East and South Asia and name separate NIOs for the Middle East and South Asia.

10. Illustrative examples include reaching out to the best experts on a given subject for drafting and evaluative assistance, and identifying dissenting views on important questions.

11. This was one of the factors that pushed me toward a strategy of restoring confidence in IC analysis by demonstrating improved performance rather than through high-profile changes of personnel and procedures.

12. In addition to meetings of the National Security Council (NSC) per se, the NIC was henceforth to provide intelligence briefing materials for Principals Committee (PC) and Deputies Committee (DC) meetings. For more on this new responsibility, see Thomas Fingar, "New Missions, New Challenges, 2005–2008," in *Truth to Power: A History of the National Intelligence Council*, ed. Robert Hutchings and Gregory F. Treverton (Oxford, UK: Oxford University Press, 2019), chapter 6.

13. See SSCI Report; WMD Commission Report; and Fingar, *Reducing Uncertainty*, chapter 6.

14. For Hoekstra's comments on the need for speed, see "Blank White Board," note 5.

15. Decision making and policy development in Washington, in my experience, often resemble the description in Michael D. Cohen, James G. March, and Johan P. Olsen, "A Garbage Can Model of Organizational Choice," *Administrative Science Quarterly* 17, no. 1 (1972): 1–25.

16. Andy Shepard was the third person that expressed interest in joining the ODDNI/A. The first was Sherry Hong, one of my Foreign Service staff assistants in the INR front office; the second was Sandi Jimenez, my executive assistant in INR with whom I had worked for eleven years. When Sherry volunteered, I had such a vague notion of what I had agreed to undertake that I told her I was unsure whether I would need a staff assistant in the new position. I did, and Sherry became a major contributor to our early achievements.

17. Everything was so nascent that we did not yet have a clear definition of what being "hired" by the ODNI meant. The IRTPA legislation had moved a number of organizations and a few hundred people from CIA to the ODNI and created new ODNI positions, but we lacked clear criteria for determining which people would become permanent hires of the ODNI and which would serve on time-limited detail from their home agency.

18. See John Keefe, *Anatomy of the EP-3 Incident, April 2001* (Alexandria, VA: Center for Naval Analysis, 2002).

19. The incident, which began with the collision of a US EP-3 reconnaissance plane and a Chinese jet fighter over international waters off Hainan, occurred at the beginning of the George W. Bush administration, before many new officials had been confirmed. Secretary Powell and Deputy Secretary Armitage, with whom I had worked in the 1990s when I was director of INR's Office of Analysis for East Asia and the Pacific, asked me to play a role even though I was the carry-over Clinton-appointed Assistant Secretary of INR because they knew me but did not yet know the foreign service officers who filled positions on an acting basis pending confirmation of the new Bush team.

20. I have been frequently reminded of John's high reputation on the Hill because almost every subsequent encounter with Jane Harman, for whom I have enormous respect, begins with a ritual exchange of greetings including the statement, "But I still hate you." The reason for this good-natured but nevertheless revealing comment is that I "stole" John from her and the Committee.

21. Nancy Bernkopf Tucker, "Taiwan Expendable? Nixon and Kissinger Go to China," *The Journal of American History* 92, no. 1 (June 2005): 109–135.

22. Although the IRTPA does not use the word "Ombudsman," that is the clear intent of Section 1020 on safeguarding objectivity.

23. My response was genuine, not flippant. I had interacted with many generals and colonels when I sat in an outer office of the Deputy Chief of Staff for Intelligence in Heidelberg and had gained great respect for the four colonels and one Navy captain who were my classmates in the senior seminar.

Translating Ideas into Actions

1. Nancy Tucker did not join for a few more months, but we had identified a deputy for analytic integrity and standards from within the Intelligence Community, Becky Strode from CIA, who stepped up to the challenge from day one.

2. US Government officials face a daily barrage of information, ideas, and recommendations from bureaucratic counterparts, the media, lobbyists, foreign embassies, college classmates, Members and congressional staff, think tanks, and elsewhere. In my experience, all such inputs are assumed by the recipient to be based on less (or less carefully analyzed) information than what officials receive from the Intelligence Community, and most are assumed to be or very obviously are tied to the parochial objectives of the source. The IC is assumed to have more information and is supposed to be—and in my experience almost always is—more objective.

3. The demographic profile of IC analysts will be discussed more extensively further on, but it is worth noting here that in 2005, there was a relatively small number of very experienced baby boomer analysts, a very large number of new, mostly youthful and inexperienced people who had joined the IC after 9/11, and a small percentage of midcareer and middle grade or "noncom"-type analysts. I worried about losing people in all three categories.

4. As a general proposition, and to the extent that improving the performance of all agencies was interpreted to mean improving the ability of every agency to perform its unique missions, this part of the strategy was readily accepted. Support became less enthusiastic, and resistance intensified, when managers in a few agencies realized that that their own work would be judged in comparison to now better-performing counterparts.

5. I recalled this statement a few years later when thinking about how to expand collaboration among IC analysts because I found it difficult to believe that few teams existed and was determined to greatly expand multi-agency collaboration.

6. He conveyed more specific information in a subsequent meeting with Assistant Secretary Carl Ford and me than is contained in his formal report. See J. R. Hackman and M. O'Connor, "What Makes for a Great Analytic Team? Individual vs. Team Approaches to Intelligence Analysis" (Washington, DC: Intelligence Science Board, Office of the Director of Central Intelligence, 2004), https://fas.org/irp/dni/isb/analytic.pdf.

7. See, for example, J. Richard Hackman, *Leading Teams: Setting the Stage for Great Performances* (Cambridge, MA: Harvard Business School, 2002).

8. This was more than a theoretical problem because as soon as I began to recruit people, new staff in the ODNI/Management directorate began to demand formal job descriptions with specific tasks and criteria to be used when conducting mandatory performance reviews.

9. During the first month or so in my new position, I was bombarded with

papers and meeting requests from former IC officials, think tank researchers, and members of various study groups eager to inject ideas into the reform process. I genuinely appreciated their desire to help and was eager for ideas, but I had already become convinced that it would be difficult to obtain "buy-in" from IC analysts and managers for any plan that they had not helped to shape.

Think Big, Start Small, Fail Cheap, Fix Fast

1. The flip side of having wide latitude to develop an implementation plan was that staff and some Members of Congress, the President's Intelligence Advisory Board, and others pressed for an early and reasonably detailed blueprint describing what I intended to do.

2. For a more extended discussion of this point, see Thomas Fingar, "Building a Community of Analysts," in *Analyzing Intelligence: National Security Practitioners' Perspectives*, 2nd ed., ed. Roger Z. George and James B. Bruce (Washington, DC: Georgetown University Press, 2014), 287–301.

3. In Washington, an "elevator speech" is a very brief—a few sentences or a few minutes in duration—statement summarizing key developments, judgments, and requirements germane to a particular account or policy issue.

4. The earliest versions of my parish stump speech were not recorded, but the content was essentially the same when I spoke to "The DNI's Information Sharing Conference and Technology Sharing Expo" in August 2006. My talk at that IC-wide meeting can be found at https://www.dni.gov/files/documents/Newsroom/Speeches%20and%20Interviews/20060821_2_speech.pdf.

5. Very early in the process, we began to produce updates that we informally referred to as "good news grams." These were (mostly) unclassified one-to-two-page summaries of recently taken steps indicating progress implementing mandated reforms that we prepared primarily for Hill staffers on the oversight committees but had available to share with others as well.

6. On the authority of the DNI to transfer personnel, see IRTPA, Sec 102A.

7. How we intended to do that will be discussed further on. Almost four years later, I mentioned to President Bush that this had been my first priority after being named DDNI/Analysis. He interrupted me to say, "You did."

8. See, for example, Scott Shane, "Year into Revamped Spying, Troubles and Some Progress," *New York Times*, February 28, 2006, http://www.nytimes.com/2006/02/28/politics/year-into-revamped-spying-troubles-and-some-progress.html?_r=0.

9. In addition to the NIC and PDB staffs, I had "inherited" the staff of the now-disbanded Assistant DCI for Analysis and Production. Some members

of the former Analysis and Production staff moved into subdivisions of the ODDNI/A, but most soon returned to their home organizations.

10. Extensive, but partial lists of reform proposals can be found in Best Jr., *Proposals for Intelligence Reorganization, 1949–2004*; and Warner and McDonald, *US Intelligence Community Reform Studies Since 1947*.

11. Key elements of then current conditions included the need to demonstrate results quickly, ambiguity and animosity in the relationship between the ODNI and the Intelligence Community, and the imperative that there be no deterioration of current capabilities and support to national security customers while striving for improvement.

12. Although the ODNI staff continued to grow during my tenure, that of the ODDNI/A remained both stable and small. The fact that I was double-hatted as Chair of NIC enabled me to utilize NIC personnel with nonanalytic functions (such as contract monitors) as needed for ODDNI/A tasks—a capacity that terminated after my departure—but the primary reason for limiting the size of my staff was my reluctance to add people. In my experience, adding people tends to increase bureaucratic overhead (personnel reports, coordination, turf disputes, and so on). Excluding the NIC and the PDB, the analysis directorate had a staff of only thirty to thirty-five during my tenure. This was adequate to pursue integration of sixteen IC agencies and collaboration involving thousands of analysts.

13. Each of these matters will be discussed further on, but, briefly, originator-controlled (ORCON) limitations on which agencies and analysts would receive or have access to particular reports had existed for decades and effectively left "need to know" decisions in the hands of collectors, who seldom had a basis for knowing what analysts wanted or needed to analyze subjects in their portfolios or to support their primary customers.

14. See, for example, Perrow, "A Symposium on *The 9/11 Commission Report*."

15. See, for example, Fingar, "Office of the Director of National Intelligence: Promising Start Despite Ambiguity, Ambivalence, and Animosity," 139–155; and Calvert Jones, "Intelligence Reform: The Logic of Information Sharing," *Intelligence and National Security* 22, no. 3 (June 2007): 384–401 and works cited therein.

16. IRTPA, Sec. 1016.

Taking Stock

1. Limited knowledge about other components of the IC was more a function of the confederal character of the Intelligence Community than of disdain or willful disinterest.

2. I do not remember exactly how we explained the purpose of the survey to the agency analytic managers but think that we did so by noting that it was a pilot to get at the kinds of information we had judged to be useful in discussions that began informally and moved forward in one of the first meetings of the Analysis and Production Board. I note this because I believed we had buy-in for the survey and that the difficulties we encountered were the result of unclear guidance and lack of experience responding to the kind of questions we asked, not to passive-aggressive resistance to what we were trying to do.

3. These points will be elaborated further in the discussions of training, evaluative criteria, and the results of formal evaluations of the work done in all agencies.

4. For more on my view of collaboration, see Fingar, "Building a Community of Analysts," 287–301.

5. I confess that, as a senior manager in INR at the time, I viewed the ARC as both a tool that could be used to facilitate collaboration and a repository of potential replacements for my own aging workforce.

6. In my presentations during early town meetings and parish calls, I often noted that we envisioned collaboration as something analysts would want to do because it made their jobs easier and their products better. I illustrated the point by saying that I never liked it when my parents told me to "cooperate" with my siblings or when bureaucratic requirements forced me to "coordinate" my assessments with people in other agencies who had little knowledge of why the assessments had been written and did not necessarily know very much about the subject. Most got the point immediately and heads moving from north to south indicated approval.

7. One reason it was possible for INR analysts to maintain contact with colleagues in other agencies who had moved on to new positions is that INR analysts typically remained on the same account for many more years than analysts in other IC components.

8. We employed the same approach later when we established criteria for interaction in "A-Space." By that time, we were referring to the use of "ebay" methods to demonstrate expertise and reliability.

9. IRTPA, 118 STAT.3644-3648.

10. See discussion of town meetings and parish calls in the chapter "Organizing Themes and Goals."

11. I realize that the term "substantive expertise" means different things to different people and in different contexts. As used here, it refers to subject matter expertise about places, people, issues, relationships, and so on. Other

forms of expertise include disciplinary or process expertise, and expertise on particular USG and/or IC missions and methods. These types or categories of expertise are not mutually exclusive. Indeed, the best analysts and analytic managers have all three types. But for purposes of the ARC, what I had in mind—and what we used as our working criterion—was subject matter expertise.

12. For additional information on who is an analyst, see Thomas Fingar, "A Guide to All-Source Analysis," in *AFIO's Guide to the Study of Intelligence*, ed. Peter C. Oleson (Falls Church, VA: Association of Former Intelligence Officers, 2016), 297–303.

13. This insight contributed to the decisions to establish A-Space and the Library of National Intelligence (see further on).

14. Nobody raised the issue at the time, but two years later I briefly had second thoughts about defining analysts in this way when I negotiated with security officers for permission to include all analysts—defined by membership in the ARC—in a pilot program that became known as A-Space. This point is discussed at greater length further on.

15. Some agencies and individuals were less comfortable with this approach than were others. Unsurprisingly, military components appreciated the latitude resulting from the "commander's intent" approach to guidance but also wanted authoritative guidelines or criteria for assessing individual performance, the quality of analytic products, and other "measurable" indicators.

16. See IRTPA, Sec. 1019.

17. IRTPA, Sec. 1019, states, "[T]he Director of National Intelligence shall, not later than 180 days after the date of the enactment of this Act, assign an individual or entity to be responsible for ensuring that finished intelligence products produced by any element or elements of the Intelligence Community are *timely, objective, independent of political considerations, based upon all sources of available intelligence, and employ the standards of proper analytic tradecraft*" (emphasis added).

18. The standards are incorporated in *Intelligence Community Directive 203: Analytic Standards*. Our version was issued on June 21, 2007, https://www.dni.gov/files/documents/ICD/ICD%20203%20Analytic%20Standards%20pdf-unclassified.pdf; an updated version incorporating the same standards was issued on January 2, 2015, https://www.dni.gov/files/documents/ICD/ICD%20203%20Analytic%20Standards.pdf.

19. Legacy mindsets and bureaucratic resistance from some agencies made preparation of new IC guidelines and directives an extremely slow and

frustrating process. We decided that we could not and would not wait. We cited the IRTPA legislation to justify the use of standards enumerated there for evaluation of written products. I used the authority delegated to me as Chair of NIC and as overseer of the PDB to implement the standards for products in those two flagship arenas.

20. At the time, I judged that the most important reason for acceptance of our assessment of steady improvement was that the SSCI and HPSCI staff members who read our reports had reached a similar judgment on the basis of the products and briefings they received from the Intelligence Community. Another factor may have been the fact that we endeavored to keep the Hill, which really meant key staff, informed about what we were doing and why we were doing it that way. Helping them to understand what we were doing may have given them greater confidence in the results we reported. At the margins, it might also have helped that key members and staff stated that they trusted what we said because they had confidence in us and/or me.

21. This description of eventual agency acceptance—if not embrace—of the evaluation process is accurate but obscures the degree of fear and suspicion that we had to address almost constantly. Analytic managers wanted the information we provided but did not want to be graded or made vulnerable to possibly unfavorable comparison to other agencies.

Training and Tradecraft

1. See, for example, Rebecca Fisher, Rob Johnston, and Peter Clement, "Is Intelligence Analysis a Discipline?" in *Analyzing Intelligence: National Security Practitioner's Perspectives*, 2nd ed., ed. Roger Z. George and James B. Bruce (Washington, DC: Georgetown University Press, 2014), 57–77.

2. Establishment of a "National Intelligence University" was mandated by President Bush in his directive enumerating "Actions to Implement WMD Commission Recommendations," Recommendation 6.4, June 29, 2005, http://fas.org/irp/news/2005/06/who62905-wmd.pdf,

3. Nancy's reference to my experience developing courses was based on our interactions when I was teaching at Stanford in the 1970s and early 1980s.

4. This proved to be an enduring source of tension between the ODDNI/A and agencies that effectively attached greater importance to inculcating pride in and loyalty to the agency than to instruction in common tradecraft skills and commitment to collaboration within the larger intelligence enterprise.

5. We endeavored to reinforce common training and interpersonal relationship bases for confidence in the quality of work produced by counterparts in

other agencies by underscoring that products of all agencies would be evaluated using the same criteria.

6. For greater detail on the development of tradecraft standards, evaluation of analytic products, and Analysis 101 and other training, see the following articles by members of the staff that developed and implemented them. Nancy Bernkopf Tucker, "The Cultural Revolution in Intelligence: Interim Report," *The Washington Quarterly* 31, no. 2 (2008): 47–61; Richard H. Immerman, "Transforming Analysis: The Intelligence Community's Best Kept Secret," *Intelligence and National Security* 26, no. 2–3 (2011): 159–181; and Jim Marchio, "Analytic Tradecraft and the Intelligence Community: Enduring Value, Intermittent Emphasis," *Intelligence and National Security* 29, no. 2 (2014): 159–183.

7. See *Goldwater-Nichols Department of Defense Reorganization Act of 1986*, Public Law 99–433 October 1, 1986, https://history.defense.gov/Portals/70/Documents/dod_reforms/Goldwater-NicholsDoDReordAct1986.pdf; and James R. Locher III, *Victory on the Potomac: The Goldwater-Nichols Act Unifies the Pentagon*, Rev. ed. (Texas A&M University Press, 2004).

Transforming the *PDB* into a Community Product

1. President Bush Administration Actions to Implement WMD Commission Recommendations, June 29, 2005, Recommendation 9.14, http://fas.org/irp/news/2005/06/wh062905-wmd.pdf.

2. Characterizing this judgment as widespread is based on conversations between the passage of the IRTPA and the standup of the ODNI, and on my own sense of sentiment in the IC and among staff and members of the House and Senate intelligence oversight committees.

3. The quotation is from IRTPA), Sec. 102.

4. See, for example, Walter Pincus, "CIA to Cede President's Brief to Negroponte," *Washington Post*, February 19, 2005, https://www.washingtonpost.com/wp-dyn/articles/A36532–2005Feb18.html.

5. The NIC was the only analytic component of the ODNI and, as such, was assigned responsibility for preparation of briefing materials for NSC, Principals Committee, and Deputies Committee meetings. This change and its consequences are discussed in Fingar, "New Missions, New Challenges, 2005–2008."

Management of the Analysis Mission

1. For additional detail on my perception of what analysts do, see Thomas Fingar, "Analysis in the US Intelligence Community: Missions, Masters, and

Methods," in *Intelligence Analysis: Behavioral and Social Scientific Foundations*, ed. Baruch Fischhoff and Cherie Chauvin (Washington, DC: The National Academies Press, 2011), 3–27.

2. Structuring the comparison in this way should not be interpreted to mean that any of the first three tasks listed were easy. All, especially information sharing, proved more difficult and frustrating than I had anticipated.

3. IRTPA, Sec. 1012, https://www.nctc.gov/docs/pl108_458.pdf.

4. The scope eventually expanded to include analytic components of the Coast Guard, the Drug Enforcement Agency, and the FBI-led Fusion Centers and Joint Terrorism Task Forces.

5. When Ron's tour of duty was up, he was ably replaced by Air Force Colonel Jon Wohlman.

6. Over the weekend, we prepared multiple versions of the analysis at classifications ranging from Confidential to Top Secret/Sensitive Compartmented Information.

7. The workshop was one of several organized as part of the Summer Hard Problems (SHARP) program described in the chapter "Transforming Analysis."

8. The workshop underscored the need to reduce obstacles to sharing classified foreign intelligence information with law enforcement officers, most of whom do not have security clearances. This problem had many dimensions, including the need to streamline declassification of relevant products, creation of new databases, and the need to rework training programs (including Analysis 101).

9. See, for example, Gregory F. Treverton and C. Bryan Gabbard, *Assessing the Tradecraft of Intelligence Analysis* (Santa Monica, CA: RAND Corporation, 2008), chapter 1.

10. For more on these developments, see Fingar, *Reducing Uncertainty*, chapters 2 and 3.

11. Collection capacity, especially for unclassified (open source) information is far greater than the capacity to process what is collected. Advances in information technology helped somewhat but, during my time as DDNI/A, they did more to expand the size of the information haystack than to locate important needles. The problem was less severe for clandestine collection, but the imbalance between collection and analysis was becoming worse, not better, during my tenure. Thus, for example, the volume of imagery collected increased far more rapidly than did the number of imagery analysts.

12. Prior to the advent of the ODNI, lists of collection priorities were distributed to all collection agencies and each one did its best to collect on the

highest-ranked subjects. There was some effort to rationalize collective efforts and avoid the "everyone runs to the ball" problem but improve the allocation of effort to maximize likelihood of success while minimizing duplication of effort, cost, and risk. My counterpart for collection, Mary Margaret Graham, oversaw reforms that regularized and improved deconfliction and efficiency. Authorities and procedures for setting intelligence priorities were codified in *Intelligence Community Directive Number 204: Roles and Responsibilities for the National Intelligence Priorities Framework* (Effective September 13, 2007), https://www.dni.gov/files/documents/ICD/ICD_204.pdf. This directive was superseded by *Intelligence Community Directive 204: National Intelligence Priorities Framework* (January 2, 2015), https://www.dni.gov/files/documents/ICD/ICD%20 204%20National%20Intelligence%20Priorities%20Framework.pdf.

13. National Intelligence Officers (NIOs) are senior analysts drawn from IC agencies, other USG organizations, or think tanks and universities who head the regional and transnational issue components of the National Intelligence Council. Until displaced by National Intelligence Managers (NIMs) after I had left the ODNI, NIOs functioned as the senior substantive experts and points of contact for the IC as a whole.

Transforming Analysis

1. See, for example, "DDNI/A Addresses DNI Information Sharing Conference and Technology Exposition," August 21, 2006, https://www.dni.gov/files/documents/Newsroom/Speeches%20and%20Interviews/20060821_2_speech.pdf; and "2007 Analytic Transformation Symposium Transcripts," https://www.dni.gov/files/documents/Newsroom/Speeches%20and%20Interviews/20070905_speech.pdf.

2. ORCON restrictions on distribution resulted in part from explicit limitations imposed by liaison partners (for example, injunctions not to share the information with specific agencies), but most reflected "need to know" determinations made by collectors.

3. As used here, "tools" and "analytic tools" refer to software applications sold to the IC and to IC analysts as near-miraculous ways to manage and mine "raw" data to discover patterns and linkages and generate hypotheses explaining their origins and implications.

4. The terms "raw" and "finished" intelligence refer, respectively, to information captured by collection systems (for example, signals intercepts, imagery, clandestine human intelligence, and media reporting) and to analytical assessments and judgments based on "raw" information.

5. Describing it as a pilot probably also contributed to the willingness of agencies to allow us to access "their" data through A-Space.

6. Top Secret is the highest of three levels of classification (the others are Confidential and Secret). Holding a Top Secret (TS) clearance is a prerequisite for access to specific categories of sensitive information. Eligibility for access to specific categories or "compartments" of information requires additional vetting of persons holding a TS clearance.

7. Among other reasons for wanting the new system to use commercial software was to shift responsibility for updates and upgrades to vendors who would be doing it for competitive reasons. Identifying and utilizing vendors to develop the systems we wanted provided yet another example proving that nothing is easy in the US Government. The companies best able and most eager to do what we wanted often were too small to qualify for USG contracts. We found a workaround (having the developers become subcontractors to a big company with an existing contract that could be modified to cover our project), but we also kicked this discovery and shortcoming to the Acquisition directorate of the ODNI (successor to the original Management directorate).

8. For more detailed discussion of A-Space, see Michael Wertheimer, "Remarks and Q&A by the Assistant Deputy Director of National Intelligence for Analytic Transformation & Chief Technology Officer," Transcripts from the 2007 Analytic Transformation Symposium, Chicago, Illinois, September 5, 2007–September 6, 2007, https://www.dni.gov/files/documents/Newsroom/Speeches%20and%20Interviews/20070905_speech.pdf. It was both gratifying and helpful to our credibility with analysts and overseers that *Time* magazine named A-Space one of the fifty best inventions for 2008. *Time*, October 29, 2008. A-Space ("Facebook for Spies") was number 32, http://content.time.com/time/specials/packages/article/0,28804,1852747_1854195_1854171,00.html.

9. My opposition to the traditional distinction between "white collar" all-source analysts and "blue collar" single INT analysts and willingness to make the category of analyst more inclusive and egalitarian was another manifestation of this goal.

10. One way in which closer collaboration between analysts and collectors contributed to better analysis resulted from early and intimate exchanges between drafters of NIEs and collectors familiar with the intelligence on the topics to be covered. This collaboration helped identify new information, facilitated cross-checking with other intelligence, and enabled collectors to assess the reliability of sources on the specific points analysts wanted to understand.

11. For additional detail on the Library of National Intelligence, see Wertheimer, "Remarks and Q&A."

12. ICPM 2007-200-2, "Preparing Intelligence to Meet the Intelligence Community's "Responsibility to Provide," December 7, 2007, https://www.dni.gov/files/documents/IC%20Policy%20Memos/ICPM%202007-200-2%20Responsibility%20to%20Provide.pdf.

13. For more detail and examples, see Wertheimer, "Remarks and Q&A." The expectation that at least subsets of the people assembled for SHARP workshops would continue to work collaboratively has been proven correct. Many continue to work together or exchange ideas a decade after this program was discontinued by my successors.

14. On one such source of inspiration, the Diplomatic Intelligence Support Center in Sarajevo, see Marjorie Niehaus, "Bureau of the Month: Intelligence and Research," *State Magazine*, November-December 1996, https://1997–2001.state.gov/publications/statemag/statemag_nov-dec/bom.html.

15. RASER teams deployed first in the United States after six months of full-time training. These early assignments were designed to work on real problems identified in the SHARP workshops to build end-to-end capacity to identify and track threats to the homeland. The deployments to FBI field offices and big city police departments resulted in a number of breakthroughs and adoption of new ways of doing things. Having seen RASER teams in the field (one of their exercises required collecting intelligence and avoiding capture by US Army Ranger units), the Marines specifically requested deployment of a RASER team to Kandahar. See Wertheimer, "Remarks and Q&A."

16. The value of easy interchange with USG officials outside the Intelligence Community is easily demonstrated by INR's sustained ability to bolster its small size (in comparison to other IC agencies) through regular contacts with the Foreign Service Officers (FSOs) working elsewhere in the State Department headquarters building and at overseas posts. Although INR typically has only one or a few area specialists and a handful of functional specialists working on a given country, they can easily expand the pool of expertise by drawing upon the knowledge of dozens of FSOs in the regional and functional bureaus in addition to their contacts across the IC and outside of government.

17. To make all IC products more accessible and useful to national security customers and to help alleviate the uncertainties and constraints summarized here, we pressed for and produced guidance on writing for maximum utility. The original version of this directive, ICD 208, *Write for Maximum Utility*,

was issued on December 17, 2008. A revised version, titled *Maximizing the Utility of Analytic Products*, was issued on January 9, 2017, https://www.dni. gov/files/documents/ICD/ICD%20208%20-%20Maximizing%20the%20 Utility%20of%20Analytic%20Products%20(09%20Jan%202017).pdf.

18. The original version of this IC Directive was issued in 2008 (https:// www.hsdl.org/?view&did=14891). The revised version of the ICD titled *Analytic Outreach* was signed on August 28, 2013, https://www.dni.gov/files/ documents/ICD/ICD%20205%20-%20Analytic%20Outreach.pdf.

Roads Not Taken

1. IRTPA, Sec. 1021, https://www.dni.gov/files/documents/IRTPA%20 2004.pdf.

2. For more on NIC responsibilities, see Robert Hutchings and Gregory F. Treverton, eds., *Truth to Power: A History of the National Intelligence Council* (Oxford, UK: Oxford University Press, 2019). On the new NIC responsibility to provide briefing materials for NSC-convened meetings, see Fingar, "New Missions, New Challenges, 2005–2008."

3. IRTPA, Sec. 1021, https://www.dni.gov/files/NCTC/documents/RelatedContent_documents/Intelligence_Reform_Act.pdf.

4. For more on my views of open source information, see Dr. Thomas Fingar, "Remarks and Q&A by the Deputy Director of National Intelligence for Analysis, and Chairman of the National Intelligence Council," ODNI Open Source Conference, Washington, DC, July 17, 2007, https://www.dni. gov/files/documents/Newsroom/Speeches%20and%20Interviews/20070717_ speech_3.pdf.

5. For copyright reasons, it was necessary to limit access to this unclassified database of materials published in English or translated into English. It was extremely useful, and I saw it as an inducement for scholars willing to exchange ideas with IC analysts (see previous discussion of analytic outreach).

6. See "Office of the Director of National Intelligence Announces Mission Manager for Cuba and Venezuela," November 27, 2006, https://www. dni.gov/files/documents/Newsroom/Press%20Releases/2006%20Press%20 Releases/20061127_release.pdf.

7. The estimate was the immediately contentious but subsequently oft-validated December 2007 NIE on Iran's nuclear intentions and capabilities. Redacted declassified key judgments were released almost immediately, but the estimate itself remains classified. The redacted key judgments can be found

at https://www.dni.gov/files/documents/Newsroom/Reports%20and%20 Pubs/20071203_release.pdf. For additional information on the preparation and impact of this NIE, see Fingar, *Reducing Uncertainty*, chapter 6; and Fingar, "New Missions, New Challenges, 2005–2008."

Reflections and Lessons

1. Mark was certainly right, in theory, but as is often the case in Washington and elsewhere, we had no real alternative. Guidance from the Secretary was unambiguous; we had to eliminate one DAS position and the two remaining portfolios (Principal Deputy and DAS for Intelligence Coordination) had to be preserved. Happily, Mark's prediction that successors would not be able to handle the challenges of the combined portfolio have proven wrong. Those who succeeded me (Jim Buchanan and Vic Raphael) performed magnificently in the position.

2. For more detail on relationships between the NIC and mission managers, see the chapters by Thomas Fingar, Christopher Kojm, and Gregory Treverton in *Truth to Power: A History of the National Intelligence Council*, ed. Robert Hutchings and Gregory F. Treverton (Oxford, UK: Oxford University Press, 2019).

3. The NIC functioned extremely well during my time as Chair because of my ability to rely on two superb deputies (first David Gordon and then Steve Kaplan) and NIC Councilor Mat Burrows. This arrangement was effective, but it denied all of them the recognition and stature they deserved.

4. I was uncomfortable doing this but I recognized the utility of Keefe's suggestion and recalled the admonition of a senior State Department colleague who told me, in effect, "You have a reputation to die for in this town. I hope you are going to use it to get things done."

5. Although I have written little about personnel transitions in this reprise of my thinking, I would be remiss not to acknowledge the fantastic contributions of "successor" appointees to key positions, especially Richard Immerman, Professor of Diplomatic History at Temple University, who succeeded Nancy Tucker; Colonel Jon Wohlman, who replaced Ron Rice; Joe Gartin, who succeeded Steve Kaplan as Deputy for the PDB when Kaplan became Vice Chair of NIC; Craig Gralley, who succeeded Jan Karcz as my Chief of Staff; and Kelley Shreffler, Brian O'Callaghan, and Caitlin Meehan, who succeeded Sherry Hong). Sandi Jimenez accompanied me from the State Department and remained my special assistant until I retired.

6. When thinking about the kind of meetings I should convene, I recalled the sage advice I was given by a venerable Stanford dean who had helped set up the statistical systems used by the Department of Energy. As I was about to depart for Washington, Lincoln Moses told me that I could avoid a great deal of frustration in Washington if I stopped thinking of meetings as distractions from doing my job and accepted that attending and running meetings was a critical part of my job.

7. It would be difficult to overstate the importance of these meetings. They generated ideas, built esprit de corps, connected members of my team to one another and to the thinking of other ODNI senior leaders, and enabled us to function as a team rather than as a collection of individuals. Years later, other members of the team still talk and write about how valuable they were.

Part II: Lessons for New Appointees

1. Illustrative examples of scoping activities can be found in the chapter "Taking Stock."

2. I cannot resist the need to illustrate this point with an example from early in my career when I was a German translator at US Army headquarters in Heidelberg, Germany. One of the tasks I inherited from my predecessor was to translate a biweekly report from the German police that summarized all encounters between American soldiers and German law enforcement. It was not difficult to translate, but its length made this a time-consuming task and, for reasons lost in the mists of time, it had been determined that its sensitivity mandated that only the senior translator (my position) could do it. The report was completely irrelevant to our mission and the translation was produced in only one copy for delivery to just one senior officer. I approached that officer to say that doing this translation precluded work on more important projects and that I thought it better for me to skim it in German and tell him whether it contained anything he needed to know. He responded, "Who gets this report?" I responded, "Just you, sir." "Why do I get it?" "Because you asked for it." "Who else gets it?" "No one, sir." "Do I need it?" No, sir." "Then stop translating it and just tell me what I need to know."

3. Information on how I built my team can be found in the chapter "Building a Team and Building Support."

4. Illustrative examples can be found in the chapter "Translating Ideas into Actions."

5. Examples can be found in the chapter "Blank Whiteboard and Ticking Clock."